Sample Comments from Ben Kaplan's Mailbag

"You list a wealth of information, but what may be just as important, you do it in such a way that conveys enthusiasm and fosters inspiration. . . . Many thanks for such a terrific service to future generations. Huge amounts of children will undoubtedly be indebted to you for teaching them how not to be in debt."

> —Patrick B. (Parent)
> Washington, DC

"My mom and I jointly read your book, *How to Go to College Almost for Free*. What a great book—well-written, fun to read, and full of pertinent advice . . . Using your methods, I have already won a local scholarship, which I can add to my two California state governor's scholarships . . . Thanks for all the great information"

> —Steve S. (High School Student)
> San Francisco, CA

"Last week I received my first scholarship! That reflects my tuition and books for the first semester! My elation was so immense that you'd have thought I'd won the lottery. Actually, it felt better as I felt I'd earned it with my 12-page application. . . . My goal is gaining momentum with each day and application I turn in. Bravo Ben! You are making a big difference in the world."

> —Cynthia M. (Adult Returning Student)
> Gleneden Beach, OR

"Using your book as a fundamental guideline, I have been working hard all year, and had a great success in winning a number of scholarships!"

> —Yong-Hwa L. (College Student)
> Woodinville, WA

"As a parent of a scholarship seeker, I found your book to be profound and extremely thorough. It was very informational and yet designed for us "common folk" . . . My daughter was lucky enough to be the recipient of the Target All-Around Scholarship. It was the first scholarship she had ever applied for! Boy were we thrilled! Your book was pure genius."

> —Kim D. (Parent)
> Juniata, NE

"Your book is great and your ScholarshipCoach.com website complements it so well. Congratulations on your huge success. I've read your book, told some friends, and we're starting a scholarship interest group. Your book is our guidepost!"

> —Bob H. (Parent)
> Milwaukee, WI

"My freshman year in high school was very depressing for me. I had no will power, no motivation, no ambition in life, no form of self-discipline. . . . Then I read your biography. At that point, I had an epiphany, where I had this overwhelming urge to accomplish anything and excel at everything. From there I started reading your book and didn't put it down until I finished it. . . . Because of your inspiration Mr. Kaplan, your motivating story, I am where I am today . . ."

—Mason T. (High School Student)
San Antonio, TX

"I have never read a book so closely as I have read your *How to Go to College Almost for Free* book. . . . I've jumped into this scholarship thing with both feet. Once I got my hands on your book, it's gone with me everywhere I've been—when we're taking a break at band practice or I'm not on stage at play rehearsal . . . I'm not letting one scholarship I know of get by me."

—Ben J. (College Student)
Dahlonega, GA

"I have seen a lot of other books in stores that claim to offer scholarship advice, when really there's just a bunch of tired clichés and information recycling. Your book is really fresh and different—and very readable. I finished it in three days! Keep writing and I will keep buying!"

—Sharie S. (Adult Returning Student)
Vancouver, BC

"My grandmother gave me your book for Christmas a couple of years ago. I thanked her and put it away because I thought it was one of those fake books with big titles like "How to Win a Zillion Dollars Overnight with no Money Down." Imagine my pleasant surprise when I finally looked it over! I found your book to be insightful, practical, and extraordinarily helpful. I just wanted to thank you so much for sharing your insights and experience with the millions of wannabe scholarship winners out there."

—Jennifer S. (High School Student)
Birmingham, AL

"Following advice that you provided in your book, my son and I have been searching for scholarships. Utilizing other schools' web pages, as you suggest, a local scholarship was found . . . My son received two $250 checks in the mail yesterday from the two organizations sponsoring the scholarship. We were shocked to say the least! We will keep plugging away with vigor . . . Thanks for your book!

—Rene W. (Parent)
Jackson, MS

THE
SCHOLARSHIP SCOUTING REPORT

An Insider's Guide to America's Best Scholarships

BEN KAPLAN

HarperResource
An Imprint of HarperCollins*Publishers*

HarperCollins books may be purchased for educational, business, or sales promotional use. For information please write: Special Markets Department, HarperCollins Publishers, Inc., 10 East 53rd Street, New York, NY 10022.

FIRST EDITION

Designed by: Stratford Publishing Services, Brattleboro, Vermont;
Waggle Dancer Media, Inc., Portland, Oregon

Ben Kaplan also conducts seminars, workshops, and other events. For more information visit: **www.BenKaplan.com**

Trademarks and Permissions: All brand names, product names, and services used in this book are trademarks, registered trademarks, service marks, or trade names of their respective holders. *The Scholarship Scouting Report, How to Go to College Almost for Free, Scholarship Seeker's Toolbox*, Ben Kaplan's Scholarship Trilogy, The Scholarship Coach, ScholarshipCoach.com, Coach's Comments, and Ben Kaplan Presents, along with their associated logos, are all trademarks of Waggle Dancer Media, Inc.

Disclaimers: The author, Ben Kaplan, has no affiliation with Kaplan Educational Centers or Kaplan Books, neither of which has endorsed this publication. This book is designed to provide accurate and authoritative information in regard to the subject matter covered. The author and the publisher, however, make no representation or warranties of any kind with regard to the completeness or accuracy of the contents herein and accept no liability of any kind. Furthermore, this book is sold with the understanding that neither the author nor the publisher is engaged in rendering legal, accounting, or other professional service. If legal advice or other expert assistance is required, the services of a competent professional person should be sought. Any advice given by the author about how to win specific scholarship contests is solely the opinion of the author, and is not endorsed by any individuals or organizations affiliated with these programs.

All scholarship entries, essays, artwork, and photographs have been reprinted with permission from either the organizations administering the scholarship programs or the students who applied.

Library of Congress Cataloging-in-Publication Data
Kaplan, Benjamin R.
The scholarship scouting report : an insider's guide to America's best scholarships / by Ben Kaplan.
p. cm.
ISBN 0-06-093654-1
1. Scholarships—United States—Handbooks, manuals, etc. I. Title.
IB2338 .K365 2002
378.3'4—dc21   2002068486

03 04 05 06 07   10 9 8 7 6 5 4 3 2 1

Use of Companion Web Resources

Purchasers of this book are granted access to an interactive Coach's Locker Room located at **www.ScholarshipCoach.com** on the World Wide Web. Follow the directions to register for the Coach's Locker Room, and when prompted for an access code during the registration process, enter the following code:

SCOUT 464737678B

To all the parents out there who—despite the prospect of skyrocketing tuition and excessive student loan debt—encourage, motivate, challenge, and inspire their kids to pursue bold educational dreams.

To all the students out there who are determined to make those dreams a reality.

Perhaps this book can help.

Acknowledgments

So many wonderful people have played a major role in making this book possible. It is my pleasure to take a moment to voice my heartfelt appreciation.

First of all, I'd like to thank my literary agent, Laureen Rowland, who has been a true believer in *The Scholarship Scouting Report* from the very beginning. Laureen went above and beyond the call of duty for an agent and made countless contributions to all aspects of this book.

I'd also like to recognize all of the good folks at HarperCollins who supported and championed *The Scholarship Scouting Report*. In particular, I'd like to thank Kathy Huck and Megan Newman for their exhaustive efforts on behalf of this book. I am also grateful for the special contributions made by Shelby Meizlik, Kate Stark, Nina Olmstead, Laurie Rippon, Connor Henton, and, of course, Cathy Hemming.

Many thanks to Adrian Zackheim for his leadership and vision in putting in motion the publishing plan for this book and my prior book, *How to Go to College Almost for Free.*

I'd like to give kudos to Joe Veltre, who provided useful input and comments during the initial planning stages of this book.

I'd also like to give a "shout out" to Emily Portwood and Carole Karnofski for their diligent and thorough research assistance. Helping gather and organize the material for this book was a Herculean task, and Emily and Carole were certainly up to the task. You guys rock!

"High fives" are in order for everyone at Waggle Dancer Media who served as sounding boards for virtually every aspect of this book, from cover design and interior layout to editing and typography. These fun-loving waggle dancers filled in and helped out with anything and everything that was needed.

A hearty "well done" goes out to Judith Schaeffer for her creative suggestions and masterful book production scheduling.

I'd like to express my appreciation to the hundreds of the scholarship administrators, judges, and winners who were interviewed for *The Scholarship Scouting Report*. I am deeply grateful for the many insights each of you contributed to this book.

I'd also like to thank Grandma E, Grandma Ruby, Grandpa Freddy, Uncle Skip, Aunt Ellen, and all of the other book cheerleaders in my extended family. When it comes to being supportive, my relatives are off the charts.

Most of all, I am indebted to the world's greatest dad and mom, Gary and Patana. I certainly did a good job in "choosing" my parents!

What's Inside

ICONS THAT HIGHLIGHT KEY INFORMATION

Keep an eye out for the icons shown below. They will help you locate key information throughout the text.

 Indicates important insider information uncovered through in-depth interviews with program administrators, judges, and past winners—information not readily available in program literature.

 Helps you quickly identify the scholarship amounts or college cash awarded by the program.

 Spotlights added benefits to scholarship winners beyond just the money received (such as trips, internships, and special prizes).

 Identifies text from actual essays and entry materials submitted by past scholarship winners.

 Denotes the specific keyword for each scholarship or Related Award Program ("AMLEGORA" in the example shown at left) that unlocks special bonus material in the Coach's Locker Room at ScholarshipCoach.com.

ICONS THAT INDICATE ENTRY REQUIREMENTS

The following icons help you identify, at a glance, the entry requirements for each scholarship program. They appear under the entry requirements header in the box located on the first page of each scouting report.

 Write and submit an essay of at least 300 words.

 Write a response of less than 300 words to a question posed in the application.

Prepare a list of activities and credentials (may also include awards and honors, employment, and community service).

 Submit a school transcript, grade-point average, and/or test scores.

 Send in original student art and/or computer graphics.

 Submit an outside writing sample (such as class papers, published articles, poems, or creative writing samples).

 Provide financial information or verification of financial need.

 Interview with judges or program administrators in person or by phone.

 Requires a nomination to apply.

 Perform, either live or taped, a speech, presentation, or talent (such as singing, music, or dance).

 Initiate or participate in a substantial project (such as a science, community service, or history project).

 Obtain and submit letters of recommendation.

 Include an application fee with your submitted entry.

 Submit additional documentation (such as newspaper clippings, additional recommendation letters, or class papers).

Calling All Scholarship Seekers!

Whether you're talking about the Super Bowl or the World Series, the NBA Finals or the Stanley Cup, one thing is for sure: When professional athletes show up for the "big game," they come *prepared*. With the championship on the line, you'd better believe that they've reviewed game films from previous match-ups, plotted responses to potential game-day scenarios, and studied scouting reports of the opposing teams. Losing is *not* an option!

And it's no different for those of us seriously playing the college scholarship game. If you're serious about winning college cash—and I have a strong suspicion you are, because you picked up this book—you've got to show up *ready* to play. This means doing the necessary detective work for each scholarship possibility, thinking strategically about each program's judging criteria, and reviewing past winning entries to understand how others have played the game well.

Of course, there's just one problem: Unlike sports superstars and their big league teams, most of us don't have access to the people, resources, and information that could best help us prepare. And even if we should be so fortunate, the process of gathering, distilling, and processing this essential pre-game information can be overwhelming.

But what if there were a *single* place you could go to get the genuine lowdown on many of the nation's top scholarship opportunities? Wouldn't it be great if in that single location you could not only learn the essentials of each scholarship program, but also pick up insider information distilled directly from conversations with the administrators and judges who hold the purse strings? What if that one mother lode of scouting information were also layered with insights gleaned from hundreds of scholarship winners, and then glazed with the actual scholarship application materials and sample entries that helped these winners claim such awards?

And what if I told you that such a place *does,* in fact, exist? To get there, would you walk over a bed of hot coals? Swim across a shark-infested bay? Run in the Boston Marathon wearing nothing but a goofy smile? Fortunately, you don't have to do any of these things: The book you are now holding is, quite simply, the college cash cornucopia you've been searching for.

I wrote *The Scholarship Scouting Report* because I knew first-hand how time-consuming, confusing, and frustrating it can be to do scholarship research and detective work when you're new to the college money game. So, dear reader, to make your life a lot easier, I've done much of the heavy lifting for you: I've gathered together in these pages crucial information and proven strategic analysis on many of the nation's top scholarship programs—opportunities that you can apply for, with a high degree of success, right away.

Furthermore, when used together with the other two books in my scholarship trilogy—*How to Go to College Almost for Free* (published by HarperCollins) and *Scholarship Seeker's Toolbox* (published by Waggle Dancer Books)—*The Scholarship Scouting Report* becomes the critical component that connects strategic principles and concepts with real-world applications and results.

▌ My Personal Scholarship Quest

It wasn't very long ago that I was in a situation probably very similar to yours. I was in my junior year at a public high school in Eugene, Oregon, and I didn't have a clue how I was going to pay for college. I had grown up playing competitive tennis and always dreamed of going to a top college on a tennis scholarship—but after a stress fracture in my back took me out of tennis for nearly 18 months, I suddenly needed to find another way to realize my educational dreams. . . .

When I found my first scholarship application, I didn't know it was destined to change my life. But it did. And after miraculously winning that first scholarship award, I decided to apply for three dozen more. Thanks to a combination of hard work, determination, strategic know-how

Here I am at a scholarship award ceremony. Now that's what I call a BIG check!

(the result of some serious research), and plenty of good, old-fashioned luck, I ended up winning more than two dozen of these awards and amassed nearly $90,000 in scholarship winnings—unrestricted money that I could use at the school of my choice. Coupled with some college credit I had earned in high school, I had covered—to the amazement of my entire family—virtually the entire cost of attending Harvard. (You should have seen the look on my parents' faces!)

THE BIRTH OF *THE SCHOLARSHIP SCOUTING REPORT*

After I had won enough scholarships to pay for my own college education, I wanted to help others achieve a similar success. I began by writing articles on the subject for national publications and responding to e-mails from students, parents, and guidance counselors who asked me for advice. This experience, in turn, led me to write *How to Go to College Almost for Free*. By the time I started appearing on television and radio talk shows across the country, I had acquired the nickname "The Scholarship Coach."

Although I had wanted to do a book like *The Scholarship Scouting Report* for quite some time, the project really gained momentum when I embarked on my first Scholarship Coach National Tour—a 7-week, 25-city road trip in which I conducted free scholarship workshops from coast to coast. All along the route, as well as on my website, I asked high school and college guidance counselors, scholarship program administrators, and financial aid officers which scholarship programs they felt were among the very best in the nation. I also asked students and parents at my events about the top programs they had encountered in their own scholarship quests. By the time I returned home, I had accumulated a list of well over one thousand "people's choice" scholarship programs.

Then the real work began. After assembling a research team, I began to review each scholarship program individually. I decided early on that I wanted to focus my efforts on programs that offered *portable scholarships*—college cash awards that were *not* limited to use at particular institutions. As a result, I eliminated from consideration "school-specific" scholarships that were offered by individual colleges.

I also decided to concentrate on programs that were open to a wide range of students. Anyone who has been through the scholarship search process knows that there are scholarships out there with incredibly specific criteria. For some programs, it's almost as if eligibility depends on something as random as being a left-handed, redheaded, vertically challenged twin from Macon, Georgia, with a long-standing affinity for knitting woolen garments! (This is, admittedly, an exaggeration—but not by much!) In my research, I decided to set aside such narrowly focused programs in favor of scholarships with the potential to impact a much, much wider range of students. As a result, I also excluded scholarships that were limited to students from a specific geographic region or ethnic background or were based entirely on athletic ability.

Finally, wanting to highlight scholarships that would benefit students and families from all types of financial backgrounds, I set aside those scholarships awarded solely on the basis of a student's demonstrated financial need. In general, I only kept scholarships with need-based criteria in the mix if (1) such factors were placed secondary to an evaluation of a student's merit and (2) the program methodology took into account that a family's actual ability to pay can differ drastically from the one-dimensional calculations of rigid financial aid formulas.

After eliminating school-specific, narrowly focused, and need-only scholarships from the pile, I developed a

For comprehensive information on how to win school-specific scholarships, see How to Go to College Almost for Free.

set of criteria to evaluate the remaining nominations. More specifically, in determining scholarships and college cash opportunities for inclusion in this book, I looked for programs that:

- Award a substantial amount of scholarship funds

- Have a proven track record

- Benefit students from a variety of backgrounds and geographic regions

- Are based upon a philosophy, methodology, application process, or judging approach that is innovative or noteworthy in some way

In evaluating the scholarship program candidates, I weighed each of these considerations equally and allowed excellence in some areas to make up for deficiencies in others.

To research the inner workings of each scholarship program, I spent countless hours on the phone with hundreds of scholarship administrators, judges, and past winners. (You should see my phone bill!) I also carefully examined stacks of written documents—including judges' scoring sheets, successful and unsuccessful scholarship applications, and internal program memos. By the time I had finished this exhaustive effort, I was pleasantly surprised to discover that the useful information I had uncovered had exceeded even my own considerable expectations.

Once I had this critical information at my fingertips, I worked hard to distill the knowledge I had gained into the pages you are about to read. Because of space constraints, I decided to focus my analysis on top scholarship programs that, taken as a whole, showcase the variety of awards available. For each of these programs, I prepared an in-depth scholarship scouting report. Along with each of these full-length reports, I've also included

Quite simply, there is no other book like The Scholarship Scouting Report. I've done the bare-knuckle research so that you can focus your time on implementing these proven strategies.

The vast majority of scholarship programs in this book do not consider your family's financial situation. In those instances when financial need is a factor, it is noted in the text.

concise profiles of "Related Award Programs"—additional top scholarship opportunities that are related to each featured scholarship in terms of the focus of the program, the type of student recognized, the sponsoring organization, or the application and judging methodology.

BEN KAPLAN'S SCHOLARSHIP TRILOGY

The Scholarship Scouting Report and my two other books, *How to Go to College Almost for Free* and *Scholarship Seeker's Toolbox*, are designed to complement one another as part of an essential three-volume set for determined scholarship seekers.

The Scholarship Scouting Report is my behind-the-scenes guide to America's leading scholarship programs—the ones you definitely need to know about. It provides in-depth research and exhaustive detective work on each of these programs and offers a detailed analysis of what it takes to win these specific (and lucrative) scholarship awards.

How to Go to College Almost for Free (published by HarperCollins) is a comprehensive "how-to" scholarship guidebook. It explains the broader scholarship and financial aid landscape—showing you how to locate and research scholarship opportunities perfect for you, position yourself for the best chance of winning them, produce winning application materials for any program, and manage your entire scholarship quest from start to finish.

Scholarship Seeker's Toolbox (published by Waggle Dancer Books) is a collection of next-generation tools that streamline the entire process of finding, applying for, and winning scholarships. Drawn from the latest scholarship technology, the book features strategic worksheets and exercises, calendar organizers, research questionnaires, self-analysis systems, ready-to-use templates, and a powerful troubleshooting kit for diagnosing and repairing potential problems in your application materials.

Put another way, if *The Scholarship Scouting Report* takes you on a guided tour of America's top scholarship opportunities and *How to Go to College Almost for Free* distills the critical strategies and techniques for successfully navigating the entire scholarship universe, then *Scholarship Seeker's Toolbox* assists you in actually *doing the work* you know you need to do.

▮ WHO SHOULD READ THIS BOOK

If you think you know what type of person wins college scholarships, think again. Did you know that an individual serving a prison sentence won an extremely competitive scholarship essay contest? Did you realize that someone with a GPA barely high enough to graduate high school ended up winning tens of thousands of dollars in college cash? Would you expect that a student diagnosed with dyslexia—someone who reads at the 18th percentile level—could claim one of the nation's most prestigious scholarships and be well on her way to a Ph.D. in astrophysics? All of these people are real scholarship winners. All of them won scholarships profiled in this book.

Quite simply, *The Scholarship Scouting Report* is designed to assist *any* student in search of scholarship money for higher education. The scholarship programs included in this book cover a full spectrum of scholarship awards—including scholarships for high school and college students, graduate students, nontraditional students, and even kids under 14. Whether you're a 6th grader just starting to dream about college, a high school senior in the midst of college applications, an undergraduate junior struggling with paying current tuition bills and raising funds for future grad school costs, or perhaps a 62-year-old grandma heading back to school (you go, girl!), this book will prove useful to you.

The programs described in these pages provide college cash for use at community colleges, trade and technical schools, public and private four-year colleges and universities, and graduate institutions. None of the awards are restricted for use at a particular school—thereby enabling school choice. Students with all sorts of backgrounds, achievements, and interests will find scholarships in this book that are appropriate for them.

Because parents can play hugely important roles in the scholarship game—as researchers, sounding boards, organizers, motivators, and proofreaders, for example—the research collected in this volume will prove to be an invaluable parental guide. Likewise, guidance counselors will find each scouting report to be a very useful reference tool for instructing students on how to improve drafts of their scholarship application submissions.

If you're looking for a gripping tale of suspense and drama, try John Grisham. But if you want to get other people to help pay for your tuition, then you've come to the right place.

How to Read the Scouting Reports

For ease of reference, the scouting reports in this book are listed in alphabetical order according to the name of each featured program. In addition, there is a detailed table of contents in the front of the book as well as a scholarship award index in the back of the book to help you find the specific programs you're looking for.

Each scouting report is divided into several parts. First, to provide essential information at a glance—and to help you quickly determine which scholarship programs are especially well suited for you—I've included key facts in a box at the beginning of each scouting report. The box also includes icons to help you easily identify the entry requirements for each scholarship program. Next to the box, I've written a program overview, describing eligibility requirements, application procedures, entry deadlines, the amount of scholarship money available (identified by the "Money Matters" icon, shown at left), and other essential information.

For an explanation of each icon used in the book, please see the icon key located after the table of contents on page xvi.

In the second part of each scouting report, labeled "A Closer Look," I examine each scholarship program in much greater detail. In this section, I not only thoroughly describe the complete application process and necessary application materials but also discuss official and "hidden" judging criteria, the procedure for screening applicants, and any other characteristics of the program that might influence how you should craft your application.

Pay special attention to any passages identified with the "Insider Info" icon (shown at left). Distilled from in-depth interviews with program administrators, judges, and past winners, this behind-the-scenes data is not readily available to the general public. I've devoted considerable resources to tracking down this insider information because of its ultimate importance. I know from my own experience that the strategic insights gained from such information can double and triple your chances of winning a given award.

The third section of each scouting report, the "Coach's Analysis" section, is where I get in the strategic groove—revealing the proven application strategies for each scholarship program and pointing out the most frequently made mistakes. Based on comprehensive interviews with past winners and scholarship judges for each award—as well as my own experience in crafting winning scholarship applications and coaching others to do so—this section outlines clear action steps that, once implemented, leverage your chances to win. Where appropriate, I've included quotes from scholarship winners and excerpts from their writing to support my points. If there is one section to read, re-read, highlight, dog-ear, and recite aloud on a moonlit night, this is the one.

Immediately following the Coach's Analysis, I've included additional information and documentation to further your understanding of what it takes to win each award. In many cases, I have reprinted sample entries, essays, and application excerpts that past winners of the scholarship have submitted, and I have annotated such material with my own "Coach's Comments." In other cases, I've summarized the various types of student submissions that have worked in the past—to spark your thinking about how to approach your own application entry. Both of these special sections, as well as entry excerpts included in the main text, are identified by the "Winning Entry" icon (shown at left). *Remember, because winning college scholarships is a game, the best way to master the scholarship game is to learn from those who play it well.*

At the conclusion of each scouting report, I provide complete contact information for the featured scholarship and profile the aforementioned Related Award Programs—with **ScholarshipCoach.com** "keywords" alongside. For the latest and most up-to-date contact information for each featured scholarship and Related Award Program, simply visit the Coach's Locker Room portion of the ScholarshipCoach.com website—a password-protected section of the site for readers of my books and users of my multimedia products—and type these keywords into the "Enter a Keyword" box. (In the next section, I'll give you complete instructions on how to register for the Coach's Locker Room and gain free access to all the special bonus material available online.)

GETTING THE MOST OUT OF THIS BOOK

The material in this book works on multiple levels. Internalizing and applying the specific strategies outlined in each scouting report will, of course, maximize your chances of winning each scholarship award. But doing so will also, because of inherent program similarities, significantly enhance your odds of winning each corresponding Related Award Program.

On a deeper level, these scouting reports represent a series of real-world case studies that illustrates and reinforces the fundamental (and universally applicable) principles of scholarship success—principles that are important for virtually every type of scholarship program you'll encounter. Therefore, working through the examples in this book will help you win many other scholarships that aren't directly mentioned in these pages.

I was first introduced to the power of the case study approach while working as a case writer for two professors at Harvard Business School— an institution that uses real-world case studies as the foundation of its curriculum.

For this reason, serious scholarship seekers should read, in full, *every scouting report in this book*—not just the reports for the particular scholarship programs you plan to pursue. In coaching thousands of students and parents to win the scholarship game, I've found that analyzing numerous scholarship programs—with their own peculiarities and different points of view—helps provide a deeper understanding of how to strategically appeal to the scholarship judges who evaluate your hopeful entry.

As you work through these scouting reports, also be sure to study the featured winning entries in a strategic way. Use these examples as a means of better understanding the objectives of each scholarship program and the successful strategies of past winners. Don't make the mistake, however, of trying to duplicate the style or content of these entries at the expense of your own unique voice. While there are underlying principles to be learned from these examples (I'll point them out to you), trying to copy someone else's writing style or point of view almost always backfires. (Indeed, I don't have to tell you that any form of plagiarism is a bad idea!)

Some sample essays in this book have had their bibliographies, footnotes, or in-text citations deleted. To view the complete text for such essays, visit the Coach's Locker Room and type in the appropriate keyword.

Furthermore, be inspired—not intimidated—by the quality of the sample winning entries you'll find in this book. To give you a high bar to aim for, I've chosen to reprint entries that are, in many cases, among the very best submitted to each scholarship program. Because most scholarship programs award several tiers of awards, to win a scholarship you don't necessarily need to submit application materials nearly as good as the examples you'll find in this book. My intention in providing such strong examples is to show you what's possible in the application format and to inspire you to keep honing and refining your materials until they're stronger than perhaps even you expected. As a high school coach once told me, "It's better to shoot for the stars and miss, than to aim for a big pile of dog poop and hit it right on."

SCHOLARSHIPCOACH.COM KEYWORDS AND THE COACH'S LOCKER ROOM

To get the most out of this book, you'll definitely want to take advantage of the **ScholarshipCoach.com** keywords found throughout these pages (identified by the graphic shown at left). You'll find keywords for each featured scholarship and Related Award Program (such as "AMLEGORA" for the American Legion Oratorical Contest). To use these keywords, all you need to do is register for and visit the special Coach's Locker Room section of the ScholarshipCoach.com site.

When you type these keywords into the special "Enter a Keyword" box in the Coach's Locker Room, you'll gain access to all sorts of bonus material, including additional sample winning entries, a variety of multimedia tools and resources, question and answer postings, personalized coaching sessions, and updates to information in this book. If the contact information for a featured scholarship program changes, for instance, the new information is immediately accessible within the Coach's Locker Room. Likewise, if you're interested in a particular Related Award Program, more coverage of the program is available in the Coach's Locker Room by entering the affiliated keyword.

To use the Coach's Locker Room, you will first need to complete the registration process. When you reach the ScholarshipCoach.com home page, go to the Coach's Locker Room box and click the "How do I register?"

Keyword

SCHOLARSHIP COACH.com AMLEGORA

In cases where I've had to excerpt sample winning entries due to space constraints, I've included the full text in the Coach's Locker Room.

link—which will direct you to the Coach's Locker Room registration page. (Alternatively, you could go to the left-hand site navigation menu and click on the "New Users" link within the "Coach's Locker Room" sub-menu.) On the registration page, you will be asked, among other things, to input an access code verifying that you are a reader of this book. The access code you should use is located at the bottom of this book's copyright page (found near the front of the book), under the heading "Use of Companion Web Resources."

Once you have successfully completed the registration process, you will use your e-mail address and the password you assigned yourself during registration to log in to the Coach's Locker Room each time you visit the site. When returning to the site, type your e-mail address and assigned password into the Coach's Locker Room login box on the ScholarshipCoach.com home page, or click on the "Return Users" link within the "Coach's Locker Room" site navigation sub-menu. Don't worry, this sounds more complicated than it really is!

If you have questions about any aspect of this process, send e-mail to help@scholarshipcoach.com for more detailed instructions.

A NOTE TO SCHOLARSHIP PROVIDERS

Are you a scholarship administrator or judge? Want to spread the word about your great program? All you have to do is e-mail me a brief summary of your scholarship program along with information on how I can reach you. For fastest response, send your e-mail to **info@scholarshipcoach.com** and be sure to include your name, title, phone number, e-mail address, and a list of the organizations or individuals sponsoring and administering the program.

After I receive your e-mail, I will contact you with further instructions for submitting any additional information. Your program will automatically be considered for inclusion on the **ScholarshipCoach.com** website, in future editions of *The Scholarship Scouting Report* and *How to Go to College Almost for Free,* in other books and multimedia resources, and as part of my annual Scholarship Coach National Tour.

THE WINNING ATTITUDE

After interviewing hundreds of scholarship winners for this book, one thing has become crystal clear: The most successful scholarship winners share a certain perspective on the process. It's something I've come to call "the winning attitude."

What is this attitude that separates the most successful scholarship seekers from all the rest? It has something to do with their willingness to jump headfirst into the process, their ability to move beyond small setbacks, and their all-out determination to achieve scholarship success.

First, jumping headfirst into the process means applying for as many scholarships as you possibly can. You should not only go after all of the scholarship opportunities profiled in this book that you are eligible for, but you should also pursue numerous other scholarship awards (especially local and school-specific scholarships) that turn up in your own research. (See *How to Go to College Almost for Free* for ten powerful action steps that will help you locate additional scholarship opportunities that are perfect for you.)

Applying for scholarships, after all, is partly a numbers game. To leverage your chances to win—and win big—you need to stack the odds in your favor. No matter how many times you read this book or how many times you visit the Coach's Locker Room, you will shortchange yourself if you don't give yourself enough chances to win. The vast majority of scholarship winners I've interviewed *didn't* apply for just one or two awards.

Second, when you're applying for numerous scholarships, an inevitable part of the process is getting your share of rejection letters (everyone gets them—me included). Top scholarship winners, however, have the ability to forget about each snub and move on to the next application. In fact, the students who are best able to deal

One of my goals in writing this book was to help do the detective work on these leading scholarship programs, so you can focus your own research time on unearthing additional awards that fit your profile.

The process of filling out numerous scholarship applications forced me to think critically about my career and life goals. This process helped me figure out what I wanted to do with my life and determine the steps necessary to reach my objectives.

One student I met applied for seven scholarships and didn't win a single one. But she stuck with it and applied for ten more–winning about $25,000 for college!

Applying for college scholarships teaches you to believe in yourself and to persuade others to believe in you, too. This ability will prove helpful not only in securing college funding but in virtually every other aspect of your life.

with these inevitable rejections are the ones who end up winning the most college dough.

If you know anything about baseball, you're probably aware that Babe Ruth was perhaps the most prolific homerun hitter ever. But you may not know that he also held the record for striking out the most times in a single season. Top scholarship winners recognize, on a gut level, that people never remember the scholarships they didn't get—just the ones they did. So try to have a sense of humor about the whole process and don't dwell on any one application. Whether or not you win a scholarship is never a measure of how good or talented you are; it's simply a measure of whether or not you get to claim that particular chunk of college cash.

Finally, having a winning attitude means possessing an unbridled determination to realize your educational dreams. Winning a scholarship isn't like winning the lottery; it takes work, and there will be many occasions when others may doubt your chances. It's amazing how many scholarship winners I've interviewed who were told at some point that they didn't have what it took to win a particular scholarship award. But they went ahead and took the plunge, proving the naysayers wrong.

As you work through the scholarship scouting reports that follow, it is my hope that you will embrace this winning attitude. So be excited. Get energized. And go for it! Turn the page and let's begin . . .

DON'T FORGET TO WRITE!

Was this book helpful to you? Which scholarships have you won? What lessons have you learned? Do you have any interesting scholarship stories to share? Here's a little secret: I love getting mail! So if you have a free moment, write me a note and let me know how your scholarship quest is going.

I might even include your comments and feature your accomplishments on the ScholarshipCoach.com website or in future editions of this book. (If you don't want me to use your name, just say so.)

The preferred way to contact me is via e-mail at:

Ben@ScholarshipCoach.com

Or if you're so inclined, you can snail-mail me at:

Ben Kaplan
c/o Waggle Dancer Media, Inc.
P.O. Box 23577
Portland, OR 97281-3577

I look forward to hearing from you!

American Legion Oratorical Contest

When Max Miller, then a high school sophomore in Ankeny, Iowa, first entered the American Legion Oratorical Contest, he didn't expect to get past the local level. But as a high school junior, with a determined look on his face and a year of contest experience under his belt, Miller returned from the national finals with top honors and more than $25,000 in scholarships from his two years of participation.

For students like Miller, this oratorical contest—sponsored by the American Legion, a veterans group that seeks to promote patriotism and civic duty in the nation's youth—offers the opportunity to develop and hone their oratorical skills, earn some big-time college cash, and get to know some friendly veterans.

Entrants to this competition must be in grades 9 through 12 and under 20 years of age. They also must have U.S. citizenship or be permanent U.S. residents and attend either a public, private, parochial, military, or home school in the fifty states, Washington D.C., Puerto Rico, Mexico, or France.

Two types of speeches are delivered in this competition, both of which must be delivered without notes or a script. The *prepared oration* must be eight to ten minutes long and on a topic of the entrant's choosing that is related to the U.S. Constitution. The *assigned topic oration* must be three to five minutes in length on one of four previously designated Articles and Sections of the Constitution that will be randomly selected by a contest official. All students speak on the same assigned topic and each student is given a five-minute preparation period.

TARGET RECIPIENT

■ High school students (under age 20)

ENTRY REQUIREMENTS

Performance

DEADLINES

■ Local and State: Varies
■ National: March

	Keyword
SCHOLARSHIP Coach.com	AMLEGORA

Depending on a student's state of residence, there can be up to four levels of local competition—post, district, area, and department (state)—prior to the national round. For the post, district, and area levels, cash and scholarship awards are at the discretion of local American Legion groups, and frequently total several hundred dollars. Winners are announced immediately after each round of competition.

About two-thirds of the departments provide awards to the top state winners, with award amounts averaging from $1,000 to $1,500. All state winners are guaranteed an additional $1,500 for participating in the national competition, and those who make the national semifinalist round but do not advance to the finals each receive an additional $3,000.

The first-place, second-place, and third-place national winners are awarded $19,500, $17,500, and $15,500, respectively. The American Legion will also pay travel expenses for students invited to the national contest (and expenses for a chaperone over age 21).

Other than the top three national winners, students are permitted to reenter the contest each year they are eligible. In fact, there are generally six to eight repeat winners each year on the national level.

Contest dates at the local and state level vary (contact your local American Legion post for more information), but the national contest is usually held in early March.

Some states may provide substantially larger amounts. The first-place and second-place winners in New York, for instance, receive $6,000 and $4,000, respectively.

▌ A CLOSER LOOK

As the general topic for the *prepared oration* segment of the competition is quite broad, it may help to note that past winning entries have tended to (1) address the greatness of the Constitution in its entirety, using historical examples to show how fortunate we are that our system of government was established, and (2) feature various parts of the document, illustrating how each Article is important to the whole.

The four elements of the Constitution used as *assigned topics* vary from year to year. According to Mike Buss, the program director for the contest, the specific topics do not repeat within a four-year time frame. Past assigned topics have included:

- the Second Amendment (the right to bear arms)
- the Fourth Amendment (the right against unreasonable search and seizure)
- Article 3, Section 1 (the judicial system)
- Article 2, Section 1, Paragraphs 6 and 7 (presidential compensation and oath)

The judging scorecard for the oratorical contest follows a strict 100-point scale, in which content is worth 70 points and speaking skills are worth the remaining 30 points. The content component of both the prepared oration and the assigned topics is divided into four basic subcategories: originality and freshness (16 points), skill in selecting material (16 points), logic (16 points), and comprehensive treatment of subject matter (22 points). In calculating the point totals, the content of the prepared oration is worth nearly three times as much as that of the assigned topic.

Similarly, program guidelines divide the points allocated to speaking skills into three equally weighted subcategories: voice and diction (10 points), style (10 points), and body language (10 points). The speaking skill demonstrated by the contestant when delivering the prepared oration is worth 50 percent more than that of the assigned topic.

At the department and national levels (and frequently at earlier levels as well) five judges participate in each round; however, the judges are not identified among the audience members. On the local level, judges frequently include attorneys, journalists, religious leaders, media personalities, and business professionals. At the national level, distinguished leaders—generally from the city of Indianapolis (the host city for the competition) and surrounding areas—serve on the judging panel. Recent national judges have included a leading Indianapolis TV news anchor, a retired Attorney General of Texas, and various retired military personnel.

The national competition is divided into quarterfinal, semifinal, and final rounds. For the quarterfinal round, students are randomly divided into groups of six, and the top scorer from among the six advances to the next round of competition. With nine competitors still left in the competition for the semifinal round, entrants are divided into groups of three, with the top scorer again advancing. In the final round, the three surviving entrants compete head to head for first, second, and third place.

Coach's Analysis

Choosing an appropriate prepared oration topic and presenting it in an interesting way is an essential aspect of doing well in this competition. Max Miller, for instance, learned how to choose a better speech topic after his first attempt in the competition in his sophomore year. To learn how to pick topics that maximize *your* chances of winning, let's examine Miller's choice of topics over this two-year period.

First, as a sophomore, Miller focused his prepared oration on one specific topic—freedom of religion as set forth in the First Amendment of the Constitution. Let's look at a brief excerpt:

Each time we think that religion should be forced upon a government institution, we spit on the graves of every American who has ever fought in any other American war—

fighting to protect America, fighting to defend the Constitution, and fighting for the rights of individual choice of religion. Our freedom has cost us millions of lives: To take freedom from some would mean those lives were lost in vain.

The speech was good enough for Miller to win in his home state of Iowa, but he didn't advance past the first round of the national competition. However, at nationals that year, Miller did gain an appreciation for the approach of the most successful entrants.

"In my speech I focused on one specific topic, but I noticed that the people who made it to the final round focused on the Constitution as a whole, the Constitution as an idea," emphasizes Miller. "When you focus on the big picture, you can reach your audience better. Keep in mind the American Legion's goal—they want to promote respect for the Constitution."

The following year, Miller developed an entirely new speech that incorporated the lesson he had learned. In his winning speech, he likened allegiance to the Constitution to a marriage vow, and suggested that all Americans should take a vow to respect and cherish the Constitution. Here's the key excerpt:

Because Miller's speech went on to chastise proponents of prayer in school, it also had the potential to be quite controversial. In general, tackling controversial topics in scholarship submissions is a risky proposition.

Winning Entry

When two people marry, they make a commitment to one another. They make a promise that through sickness and health, richer and poorer, till death do them part, they will love, honor, and obey one another. We, as citizens of the United States, are also involved in a marriage, which has the same duties any married couple has. Through sickness and in health, richer or poorer, till death do us part, we must love, honor, and obey the Constitution. This marriage began when the Constitution was ratified over two hundred years ago, and if we stay as committed as any married couple should, it will last forever.

Alexander Captain, of Moraga, California—a second-place national winner—also recognized the importance

Alexander Captain, shown here accepting his award plaque, says that he achieved credibility by communicating his ideas with logic and passion.

Winning Entry

of discussing the Constitution from a big-picture per-spective. Inspired by a speech given by General Douglas MacArthur entitled "Duty, Honor, Country," Captain applied MacArthur's principles to the Constitution:

> *Duty, Honor, Country. Appropriately, they represent our Constitution and our sacred bond to it, the bedrock of our nation—the foundation for all the greatness that this country can call its own. It is our* duty *to use the rights that the constitution grants us. We must* honor *the Constitution's unparalleled heritage, and we must acknowl-edge that our unique and brilliant* country *has always and will always depend on its Constitution.*

By piggybacking on MacArthur's speech, Captain had a solid skeleton from which to hang his ideas: The subsequent body of his speech devoted one paragraph each to the concepts of duty, honor, and country. Fur-thermore, Captain realized that a military theme was likely to appeal to a veterans group such as the American Legion. "I thought that the people of the American Legion would be able to associate with and relate to a mil-itary man like MacArthur," Captain stresses.

ATTACKING THE ASSIGNED TOPICS

Often referred to as the "impromptu" portion of the contest, the assigned topics speeches are anything but off-the-cuff. Quite simply, the entrants who do the best are the ones who also write and memorize these extra speeches in advance.

"I wrote out all five speeches ahead of time," states Tiffany Francisco of Chesapeake, Virginia, a third-place national winner. "I also refined my impromptu speeches every round. Once you get to the national level you have to do that."

Insider Info

According to Mike Buss, who has witnessed countless contestant speeches, at the highest levels of the competition the assigned topics portion can have an enormous effect. "Everyone seems to do well in the prepared oration. What normally gets contestants is lack of preparation for the assigned topics. How the assigned topics are handled seems to make or break pretty much everyone."

This is not to say, however, that all four assigned topics must be four entirely new speeches. Some past winners have used nearly identical introductions and conclusions for the four assigned topics speeches and varied only the body of the speech to fit the topic that is drawn. Other winners have viewed the assigned topics as an extension of their prepared oration and have tried to extend the core ideas of their prepared oration speech into all four assigned topics speeches.

Miller, for instance, used the theme of marriage for all four assigned topics, adapting it as needed. This served an added purpose: making his speeches more memorable, believable, and fully developed. "You get known by your theme because it's easier for the judges to remember," Miller emphasizes. "People called me 'the marriage kid.'"

MASTERING YOUR DELIVERY

When you practice, have a friend or family member interrupt you at inopportune times. That way, if you lose your train of thought at the event, you will be able to quickly recover.

In addition to developing the content of your speech, getting comfortable with your delivery is another critical element of success. Year after year, credibility is one of the most important things contest winners communicate. Judges don't just want to hear you pay lip service to something you don't believe in; they want to feel the conviction of your words.

According to Captain, this is one of the things that helped him to advance all the way to the final round of the national competition. "It's really important that you believe in your speech and are passionate about it. You can detect in someone's voice, body language, and demeanor their passion for the topic."

To get comfortable in your delivery, you need to be comfortable with the contest environment. The contest is run in a quite formal manner, and great care is taken to separate orators from one another; they are kept in separate rooms and are not allowed to hear what others say until their own oration is complete.

To prepare for the contest, Max Miller (right) had his mom critique his delivery and style. (Thanks, Mom!)

Remember that the other orators are just as nervous as you are. If you're still a bit anxious, try picturing the audience naked in brown socks!

To do your best, you should also be prepared for the unique aspects of the room or stage in which you perform each speech. Typically, you're allowed to inspect and try out the stage at each venue: You can have a friend or family member sit in various positions in the audience and make sure that you're speaking loudly enough and walking in the right place. "In the final round at the national competition, I didn't check out the stage enough," Captain reminisces. "I stood too far back and didn't speak loud enough for my voice to really carry."

Finally, the best way to get comfortable is through practice. Try out your speech in front of others—and possibly a video camera—before showing up at the competition. After advancing through a local round, try to refine both the content of your speech and its delivery—asking the judges for feedback on both your strengths and weaknesses.

Getting comfortable with speaking in front of people will also help you conquer the often-dreaded scholarship interview.

If you're a freshman, sophomore, or junior, take the opportunity to participate in the contest before your final year of eligibility. No matter how well you perform your first year, you'll be that much better in your second attempt. "I really improved over the years," relates Francisco. "When I started, I was okay—but I definitely got much better."

Max Miller
Ankeny, IA
First Prize
$19,500

Winning

Entry

PREPARED ORATION:
"TO LOVE, HONOR, AND OBEY"

In this excerpt from his prepared oration, Max Miller relates the constitutional obligations of citizenship to the institutional obligations of marriage.

When the Constitution was ratified, we as Americans made our way down the aisle and completed our vows of marriage. That ceremony has been over for over two hundred years, but the obligations we have as a married couple still remain—to love, honor, and obey. But as with most good things in life, we have begun to take our Constitution and the rights it gives us for granted. It's time we renew the vows we have as citizens and re-establish the fundamental obligations they have given us: to love, honor, and obey.

The basis of any good marriage is a loving relationship. We have many reasons as to why we should love our Constitution, but the most obvious is that it has provided us with a government that is run by the people, instead of over the people. Democracy is a sacred value, because it gives each and every one of us a voice: a voice to express our beliefs and a voice to choose our leaders. But the Constitution goes beyond setting up democracy in this nation; it also gives us rights as citizens that gives us security in our everyday lives. It is hard to imagine living in a world without freedom of speech, privacy, and due process by law, but we have to remember that there are people around the world who do not enjoy these basic privileges of American life. It is for this reason that we must always love the Constitution. However, these days it seems people would much rather surf the Internet or watch television than do something to show their love for their country and the Constitution behind it. What happened to the crowds of people, waving American flags, who would line the street for a Fourth of July parade? What happened to those who see Memorial Day as a day to honor those who gave their lives in battle, instead of an excuse

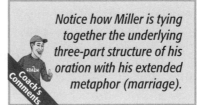

Notice how Miller is tying together the underlying three-part structure of his oration with his extended metaphor (marriage).

A helpful rhetorical device in an oration is to place special emphasis on key points by phrasing them in the form of a question or series of questions.

for a three-day weekend? Too many times marriages have failed because one spouse forgot how lucky they were to have the other person. We as Americans must never forget how lucky we are to have our Constitution. Renewing our vow of love is as simple as singing the national anthem with pride, saying the pledge of allegiance with a smile on our face, and stopping for a moment to watch in awe as our flag flies proudly in the wind.

The second responsibility our vows of marriage have given us is our duty to honor our Constitution. This out of all of our obligations is probably the easiest, considering that our sacred document is nothing short of a miracle. Never before, and probably never again, have so many intelligent and insightful minds been able to congregate and create what our Founding Fathers did in that old Philadelphia statehouse. Some may call it divine intervention, fate, or maybe just dumb luck, but whatever circumstances led to the formation of our Constitution, it remains as the bedrock of both American government and American society. If you ever visit the National Archives in Washington, D.C., you will enter into a large room with a ramp around the edge leading to an altar-like structure at the front. In the glass casing of that altar is the American Constitution. People wait in line for many minutes just to get a few-second glance at our nation's founding document. We as Americans have put our Constitution on a pedestal, not simply because of the role it has played in our nation's history, but because its ingenious structure should be considered the eighth Wonder of the World. The idea of three branches of government, each having checks on the others, is an idea that has allowed us to maintain a stable government for over two centuries. But, the real reason our Constitution stands heads above all other forms of government, is because the Founding Fathers realized that they were not infallible and gave us the amendment process. With Article 5 of the Constitution, we can correct the mistakes of the past, and change our government to meet the needs of the people in changing times. We must always honor the Constitution, or we risk someday forgetting about its beauty, and losing it forever.

To love the Constitution is great, to honor it is even better. But, the only way that we as a country can truly keep this sacred document is to obey the basic principles of democracy that it has given to us. There is an old story that

> *After observing other entrants, Miller advises against memorizing hand gestures and other body language. "Some people get too mechanical in speaking," he says. "Looking natural is as important as looking prepared."*
>
> Coach's Comments

Ben Franklin walked into a tavern after the Constitution was approved by the Philadelphia convention. He sat down and a young waitress came to him and asked, "Well, Doctor Franklin, what have we got, a republic or a monarchy?" Franklin replied, "We have a republic, madam, that is if we can keep it." Franklin knew the success of the Constitution was dependent upon the citizens partaking in the election process and getting involved in government. However, these days, voting seems to be the last priority on everyone's list. According to one study conducted by USelectionatlas.org, only 49 percent of eligible voters voted in the 1996 presidential election. Less than half of the voting population in America cared enough to take a few minutes out of their day and cast their vote. It is a sad day in America when we refuse to partake in the democracy that we value so much. Just as Franklin pointed out to that young waitress in Philadelphia, we have a republic, but we can always lose it, especially if we are lazy, if we just don't care, and if we don't obey the duties of democracy that the Constitution gave us.

A vow of marriage is a vow of commitment, duty, and responsibility. When our Founding Fathers created the Constitution, little did they know that they were engaged to the greatest form of government known to man. When we walked down that sacred aisle of marriage, we walked toward our freedom, and to our destiny. But, the reception is done, the honeymoon is over, and all that remains is the vows of marriage that we took so long ago: to love, honor, and obey. What God and fate hath brought together, let no man put asunder.

> *Many successful American Legion speeches have featured a conclusion that ties directly back to the theme (in this case the concept of marriage) introduced at the beginning of the oration.*
>
> Coach's Comments

To read more from Max Miller's prepared oration, visit the Coach's Locker Room at ScholarshipCoach.com (Keyword: AMLEGORA).

Max Miller
Ankeny, IA
First Prize
$19,500

Winning
Entry

ASSIGNED TOPIC:
ARTICLE 3, SECTIONS 1 AND 2

In this second oration excerpt, Miller likens the U.S. Supreme Court to a marriage counselor who intervenes when disputes arise between the Constitution and the American people.

What separates the good marriages from the bad is how the couple handles the dispute. Bad marriages end in divorce, and good marriages learn from the experience and grow stronger. In American life, the hot topics of the day can get out of hand and disrupt the marriage we have with our Constitution. Fortunately for us, the Constitution has provided an ultimate marriage counselor, the Supreme Court, to interpret the Constitution and work America through its own domestic disputes, and marriage problems.

The ultimate power of the Supreme Court of the United States is judicial review. This is the process where the justices of the Supreme Court examine the constitutionality of state and national laws. This is probably the most accepted function of the Supreme Court, yet it was never intended underneath our constitution. Article 3, Section 1 of the Constitution simply states that a Supreme Court will be formed and will consist of justices who will be paid for their services. Section 2 of this article goes on to list the jurisdiction of the Supreme Court and lists its duties, but nowhere does it outline the power of judicial review. This process of the Supreme Court is the direct result of one Supreme Court case in America's early history.

In the landmark case of *Marbury v. Madison*, John Marshall, chief justice of the Supreme Court, practiced judicial review for the first time in our nation's history. The case came at a time where leadership in our nation was switching from federalists to republicans. The story goes that

When referencing historical details in your speech, it's a good idea to confirm these details with a history or government teacher.

Coach's Comments

John Adams, a federalist, stayed up until midnight on his last day in office issuing new appointments of federalists to high positions of power. One of those appointments was William Marbury to a federal judgeship in Washington, D.C. However, Marbury's appointment was not delivered to him once republican Thomas Jefferson took office. Secretary of State James Madison, who was in charge of delivering the new appointments, refused to give Marbury his position. William Marbury then sued James Madison, claiming that the Supreme Court should force Madison to deliver the appointment. Technically, the court had this power under Section 13 of the Judiciary Act of 1789. John Marshall was in a dilemma in this case because although he believed that Marbury deserved the appointment he had been given, he also believed that the Constitution had not given him the power to interfere with another branch of government. After much consideration, Marshall ruled in favor of Marbury, but also added in the decision that Section 13 of the Judiciary Act was unconstitutional, and therefore the court could do nothing to enforce its decision. At face value, it may look as though Marshall decreased the power of the Supreme Court, but in actuality, he had declared an act of Congress void, and gave the Supreme Court more power than had ever been intended.

Out of the *Marbury v. Madison* case our marriage with the Constitution gained an important tool. Whenever arguments erupt between the people of this nation and our founding document, we have a third-party body that can examine the disagreement and settle it.

To read more from Max Miller's prepared oration, visit the Coach's Locker Room at ScholarshipCoach.com (Keyword: AMLEGORA).

CONTACT INFORMATION

Keyword **AMLEGORA**

For more information on local, district, and state competitions, contact individual American Legion posts in your area.

The Americanism and Children & Youth Division
The American Legion
P.O. Box 1055
Indianapolis, IN 46206

Phone: (317) 630-1249
E-mail: acy@legion.org
Website: www.legion.org

RELATED AWARD PROGRAMS

For more information on a Related Award Program, enter the associated keyword in the "Enter a Keyword" box located in the Coach's Locker Room section of ScholarshipCoach.com

■ Fleet Reserve Association Americanism Essay Contest

Sponsored by another military-affiliated organization, this essay contest invites students in grades 7 through 12 to submit patriotic essays of less than 350 words. Multiple national awards range from $2,000 to $5,000 plus a top prize of $15,000. Entries must be submitted to local FRA branches by an early December deadline.

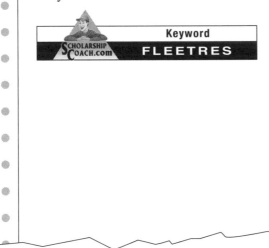

Keyword
FLEETRES

■ Angelfire Scholarship

This program, sponsored by the Datatel Scholars Foundation, is for any student who is a Vietnam veteran, or a child or spouse of a Vietnam veteran, who is attending (or will attend) a Datatel client college. The application includes a personal statement discussing how the Vietnam War personally affected the applicant and their educational goals, as well as how the scholarship will help achieve the outlined goals. Awards are $700, $1,300, or $2,000 (actual amount based on school tuition). Applications must be endorsed by a client college and submitted before the deadline in mid-February.

Keyword
ANGEFIRE

America's Junior Miss

What do *Good Morning America* host Diane Sawyer, television broadcaster Deborah Norville, and *Newhart* actress Mary Frann all have in common? Besides being TV personalities, they were all participants—and scholarship winners—in the America's Junior Miss Program. While the program has evolved considerably over the years, the organization continues to recognize high school girls for their initiative, enthusiasm, poise, and intelligence.

In the modern-day competition, judges evaluate entrants in five major categories: scholastic achievement, fitness, poise, interview skills, and talent. Although the program has elements that resemble a traditional "pageant"—entrants are interviewed in eveningwear on stage and participate in a choreographed "fitness routine" to a cheering crowd—the program has no swimsuit competition, and physical attractiveness is *not* a specific judging criterion.

TARGET RECIPIENT

- High school juniors

ENTRY REQUIREMENTS

DEADLINES

- Varies by state

	Keyword
	AMJUNMIS

Money
$
Matters

Of special note to this program is the generous amount of scholarship money awarded to participants. In addition to the top three national prizes of $50,000, $25,000, and $15,000, four participants on the national level who excel in specific judging categories (scholastic, talent, fitness, and poise) each earn a cool $10,000. Also available on the national level are five finalist scholarship awards ($3,000 each), 16 awards for success in preliminary judging rounds ($2,500 each), and numerous "satellite" awards—given for various endeavors ranging from community service to party planning ($1,000 to $5,000 each).

Each entrant is eligible to win multiple awards. Many participants earn thousands of dollars on the local and state levels alone (the amount of money varies by state) and also become eligible for school-specific awards at more than 20 colleges.

In order to compete in the America's Junior Miss program, applicants must enroll for the competition by their state deadline—typically during the summer between their sophomore and junior years in high school or at the beginning of their junior year. In most cases, entrants compete in the local contest during their junior year or during the first half of their senior year—with subsequent state competitions usually scheduled for the summer before their senior year or during their senior year. Students who advance to the national competition level are sent by their sponsoring states, all expenses paid, to compete for the title of America's Junior Miss. The national finals occur in June each year, soon after high school graduation.

In a recent contest year, the eight national finalists each earned, on average, $1,175 on the local level, $6,675 on the state level, and $21,250 on the national level.

Added
Bonus

There are no application fees for the competition, but entrants are responsible for providing their own clothes (although some outfits may be provided by sponsors).

∎ A Closer Look

The America's Junior Miss program generally has three levels of competition: local, state, and national. Within each level, the competition usually has two separate rounds, the preliminary round and a finalist round. The contestants with the highest overall scores, taking into account all five categories, advance to the finals. Out of the eight finalists at the national level, the top overall scorer is named America's Junior Miss.

All levels of the competition use the same weighted scoring formula: scholastic achievement (worth 20 percent of the overall score), interview (25 percent), fitness (15 percent), talent (25 percent), and poise (15 percent).

On the national level, judges have included representatives from corporate sponsors, past America's Junior Miss winners, star athletes, and arts professionals from such groups as the New Actors Workshop and the National Conservatory of Dramatic Arts.

Two of the five categories, scholastic achievement and the interview, are scored during the week before the on-stage competition begins. Judges score scholastic achievement according to a strict formula that includes points for GPA, standardized test scores, advanced coursework (such as honors or advanced placement classes), and the academic reputation of the high school (as determined by school data supplied by a guidance counselor). For the interview portion of the competition, each competitor answers questions for ten minutes in front of the five-judge panel. For the most part, judges ask questions based on a biographical questionnaire filled out by the contestant prior to the interview.

Judging for the fitness, talent, and poise categories occurs during the on-stage portion of the program. To evaluate fitness, all entrants learn a choreographed routine and perform the routine as a group. The choreographer at each competition briefs the judges before the fitness routine is performed on what they should look for. Typically, entrants who receive higher fitness scores display strong muscle tone during key portions of the routine, land with their feet together at the end of a move, display agility, and have the stamina to refrain from heavy breathing. (Hint: Being keeled over an oxygen tank on the side of the stage is *not* a good sign!) To help the judges make individual evaluations, each competitor is spotlighted alone during a specific portion of the music; at this time, the individual scoring is done.

During the talent portion of the competition, each contestant is given 90 seconds to showcase a talent of her choosing. Talents commonly demonstrated during the competition include singing, dancing, and playing a musical instrument. Contestants who advance to state or

Program administrators emphasize that America's Junior Miss is not a pageant. Rather, it's intended to be a scholarship program that recognizes excellence in young women.

Each contestant is given 90 seconds only. If any contestant takes longer than 90 seconds, she is disqualified.

national competitions are allowed to change their costume, their routine, and even their chosen talent before competing in the next round of judging.

Kentucky Junior Miss Erin Pettigrew dances her way to a third-place finish in the national competition. Pettigrew also took top honors in the scholastic achievement category.

Poise is a combination of two separate judging criteria: confidence on stage and impromptu speaking ability. To demonstrate confidence, contestants walk out on stage dressed in eveningwear. They then demonstrate impromptu speaking ability by delivering a 30-second response to a question based on their biographical questionnaires. The judges listen for content as well as for the confidence and clarity of each competitor's response.

At the national competition, additional "satellite" scholarship awards are also available. To win such awards, contestants submit individual materials for judging. Available scholarship awards include the $1,000 community service award (best essay about a community service activity); the $5,000 "hostess" award (most original and complete plan for a party); the $1,000 "daily journal" award (best written diary entry on the week's events); and the $1,500 "be your best self award" (awarded to the entrant with the finest essay on the "best self" contest theme).

SCHOOL-SPECIFIC SCHOLARSHIP OPPORTUNITIES

Several colleges and universities, such as those schools listed below, provide additional scholarships for America's Junior Miss contestants, finalists, and winners at the local, state, and national levels.

- Albright College
- Averett College
- Campbellsville University
- Columbia College
- Gustavus Adolphus College
- Huntingdon College
- Judson College
- Keystone College
- Lindenwood University
- Marymount University
- Mississippi University for Women
- Missouri Valley College
- Ouachita Baptist University
- Salem-Teikyo University
- Savannah College of Arts and Design
- Spring Hill College
- St. Olaf College
- Troy State University
- University of Alabama
- University of Mobile
- University of South Alabama
- University of West Alabama
- Western Maryland College

▌ COACH'S ANALYSIS

Approach this scholarship competition as if you're auditioning to be a spokesperson for the America's Junior Miss program. This is because the entrant chosen as America's Junior Miss serves exactly in this capacity: Even while embarking on her freshman year in college, she represents the program at numerous public and private functions, schmoozes with current and potential corporate sponsors, and promotes the program's "Be Your Best Self" platform in media appearances.

According to Lynne Bellew, executive director of the program, the judges are instructed to select America's Junior Miss based on an evaluation that goes beyond a direct interpretation of the five judging categories to some extent. "We talk to them [the judges] about what America's Junior Miss is about, the characteristics we look for and the qualities we look for," Bellew emphasizes. "Is she somebody who's working every day to be her best self? If she were walking into a room with reporters for an interview or going to work with a national sponsor, is she personally comfortable with herself in any situation?"

Carrie Colvin, a recent America's Junior Miss first-place national winner from Birmingham, Alabama, agreed that there is a set of hidden judging criteria underlying the five official judging categories—criteria that have a big impact on the eventual outcome. "The judges, as well as looking at the five categories, look at the personality of the girl and her spirit," notes Colvin, now a student at Vanderbilt University. "They know that this girl has to represent either her county, or her state, or the nation, and they want a good representative who can be comfortable in social circumstances where she has to meet people. . . . You have to represent the organization and what it stands for. It's just as much about your personality, spirit, and genuine attitude as it is about those other things."

What specific underlying qualities are judges looking for? According to both program administrators and past participants, these qualities center on traditional American values—things like enthusiasm, character, wholesomeness, civic duty, work ethic, and compassion for others.

How can you best communicate such qualities? Due to their more personal nature, the interview and poise portions of the competition may be your best opportunity to demonstrate these core character traits. Because judges base questions during both the interview and poise portions of the contest on your biographical questionnaire, make sure that your responses to the questionnaire highlight areas of your personality and background that clearly demonstrate such qualities. If you're not sure, for instance, about which of your favorite television shows to include on the form (you're asked this on the questionnaire), select the one that gives you the best lead-in to a topic that highlights your unique and compelling personal perspectives, values, and attributes. (Incidentally, one recent finalist who selected *Friends* as her favorite television show was asked about how popular shows influence young people's behavior.)

Not only should you be prepared to discuss every item on your questionnaire, but you should also be ready to field some current events, issue-oriented, and general knowledge questions. Recent questions have included:

■ Do you feel the Electoral College is necessary in America today?

■ How do you feel about random drug testing in schools?

■ Who are Condoleezza Rice and Donald Rumsfeld?

With one minute left in the interview, Bellew notes, the judges usually ask each competitor if there is anything else she wants to make sure the judges know. Suffice it to say, you should prepare for such a moment ahead of time. The key to preparing this type of response is to try to be specific, to focus on personal experiences and perspectives, to take into account the hidden judging criteria outlined above, and to avoid generic-sounding statements. Avoid the type of statement given all too often by beauty pageant participants—responses that are perceived as little more than lip service to what the judges want to hear. ("My goal for the future is to single-handedly bring about world peace!") It's perfectly fine to give idealistic and optimistic answers, but the key is to back up these statements with concrete and specific examples that demonstrate you truly mean what you say and have thoughtfully considered the statement you are making.

To get an even better understanding of the personal qualities that distinguish the top contestants in the program, make an effort to attend local America's Junior Miss

Insider Info

During the interview, especially at the local or state level, contestants are commonly asked questions about noteworthy government officials in their particular state.

For more interview strategies and techniques, see the first book in my scholarship trilogy, How to Go to College Almost for Free.

competitions in your area and watch the national competition on the TNN cable television channel in late June of each year. (Videotapes of the national competition are also available from the America's Junior Miss organization.) Keep in mind, however, that because two of the five components of the competition (scholastic achievement and the interview) occur prior to the event, the contestant who delivers the best on-stage performance is not always the overall winner.

Q&A WITH AMERICA'S JUNIOR MISS CARRIE COLVIN

To get more details on how best to prepare for the competition, I asked America's Junior Miss Carrie Colvin some additional nuts and bolts questions. Here's what she said:

THE COACH: How should entrants best prepare for the fitness portion of the competition?

COLVIN: The fitness portion of the competition is meant to specifically test the stamina of the girls competing, as well as to be certain that the girl chosen to represent the Junior Miss Program maintains a healthy physique. A girl who is physically fit doesn't need to change her fitness routine; no one is expected to alter her body type or physical capabilities. Personally, I continued dancing and also continued to run to keep up my endurance level.

THE COACH: How did you decide what talent piece to perform?

COLVIN: I wanted to perform a piece that would both appeal to the audience and display my dancing ability. The talent portion is the contestant's chance to shine in her own way! I chose the song "America" from *West Side Story* because it is lively, entertaining, and it seemed to match my personality. Most importantly, though, it was a song that I truly enjoyed listening to and felt like I could hear over and over without growing tired of it.

THE COACH: Were you nervous for the interview or poise segments? How did you overcome your nerves?

COLVIN: The interview and poise portions make me more nervous than any other area of competition. I do not consider myself a natural public speaker and I'm often shy about my ability to communicate. However, the most comforting thought that ran through my head during both events was that the judges were only looking to know me better, and what do I know more about than myself? With that thought in mind, I was able to calm my nerves and speak confidently.

THE COACH: Did you do anything special to prepare for these portions of the competition?

COLVIN: I had my mother and other friends ask me questions from time to time, just to make sure I was comfortable answering questions on the spot. I truly feel like that little bit of practice made a big difference in my interview. Also, though, I tried to stay up to date with major current events in my community and in the nation. The judges are simply looking for a girl who is well informed and can speak plainly about herself and her surroundings. There is no pressure to sound like a politician or professional speaker!

THE COACH: How did you pick what to wear for the poise competition? What type of outfit should an entrant look for?

COLVIN: When I was choosing a dress for the poise competition, I was looking for a dress that I would feel comfortable wearing on stage in front of an audience. I definitely looked for dresses that were not too revealing or too flashy. I think the most important thing to remember when choosing an outfit for poise is that you want the attention to be on what you're saying; the dress is just meant to complement you.

THE COACH: What, in your experience, are the differences between the local, state, and national competitions?

COLVIN: One of the many wonderful aspects of Junior Miss is that there is not much difference between the local, state, and national competitions! I found that I knew exactly what to expect when I moved from local competition to state, and from state to national. The same five areas of competition run throughout all three levels. The one difference could be the size of the competition and the publicity that the competitions attract at each higher level.

THE COACH: What is your best memory from America's Junior Miss?

COLVIN: This is the hardest question of all! The America's Junior Miss Program is much more concerned with making memories than it is with choosing a winner. When a number of girls are brought together, and each of them has the same dreams and aspirations, it is inevitable that strong bonds will form and lifelong friendships will begin. My favorite memory could be the final night of competition when we were all waiting to go on stage. We had reached the culmination of two weeks of rehearsals, parties, special events, and competition, and we were full of anxious excitement and genuine love for each other. It was a great moment!

*Nicole Swanson
Lakeville, MN
Satellite Award
$1,000*

DAILY JOURNAL:
TUESDAY, JUNE 19

Winning
⭐
Entry

In this winning journal entry, Minnesota Junior Miss Nicole Swanson describes a day at the national competition in a fun and conversational way.

"Guys this is the best part of the trip!" I've heard this exclamation at least three times already. We enjoyed the first "best" part at the uppseedaisees slumber party, the second at the Salon Selectives Prom, and today, we

experienced the third thus far: the Coca-Cola beach party. But the phrase "best part" implies singularity—one activity, one speaker, rehearsal, etc. You simply can't use "best" to describe multiple things.

Throughout the afternoon, I tried to pick a single thing that stood out above everything else. And I couldn't. Then, while rinsing the sand out from behind my ears in the shower after returning home at about 8:15 P.M., I had a revelation. The best thing about Junior Miss isn't the fact that we get to eat lots of free food, be celebrities for two weeks, and party every night. (Although I certainly don't mind any of that!) I realized that even though that memory of eating a really good ice cream cone after running around in the Gulf Coast sand probably will stay with me for a while, the things I have learned as a result of these activities will last forever.

Just within the past 24 hours, I have made the following discoveries:

> *When submitting an entry of this type, make it personal, fun, and upbeat. Instead of approaching it as an essay, treat it like a personal letter to a friend.*

- If you have extremely white skin, IT WILL BURN! Even if you wear sunscreen.
- Denim shorts don't air-dry very quickly.
- Time flies when you're competing in a timed sand sculpture competition. And it goes really slowly during a car ride to the beach.
- It is possible to stay up until 2:30 A.M. talking to your host brother and survive the next day on just over four hours of sleep.
- Even if the above situation occurs, you will hear your roommate's alarm clock when it goes off at 7:09 A.M. in the next room.
- Alabama strawberries are delicious!
- You can step on jellyfish at least seven times and not get stung, but don't try this one at home!
- Southern accents are contagious, y'all!
- When you think nobody's looking at you, someone is probably taking your picture.

All of that happened in one day! I can't even begin to fathom how many fragments of wisdom will deposit themselves in my head by the time I leave Mobile. Thanks to the kindness and generosity of everyone involved in every facet of the Junior Miss program, I'll return to Minnesota with a deeper understanding of Southern hospitality, good ol' home cooking and what it truly means to "be your best self."

Dawn Bentz
Hope, KS
Satellite Award
$1,500

BE YOUR BEST SELF

Winning
Entry

In her winning essay, Kansas Junior Miss Dawn Bentz relates how overcoming an eating disorder led her to "be her best self."

The year was 1999, and I was about to start my junior year at Hope High School. For most, it was the beginning of another school year, but for me, it was the beginning of a new life! I was a new person with new energy and new goals and dreams.

My first two years of high school had been very difficult for me. My dad had been killed in a farming accident the summer before my freshman year. My family decided to remain on the farm, and Mom took over the operation of the farm completely. The first year was hard on all of us. I distracted myself with gymnastics and spent as little time as possible at home. I qualified for Nationals as an Optional Level 8 gymnast that year. It was a dream come true. However, the sport was becoming too time consuming for the family as a whole. The long drive and the 20 to 24 hours of required practice a week became too much to handle with only one parent. I do not regret quitting gymnastics, because my dream now had an ending. I was a nationally ranked gymnast.

Everything seemed to be perfect for the outsider looking in. The farm was doing well. I was becoming more involved with school sports and activities, and everyone seemed to be

> According to Bentz, the strength of her essay doesn't reside in a particular sentence or paragraph. "It's strong because it's real," she emphasizes. "It's a true story about a girl finding out who she is and the power she possesses."
>
> Coach's Comments

adjusting to the drastic change in our household, but not everyone was. I had refused to deal with Dad's death when it happened. I had kept myself busy so I would not have to face the drastic changes it caused in our lives. Now I had plenty of free time and was being forced to live and deal with it.

I settled into a silent depression, drawing myself into an invisible shell so no one could know that "the perfect girl" was weak and hurting. I was losing my appetite, sleep, and my drive and determination to do anything. I started to lose weight and my stomach eventually shrunk. My condition only grew worse.

More and more meals were being skipped and less and less sleep was being attained.

I hid it all very well. But in April, I realized that I had a problem. I confidentially went to my counselor, Mrs. Burkholder, and told her that I thought I was anorexic. I did not want anyone to know, including my mom and family. Mom had enough to deal with, and I did not want to add another burden to her shoulders or make her feel like she failed me. I had always been viewed as the talented, strong individual and felt like my anorexia was a weakness that society would not allow.

Bentz says that she wasn't sure if she should write about her experience with anorexia. But in the end, she decided to discuss it because "maybe there was a person out there struggling with a similar situation and by some miracle my essay might help them."

That summer I began the painful, silent road to recovery by myself. My only allies were a book Mrs. Burkholder had given me, and a journal. I hid them between my mattresses to insure no one would ever find them. When rehabilitated at the end of the summer, I told my mom, my older sister, and my brother-in-law about my anorexia.

I was a new person my junior year of high school! I had come to terms with my dad's death and learned to deal with it properly. I was no longer anorexic and I had no desire to skip a meal. I possessed a new energy that came from this wonderful feeling of freedom.

This was when I really began to "Be My Best Self." I re-dedicated myself to my schoolwork and my name returned to the Distinguished Honors List. My life had a healthy balance of diet and exercise. I read about nutrition, exercise, and eating disorders and became informed on all of the topics. I played sports at school or worked out three times a week and properly fueled my body with three balanced meals a day. I also became more involved with the school's organizations and the church's community service projects. This wonderful emotion of hope was overflowing in my life, and I viewed community service as a chance to pass it on. I continued to get better and better. My drive and determination were strong as ever. So many goals were established that year. Many of them have been accomplished, but the most important one is still in the making. I made a decision that I was going to dedicate my life to helping people with the same problem I once had. If I had a companion or mentor who I felt I could confide in and would completely

What makes this essay stand out is its honesty and use of personal details. "Be completely honest with yourself and your audience," Bentz suggests. "Write about what you know . . . you!"

understand what I was going through, my recovery would have been a lot easier.

The greatest discovery I made that year was myself. I had lived my life trying to please everyone else, being their ideal of my best self. I learned I could "Be My Best Self" for me. This is the key: believing in yourself and giving 110 percent all of the time. I can possess joy every day now, knowing I am achieving my dreams for me.

CONTACT INFORMATION

To participate in the program you must first contact your state AJM representative.

America's Junior Miss
P.O. Box 2786
Mobile, AL 36652-2786

Phone: (800) 256-5435, (334) 438-3621
Fax: (334) 431-0063
E-mail: ajmiss@ajm.org
Website: www.ajm.org

RELATED AWARD PROGRAMS

For more information on a Related Award Program, enter the associated keyword in the "Enter a Keyword" box located in the Coach's Locker Room section of ScholarshipCoach.com

■ America's National Teenager

Following the "not-a-pageant" format, young women ages 12 to 18 compete in the areas of scholastic achievement, community service and leadership, communications skills, talent, and poise. Various awards from $1,500 to $10,000 are provided. Additional awards for talent and delivering a winning oral essay on a topic related to "What's right about America"

are also given. The national competition is held in July.

■ Miss Active Teen Across America

Young women ages 13 through 19 with a GPA above 2.5 are eligible for this competition. Entrants are judged based on six criteria:

goals, family involvement, an essay, activities and accomplishments, a volunteer project, and scholastic record. State awards can range up to $1,000; national awards vary by year. Preliminary applications are due in June.

Keyword
MISACTIV

■ Pre-Teen America Scholarship and Recognition Program

This award program spotlights the accomplishments of girls ages 7 through 12. The selection criteria includes academic achievement, school and volunteer activities, development of personal skills, communicative ability, general knowledge, and on-stage talent. More than $25,000 is divided among winning national contestants, with additional awards available on the state level. Because the program is offered in over 40 states, with each state having different deadlines, students should check with their state representatives for location-specific entry due dates (generally July or August).

Keyword
PRETAMER

Arts Recognition and Talent Search

TARGET RECIPIENT

- High school seniors
- College freshmen

ENTRY REQUIREMENTS

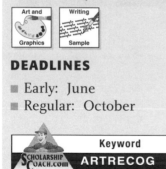

Art and Graphics

Writing Sample

DEADLINES

- Early: June
- Regular: October

Keyword
ARTRECOG

Put another way, if you haven't yet turned 19 on December 1, you're good to go!

Money Matters

Each year, a crowd of creative students from all over the country descends upon the pastel-colored glitter and glamour of one of America's most exciting cities. Welcome to Miami, Florida—where talented student musicians, dancers, artists, and writers engage in a weekend packed with workshops, performances, exhibitions, and, uh, election vote recounts.

Sponsored by the National Foundation for the Advancement of the Arts, a group dedicated to encouraging and supporting young artistic talent, the Arts Recognition and Talent Search (ARTS) program awards a number of lucrative cash prizes. To participate in the ARTS competition, students must either be graduating high school seniors or else be age 17 or 18 on December 1 of the year they are applying. (As a result of this age eligibility rule, many college freshmen are also able to enter.) Entrants must also be citizens or permanent residents of the United States or official U.S. territories.

There is no shortage of monetary awards offered to participants in the ARTS competition; prizes range from $100 to $3,000. In addition to the monetary awards, the top 125 entrants receive an all-expense-paid week in Miami, where they participate in classes taught by professionals in their disciplines, go through an interview or audition process for various awards, and showcase their artistic talents in performances and exhibitions. Top ARTS week participants in music-related disciplines are eligible for an additional

Painted in vivid blues, oranges, and greens, Allison Hult's *Ants Picnic* entry (right) was recognized as a Level 1 winner in the visual arts category. To view a color version of her winning entry, visit ScholarshipCoach.com (Keyword: ARTRECOG).

$25,000 prize from an affiliated program.

Students may submit work in the following nine categories: dance, music/instrumental, music/jazz, music/voice, theater, visual arts, film and video, photography, and writing. There are specific requirements for each of the nine categories, as well as general requirements for all entrants.

Students may enter in as many categories as they wish, but there is a nonrefundable fee of $25 per entry if application packets are sent in before the early June deadline and a fee of $35 per entry for the early October deadline. Fees must be paid for each category or subcategory in which a student wishes to compete.

There may be earlier deadlines for the ARTS regional programs.

▌ A CLOSER LOOK

After sending in a preliminary application (listing general contact and biographical information), students receive another application packet that details specific entry requirements for each artistic discipline (including formatting instructions for manuscripts, audio and video tapes, and slides). Students may enter and win in multiple categories.

Historically, the ARTS competition has been a national competition, but the National Foundation for the Advancement of the Arts has recently created some regional programs as well. Depending on their home state, students will either enter a preliminary regional competition first or else have their entries forwarded directly to the national program.

Within the nine major artistic categories, students may submit work in more than 60 disciplines that span a

Utah State University's Ben Francisco submitted this *Quartet*, showing judges his artistic vision and skill. (Is it just me, or would these ceramics look great in my house!)

Consult the official application for any newly recognized disciplines.

wide range of artistic pursuits. (The program includes new artistic disciplines as demand for them increases.) A complete listing of these disciplines is shown in the following box. Typically, the largest number of entries is in the music and visual arts categories.

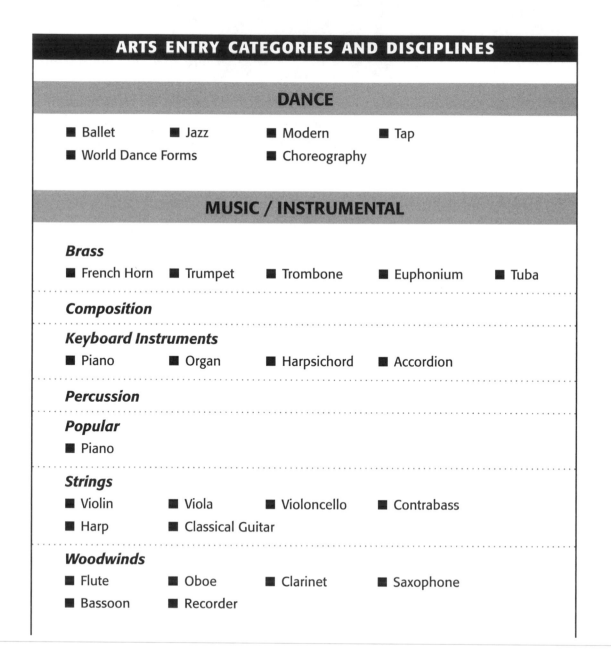

ARTS ENTRY CATEGORIES AND DISCIPLINES

DANCE

- Ballet
- Jazz
- Modern
- Tap
- World Dance Forms
- Choreography

MUSIC / INSTRUMENTAL

Brass
- French Horn
- Trumpet
- Trombone
- Euphonium
- Tuba

Composition

Keyboard Instruments
- Piano
- Organ
- Harpsichord
- Accordion

Percussion

Popular
- Piano

Strings
- Violin
- Viola
- Violoncello
- Contrabass
- Harp
- Classical Guitar

Woodwinds
- Flute
- Oboe
- Clarinet
- Saxophone
- Bassoon
- Recorder

MUSIC / JAZZ

- Jazz-Keyboard
- Jazz-Violin
- Jazz-Viola
- Jazz-Cello
- Jazz-Db. Bass
- Jazz-Guitar
- Jazz-Flute
- Jazz-Oboe
- Jazz-Clarinet
- Jazz-Saxophone
- Jazz-Trumpet
- Jazz-Trombone
- Jazz-Percussion
- Jazz-Vocal
- Jazz-Composition
- Jazz-Other

MUSIC / VOICE

- Soprano
- Mezzo Soprano
- Contralto
- Tenor
- Baritone
- Bass
- Popular Voice

THEATER

- Spoken
- Spoken and Musical Theater

Note: Students may enter only one of the two theater disciplines.

VISUAL ARTS

- Ceramics
- Costume Design
- Drawing
- Graphic Design
- Jewelry Making
- Painting
- Prints
- Sculpture
- Textile Design
- Theater and Set Design
- Other

Note: In the visual arts category, all artistic disciplines are grouped together, and entrants may include works in different disciplines as part of the same visual arts entry. A separate entry fee is not required for each discipline.

FILM & VIDEO

Note: There are no distinct disciplines within this category. All entries are grouped together.

PHOTOGRAPHY

Note: There are no distinct disciplines within this category. All entries are grouped together.

WRITING

- Poetry
- Short Story
- Selection from Novel
- Play or Script for Film or Video
- Expository Writing

During their week in Miami, Jennifer Forsythe and Isaac Oliver participated in intensive workshop sessions. Their dedication and talent earned them both Level 1 awards.

Once the submitted applications are collected, preliminary judging begins: A group of Florida educators and professionals—including arts instructors from the University of Miami and Florida International University as well as members of the Florida Philharmonic—cull through the applications, eliminating those applicants who don't meet a minimum standard of excellence for 17- and 18-year-olds. According to program officer Gena Kuczwanski, at this stage in the competition typically about 25 percent of the applicants make the initial cut.

In the intermediate judging round, a national judging panel comprised of well-known professionals in each artistic discipline descends on Miami in a sea of pastel-colored shirts. (Play "Miami Vice" theme song here.) At this phase of the judging, each entry is reviewed by a minimum of two judges, with a third judge consulted if there is a great disparity in scores.

Insider Info

Those who don't qualify for the ARTS weekend may still receive a $100 honorable mention award.

Each year, 125 entrants are invited to participate in the Miami ARTS week: The breakdown typically consists of 20 actors, 20 classical musicians, 5 jazz musicians, 20 dancers, 10 singers, 20 visual artists, 5 photographers, 20 writers, and 5 filmmakers.

The judges for the national round are the same

Jill Penney's creative use of multiple media helped her stand out from other entrants. Penney combined plastic, wire, fabric, and paint in this untitled work.

professionals who teach the classes and workshops in each discipline. A recent ARTS week, for instance, featured four writing judges—two playwrights, a poet, and a short-story writer. For the classical music category, the judges included a violinist, a pianist, a clarinetist, and a composer. Recent notables have included Poet Laureate David Lee, dancer Lupe Cerano, jazz musician Justin Dicioccio, theater professional Anthony Rapp, and photographer Bruce Weber.

Based on the performance critique of the judges at ARTS week and a 20-minute, one-on-one interview, judges rate each finalist on a five-tier scale—with each tier assigned a different cash award amount. Students may either be rated Level 1 ($3,000), Level 2 ($2,000), Level 3 ($1,500), Level 4 ($1,000), or Level 5 ($500). Unlike many other art-based awards programs, students are compared to a level of achievement instead of competing directly against one another. In a recent year, for instance, all five jazz finalists received Level 1 awards. According to program officer Gena Kuczwanski, the average award for all 125 finalists was $1,800.

Because students may enter and win in multiple categories, there is a potential to win considerably more than $3,000. Isaac Oliver of Bronxville, New York, for instance, won a total of $6,100 in college cash—$3,000 in the short-story subcategory, $3,000 more for playwriting, and another $100 for his honorable mention in poetry. In addition to the categories he was recognized for, Oliver also entered the personal essay and musical theater categories.

Success in the ARTS program also makes one eligible for other prestigious awards. The Music for Youth organization provides three prizes of $25,000 each to the top voice, music, or jazz participants at national ARTS week. In addition, up to 20 students attending the ARTS week competition also have the opportunity to be nominated as Presidential Scholars—an honor that is given to only 141 high school students each year in the United States. To be eligible for this honor, students must receive a Level 1 or 2 rating.

This unique photograph was taken by Mara Soldinger, a Level 1 award winner.

CATEGORY-SPECIFIC JUDGING CRITERIA

The following are judging criteria for each main artistic category of the ARTS competition.

DANCE

Performance

- **Artistry:** Causes a response in the audience through creativity and sincerity.
- **Musicality and phrasing:** Physical expression of the melody, rhythm, nuance, and character of the music.
- **Presentation:** Physical presentation of the artist up to the standards of the style.
- **Technique:** Ability to convey choreography with ease and proficiency.

Choreography

- **Concept:** Clarity of purpose expressed in the dance.
- **Movement invention:** Exploration of movement as presented in the dance.
- **Development of thematic material:** Elements that link the performance together.
- **Choreographic texture:** Variety in the expression of ideas.
- **Individuality of creative voice:** Original ideas, form, and presentation. Students using a traditional dance form need to demonstrate both new ideas within the traditional form and originality of conceptual ideas.

MUSIC

- **Interpretation:** Ability to present a clear, convincing concept of the piece.
- **Intonation:** Playing or singing in tune/proper tuning of the instrument.
- **Phrasing:** Recognition of the need for phrasing and ability to use it.
- **Rhythm:** Able to establish, maintain, and project complex rhythms.
- **Technique:** The level of control of the voice or instrument.
- **Tone production:** Quality of sound appropriate to the music style and the instrument or voice.
- **Diction** (voice only)**:** Clear and accurate articulation and pronunciation.

■ **Improvisation** (jazz only): Ability to use the chord progression of the music to create new melodies, rhythms, and motifs.

Composition

■ **Control of medium:** Idiomatic use and understanding of instruments and voices.

■ **Musical ideas:** The quality of the material.

■ **Musical structure:** Existence and apparentness of an underlying structure.

THEATER

■ **Flexibility and versatility of voice, movement, and expression:** Ability to interpret different forms of theatrical expression.

■ **Vocal and physical phrasing and articulation:** Use of voice and physical expression to convey the reality of the role.

■ **Concentration:** Commitment to the performance.

■ **Control of material:** Ability to make the performance believable to audience.

■ **Knowledge of context of material:** Appropriate performance of a piece based on its context in a larger work.

VISUAL ARTS, PHOTOGRAPHY, FILM & VIDEO

■ **Competence:** Ability to use the chosen medium to express original ideas.

■ **Imagination:** Creativity and freshness of ideas, readiness to take creative risks.

■ **Skillful use of materials:** Clear expression of intent of work.

■ **Creation of emotional interest in the audience:** Conveys artist's feelings clearly.

■ **Development of original ideas:** Quality extent of the body of work.

WRITING

■ **Imagination:** Creativity and freshness of ideas.

■ **Language:** Use and appropriateness of language.

■ **Originality:** Unique way of presenting the material.

■ **Overall excellence:** Talent and promise as a writer.

❚ COACH'S ANALYSIS

To maximize their chances to win, entrants must carefully choose their submission material—exhibits that showcase unique talents. According to Isaac Oliver, a winner in three different writing disciplines, you should pick submissions that illustrate your artistic range for categories that require multiple examples of your work. "I tried to pick three stories that were very different from each other," Oliver explains about his winning entries in the short-story category. "Each story revealed something different about me."

Edith Hines, a violinist from Kalamazoo, Michigan, who received both the Level 1 award and the $25,000 Music for Youth prize, suggests following a similar strategy for performance categories. "I chose to perform a concerto because it was fiery and a Beethoven sonata because it was very lyrical. I found pieces that could demonstrate the entire range of my ability."

Once the work is selected for submission, the primary task then is to create the best version of the work. Many past ARTS winners have received substantial feedback from teachers, fellow students, and professional

Edith Hines dreams of being a professional chamber musician. Hines is saving her winnings from this and other contests to purchase a new violin.

artists in their communities on how to improve their work. For each of Oliver's writing submissions, for instance, he created a chart that listed what he intended to communicate on one side of the paper and what his readers thought he communicated on the other side.

"My work changed virtually 100 percent through the revision process," relates Oliver. "The week before the submission deadline was one of the most creative periods of my life."

For those in the performing arts fields, putting together a best-work exhibit also means creating a quality audition tape. "When a judging committee listens to your tape, they assume it's your best work," explains Kevin Rivard, a French horn player from St. Petersburg, Florida, who received a Level 1 award as well as the $25,000 Music for Youth prize. "Find a room that's suitable, get a good accompanist, and purchase a quality audiotape. If you miss a note, stop and do

Striving to capture his best performance, French horn player Kevin Rivard spent four hours recording his audition tape to get a 15- to 20-minute submission.

it again. Since you have unlimited takes to get it right, your tape better be perfect." Although some student musicians decide to go into professional recording studios, others have been equally successful finding suitable areas at their school (such as an auditorium or concert hall) and using rented or borrowed recording devices.

Insider Info

As for ARTS week itself, attendees should come to the event not only with open minds but also with heartfelt enthusiasm for their craft. Because judges are evaluating artistic potential, they are also considering each student's ability to take instruction and handle constructive criticism. Level 1 vocalist Charles Jones, a freshman at the University of Southern California when he participated in the ARTS program, credits his ability to work with ARTS instructors as an important reason he received the program's top rating and $3,000 prize.

"I did exactly what they [the instructors] told me to do, and they liked that I could change singing styles on the spot," Jones emphasizes. "The people who were like, 'I'm doing it my way, I'm not changing,' seemed to get the lower scores. The people who really listened and were flexible got the higher scores because they were easy to work with and showed a willingness to learn."

*Jennifer Forsythe
Birmingham, AL
Level 1 Award
$3,000*

Winning

Entry

SELECTION FROM A NOVEL: "MURRAY"

In this excerpt from her winning ARTS entry, Jennifer Forsythe tells the story of an unconventional protagonist named Murray.

My name is Murray, and I am a coat rack. Needless to say, I do not have many friends. My mother, who sighs and says she loves me, is not even my friend.

I guess the moment I first realized this was about four summers ago. I was sent home from camp on charges of alleged homesickness. The counselors

thought that because I was not interested in the itinerary Camp Ruddy Pines had to offer I was surely seized with a vitriolic longing for . . . my home. I hadn't the emotional scope, at the time, to find my situation amusing. Not everyone enjoys riflery. And, being a coat rack, I am incapable of riding a horse.

When I asked the children if they wanted me to hold their coats they refused me. I do not understand children. Why would anyone be satisfied with wrinkly clothing? I secretly suspect that the children complained about me to their supervisors, but it is no secret that camp counselors are prejudiced against coat racks.

My mother was silent and hollow-cheeked when she came to pick me up. She demanded a conference with the camp's director. I deducted that he was unrelenting to her pleas, as I returned home with the squinty-eyed woman, who was obviously sucking in her cheeks. People do not always accept unchangeable circumstances as coat racks do. My mother, besides being unnecessarily confused, is not a coat rack. She is human. I secretly suspect that I was adopted. Either that or my father was a coat rack. This could be true, but I doubt it. I feel that I am only a coat rack.

> *Forsythe says that the inspiration for this piece came from a choir bus trip. "Everyone was taking their robes and throwing them on me,"* she notes. *"I said 'I'm not a coat rack!'"*

I have never met my father, and my mother has never spoken of him. Though it is possible, I think it is less than likely that my mother had an inappropriate relationship with a coat rack. However, I am not going to completely discard the idea. Nothing is impossible. The world does not make sense.

I attempted to impart this wisdom to my mother but she remained closed-minded. I explained to her the deeply rooted prejudices of the Camp Burry Pinecone staff, and she refused to talk to me until Thursday.

I do not think my mother is cruel. Her exasperation is a natural human reaction. Why are people scared of me? I am not hard to understand. I am a place to hang coats. It is my purpose. Had my mother not spoken to me for months, I could have accepted my situation. What many people do not know is that coat racks are extremely adaptable.

> *Because Forsythe didn't have a background in creative writing, she didn't want to enter* Murray *in the ARTS contest. Her mother, however, made her apply anyway. (Good call, mom!)*

To read more from Jennifer Forsythe's winning entry, visit the Coach's Locker Room at ScholarshipCoach.com (Keyword: ARTRECOG).

Isaac Oliver
Baltimore, MD
Level 1 Award
$3,000

SHORT STORY: "DIRECTION"

In this very short story, which numbers fewer than 400 words, Isaac Oliver demonstrates that one can communicate a great deal in a small amount of space.

The little things told me I was losing Zachary. He never came out and said it. We never fought about it. There was less eye contact over cold cereal in the morning. He learned how to tie his own tie. He started asking for directions.

I would look out the car window and feel my stomach sink as we turned onto the correct street. There was something about following the same route home in a city filled with roads and right turns.

We started talking. Not really about anything, just vocalizing. It was as if what floated around us so gently before now needed to be said—I was suddenly afraid that he would miss it. Little things like "Excuse me," or "Pass the business section," or maybe even a "Sorry, I didn't mean to kick you," in the middle of the night. In our suddenly empty midnight silence, I would look up to see if there was anything unspeakable left, only to find a dark ceiling wishing the moon would look its way.

His touch was very gentle. That was the first thing I noticed about him. In the mornings I would feel it on my shoulder, whether he was brushing something off of my shirt or just checking to see if I was still there. In the evenings his touch was like a universe of unknowns—I could never predict it; I would never tame it. He molded me each time in some new direction, as if I was some piece of clay, soft in his hands.

> **Coach's Comments**
>
> Oliver says the story started out much longer but his teacher told him "less is more." He wound up cutting two-thirds of his initial draft because he wanted to capture the loneliness of the protagonist by having the story limited to "one lone page."

I reached for his hand the other night on the subway. I guess you could say I needed it—I needed him to give me shape. Eyes slid down our bodies. And he let go. I could feel one finger at a time slipping from his, out into the air, out into the open, out into the streets and the vendors and the lights and the cracks of the sidewalks.

Suddenly liquefying in a million different directions. I turned to him and his eyes were pallid—frozen and unmistakable. I gripped the seat below me, trying to find something solid, but suddenly I couldn't hide anymore—I was alone and shapeless in a city full of wrong ways home.

As a multi-category winner, Oliver advises submitting work in as many artistic disciplines as you can.

CONTACT INFORMATION

Keyword
ARTRECOG

Students from Illinois, Iowa, Minnesota, North Dakota, South Dakota, and Wisconsin must apply through the Regional ARTS program.

National Program:
NFAA/ARTS
800 Brickell Avenue, Suite 500
Miami, FL 33131

Phone: (800) 970-ARTS
E-mail: info@nfaa.org
Website: www.ARTSawards.org

Regional Program:
NFAA/Regional ARTS
150 E. Gilman Street, Suite 1250
Madison, WI 53703

E-mail: Elliott@nfaa.org
Website: www.ARTSawards.org

RELATED AWARD PROGRAMS

For more information on a Related Award Program, enter the associated keyword in the "Enter a Keyword" box located in the Coach's Locker Room section of ScholarshipCoach.com

■ **BMI Student Composer Awards**

Students under 26 who are currently studying music and are citizens of a country in the Western Hemisphere are eligible for these awards from the BMI Foundation, a division of the American performing rights organization that represents songwriters, composers, and music publishers in all genres of music. Each applicant should submit a musical score written in the classical tradition. There are no limitations on the length of each score, nor are there restrictions as to style or instruments to be used. A total of $20,000 is divided among the winners in increments of $500 to $5,000. The number of winners varies each year. The musical scores are due in early February.

	Keyword
SCHOLARSHIP COACH.com	**BMISCOMP**

■ **Donna Reed Performing Arts Scholarships**

Honoring the Academy Award–winning actress who starred in movies such as *It's a Wonderful Life* and *From Here to Eternity* and television programs such as *The Donna Reed Show,* these scholarships recognize students who excel in the performing arts. High school senior and undergraduate actors, singers, musical actors, dancers, and musicians compete for five $4,000 scholarships and ten $500 awards. They are also invited to participate in a week-long performing arts festival. Entries in each category require separate video or audiotapes. The application deadline is in mid-March.

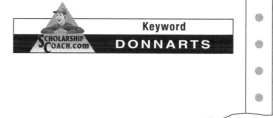

	Keyword
SCHOLARSHIP COACH.com	**DONNARTS**

Ayn Rand Institute Essay Contests

With the publication of such thought-provoking novels as *The Fountainhead* and *Atlas Shrugged*, Ayn Rand established herself as a talented, controversial, and often-mispronounced writer and philosopher. ("Ayn" rhymes with wine.) Decades later, the Ayn Rand Institute—an organization dedicated to promoting Ayn Rand's philosophy of objectivism—seeks to award substantial cash prizes to a wide range of younger and older students for writing compelling essays on Ayn Rand's multifaceted works of fiction.

The Ayn Rand Institute sponsors three separate essay-writing contests: one for ninth and tenth graders, another for eleventh and twelfth graders, and a third contest for college undergraduates.

Money $ Matters

Students in the ninth and tenth grades write and submit a 600- to 1,200-word essay on Ayn Rand's novelette *Anthem*. The institute selects one first-prize winner ($2,000), 10 second-prize winners ($500), 20 third-prize winners ($200), 45 finalists ($50), and 175 semifinalists ($30).

Money $ Matters

Applicants for the eleventh- and twelfth-grade contest write an 800- to 1,600-word essay on Ayn Rand's novel *The Fountainhead*. One first-prize winner receives a $10,000 award, five second-prize winners receive $2,000 each, and ten third-prize winners each receive $1,000. In addition, the program doles out smaller awards to 35 finalists ($100) and 200 semifinalists ($50).

Money
$
Matters

Winners of the Anthem
and The Fountainhead
*competitions are typically
notified by early June;*
Atlas Shrugged *award
recipients are notified
by late October.*

Students of any age who are currently enrolled in a full-time undergraduate degree program may enter the *Atlas Shrugged* contest by submitting a 1,000- to 1,200-word essay. Applicants compete for one first-place prize of $5,000, three second-place prizes ($1,000), and five third-prize awards ($400).

All prizes are unrestricted cash awards. Applicants are permitted to submit essays to the competition year after year—and may even win in multiple years—with the one exception being that past winners of the *Atlas Shrugged* essay contest are not eligible to reapply.

Anthem contest entries are generally due in mid-March. Essay submissions for *The Fountainhead* competition are due in mid-April. Applicants must submit their *Atlas Shrugged* essays by mid-September of each year.

▮ A CLOSER LOOK

For each contest, students may choose to write on one of three essay topics; the topics vary from year to year. Recent essay topics for each contest have included:

For *Anthem*:

▮ *Anthem* depicts a world of the future, a collectivist dictatorship in which even the word "I" has vanished. How does this collectivist system maintain power and control over its subjects? Discuss the hero's struggle to free himself from collectivism. What makes his victory possible?

▮ Compare the story of Adam and Eve's expulsion from the Garden of Eden to the story of Prometheus and Gaea in *Anthem*. For what "sins" was each condemned?

For *The Fountainhead*:

▌ In his climactic courtroom speech Howard Roark states, "The creator's concern is the conquest of nature. The parasite's concern is the conquest of men." Explain this quote's relationship to the theme as dramatized through the characters of Howard Roark, Peter Keating, and Ellsworth Toohey.

▌ *The Fountainhead* offers a vision of a totally independent man, an uncompromising innovator "standing alone against the world." How do the events of the story dramatize the conflict between independence and conformity? Explain how the novel's message is opposed to the conventional view that life requires compromise.

For *Atlas Shrugged*:

▌ Ayn Rand described the theme of *Atlas Shrugged* as the role of the mind in man's existence. How do the events and characters in the novel dramatize this theme? Discuss how the role of the mind is regarded in today's world.

▌ Many people try to defend capitalism solely on the grounds of its economic efficiency. Using the events and characters in the novel, contrast this with Ayn Rand's moral defense of capitalism as dramatized in *Atlas Shrugged*.

Regardless of the specific essay contest, the first phase of judging examines the quality of writing, to rule out entries that have obvious spelling, grammatical, and organizational problems. Screeners in this initial round don't spend much (if any) time evaluating the *content* of the essay; the focus is on the overall mechanics of the writing itself.

There are either one or two intermediate rounds, depending on the specific essay contest.

Once essays have advanced beyond the first round of judging, the focus shifts to content during the intermediate judging rounds. In this phase of the judging process, two separate graders—including both graduate students and college professors from around the country—read each essay. These judges examine the depth of each essay writer's understanding of the text. Although each judge employs his or her own methodology, judges frequently separate essays according to essay topic so that essays on similar topics can be evaluated together. If there is an extreme grade differential between the two judges for any given essay, they are required to discuss the essay and reach a scoring consensus.

A single final-round judge selects the winners for each essay contest, including the level of the prize awarded to each entrant. For the *Fountainhead* competition, John Ridpath, a retired former professor at York University and a recognized scholar of Ayn Rand's work, has been serving as this final decision maker. Each year he reads through the top 20 papers as determined by the initial rounds of judging, disregarding all points assigned by earlier judges. He then groups the essays into four piles: (1) definite winners, (2) acceptable papers, (3) weak papers, and (4) definite nonwinners. Those papers that make the top pile typically receive the first- and second-prize awards.

Darryl Wright, a Professor of Philosophy at Harvey Mudd College, has served as the single final-round judge for the *Anthem* competition (as well as a third-round judge for the *Fountainhead* contest). When evaluating essays, Wright makes notes on the back of the actual essay—jotting down what he likes and doesn't like—after his initial reading. He later comes back and re-reads the essays, comparing his second reaction to his initial reaction, and then ranks all of the essays in his pile in order of strongest to weakest.

▌ COACH'S ANALYSIS

To help with their analyses of Rand's literary works, many past winners have found it valuable to read some of her nonfiction writing. This approach can provide a better understanding of some of the more veiled concepts underlying her fictional stories. Don't spend a lot of time reading these other books at the expense of composing your essay, but do scan them for potentially useful information.

In preparation for his essay on *Atlas Shrugged,* first-place winner David Press, who attends Wichita State University, read Rand's nonfiction work *Capitalism: The Unknown Ideal.* "The nonfiction book gave me a lot of ideas about where to go with my essay," states Press. "By reading the nonfiction book and learning about the philosophy behind *Atlas Shrugged,* I learned what the Ayn Rand Institute would think is important in her fiction."

Program judges agree that familiarizing yourself with some of Rand's nonfiction can make the themes in her fiction more transparent. "Being familiar with Ayn Rand's other writings is helpful," Ridpath offers. "If you have some understanding of Ayn Rand's views from a philosophical perspective, then you would have a framework of knowledge to appreciate her fictional characters."

When you scan her nonfiction writing as background information, use it to help your comprehension and analysis, but avoid quoting her nonfiction work directly in your essay. Your essay should focus on the fiction work itself. "Too often I find students trying to impress the reader with their knowledge of objectivism, instead of explicating the novel," emphasizes Andrew Bernstein, another essay judge. "The best papers usually don't directly mention or quote from Ayn Rand's nonfiction."

Insider Info

Once you've developed this knowledge base, it's time to tackle the essay itself. To start with, be strategic about the essay question you choose to answer. Because essays on the same topic are usually compared to one another in the judging process, you want to make sure to pick a topic that gives you enough room to demonstrate your analytical skills. "One of the topics seemed a little too easy, there wasn't enough to talk about," explains first-place *Anthem* winner Daniel Higginbotham of Lynchburg, Virginia. "Another topic seemed like it would take too much work." Higginbotham chose the third option, and ended up taking home the $2,000 prize.

As you begin writing, don't commit the common error of retelling the story. After all, the judges for these essay contests have likely read Ayn Rand's books more times than Britney Spears has bared her midriff. (In fact, one of contest's judges actually *wrote* the CliffsNotes!) "Retelling the story is a good reason for getting eliminated at an early stage," says Wright, who has served as a judge for more than a decade.

To put yourself in the winner's circle, make sure your essay accomplishes three major objectives. First, don't neglect to analyze the books on a metaphorical level. According to Ridpath, one of the biggest mistakes entrants make is taking a *literal* view of a character's motivation instead of developing a deeper *metaphorical* understanding. "It is very common for students to say Howard Roark is driven by his love for architecture," Ridpath explains in reference to the main character of *The Fountainhead*. "This is not some inexplicable drive, but his passion for architecture is representative of something deeper—an independent mind."

Second, don't just make broad statements; back them up with specifics from *Anthem, The Fountainhead*, or *Atlas Shrugged*. "It's easy to work up some raw generalities," Wright comments. "The top students use details from the text to support their statements. They go to the text and show where the evidence lies."

Third, when you analyze the books, pay special attention to the role of each character in fortifying Rand's objectivist philosophy. To further distinguish yourself,

Focus your essay on your understanding of what Ayn Rand is trying to communicate. Your essay shouldn't be about whether or not you agree or disagree with Rand. (In fact, many people disagree with her views.)

Insider Info

try to communicate your understanding of Rand's more subtle nuances by discussing the significance of some of the relatively minor characters in the story. "What distinguishes the top papers is a demonstrated understanding of multiple characterizations," Bernstein stresses. "These students see how each of the characters is in some way a variation of Ayn Rand's theme. Showing your understanding of the secondary and more minor characters demonstrates even more."

Follow through on these strategies and Atlas won't be shrugging. He'll be cheering you on—all the way to the bank.

Daniel Higginbotham
Lynchburg, VA
First Place
$2,000

Winning
Entry

ANTHEM
ESSAY SUBMISSION

In this excerpt from his winning essay, Daniel Higginbotham analyzes the role of collectivism in the story of Prometheus.

Every collectivist tenet rests on the idea that the many are good and the one, evil, from the law that none may have a personal preference for a type of work ("For the Council of Vocations knows . . . where you are needed by your brother men . . . And if you are not needed by your brother men, there is no reason for you to burden the earth with your bodies") to the aversion towards considering one's own body ("for it is evil to have concern for [one's own face or body]"). It is with this doctrine that Prometheus struggles. Everything he takes pleasure in is self-serving and self-centered and therefore evil. For instance, he likes the Science of Things for the enjoyment it gives him, not for the benefits that others can derive from his studying.

Plan on applying to the Ayn Rand contest over several years. Higginbotham was named a semifinalist as a ninth grader, won first place as a tenth grader, and plans to apply again in subsequent years.

Coach's Comments

At first, Prometheus completely accepts the collectivist morality and consequently struggles to subdue his desires. The heavy influence of the doctrine is shown through his profound sense of guilt at committing the Transgression of Preference and his relief and pride at being able to suffer for it as well as his constant self-chastising, which, in fact, the books opens with.

Gradually, however, Prometheus's emotions contradict his conscious premises. As he commits more acts that he thinks to be immensely evil, like being alone and doing work for the sole reason that he wants to, he is untroubled. As he writes at the end of the first chapter, "The evil of our crime is not for the human mind to probe. . . . And yet there is no shame in us and no regret." His writing shows, however, that he still accepts the legitimacy of collectivist morality, if only consciously. Prometheus's stance towards collectivist morality evolves from utter belief to mere conscious acceptance.

Prometheus does not begin to actually struggle against collectivist morality until he meets the Golden One. After coming to know her, he begins to feel glad to be living, writing, "If this is a vice, then we wish no virtue." Here he still gives credence to collectivist morality but decides that he would rather not follow it if it means sacrificing his happiness.

What follows is his progressive rejection of various tenets of collectivist doctrine as they conflict with his observations and his happiness. As Prometheus becomes increasingly aware of his power, his being, and the enjoyment he can have, he loses respect for the ideas and laws that have governed his life, as when he discovers electricity, writing, "No single one can possess greater wisdom than the many Scholars. . . . Yet we can. . . . We forget all men, all laws, and all things. . . . So long a road lies before us, and what care we if we must travel it alone!" Prometheus, however, never questions the validity of collectivist morality. His attitude is still like that of a precocious, rebellious child—he consciously thinks the ideas he is struggling with to be right but chooses to act on his intuitions. The last vestige of his acceptance appears at the end of chapter seven, after his flight from his community. He writes, "We have torn ourselves from the truth which is our brother men. . . . We know [this], but we do not care."

Prometheus is able to fully reject collectivism when he realizes the immense delight that he can have in living for himself. When he awakens the first morning in the Uncharted Forest, completely free to do as he wills, he feels the urge to frolic, to jump and roll and laugh. Then, the Golden One joins him, consummating his happiness, and in the face of such joy he says, "Let us forget their good and our evil, let us forget all things save that we are together and that there is joy as a bond between us." This event marks Prometheus's complete, conscious rejection of collectivism. In experiencing such profound happiness he does not attempt to sacrifice it as he originally did but embraces it, renouncing the ideals that would condemn his joy.

For the complete text of Daniel Higginbotham's winning essay, visit the Coach's Locker Room at ScholarshipCoach.com (Keyword: ARANDESS).

David Press
Wichita, KS
First Place
$5,000

Winning
Entry

ATLAS SHRUGGED ESSAY SUBMISSION: "CAPITALISM: THE ONLY MORAL ECONOMY"

In this essay excerpt, David Press explores the morality of capitalism as set forth by Ayn Rand.

Capitalism, according to John Galt, is "mutual trade to mutual advantage," or as Adam Smith put it: "[trade] by mutual consent and to mutual advantage." In true capitalism, the economy is strictly separated from the state, just as there is a separation between church and state in the USA. This basic tenet of capitalism describes the only economic system that can be morally justifiable. Communism, fascism, socialism, dictatorships and "regulated capitalism" are all systems that breach upon an individual's basic rights, while capitalism respects and recognizes a man's right to control the product of his mind. In her philosophical treatise *Atlas Shrugged*, Ayn Rand uses fictional characters and events to dramatize the only economy that is consistent with man's rights and virtues.

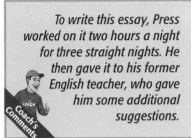

To write this essay, Press worked on it two hours a night for three straight nights. He then gave it to his former English teacher, who gave him some additional suggestions.

Before Ayn Rand, no one had ever seriously attempted to justify capitalism on moral grounds. It was a given that capitalism was immoral; the proponents of capitalism merely tried to exhibit the efficiency of the system (i.e., it is a "necessary evil"). Economists did this because they focused only on the people who would be helped by an anti-capitalist society: the "needy." What Ayn Rand presents so masterfully through *Atlas Shrugged* is the objective perspective of what is occurring in societies where people may take from others for the "public good"; in the novel, she repeatedly begs the question: "At whose expense?" When the People's State of Mexico nationalizes the San Sebastián mines, Ayn Rand clearly presents what is really happening: a gang of looters is robbing an honest business for their own benefit. In any other case, this would be deemed highly immoral, but when it is done in the name of the "public good," the action suddenly becomes noble. By utilizing hard-working and honest heroes and heroines such as Hank Rearden and Dagny Taggart, Ayn Rand presents what really happens to the victims of the "needy."

> *Keep in mind that the Ayn Rand Institute is a staunch supporter of capitalism. "If you start criticizing capitalism a little bit, I don't think they would take that kindly," says Press. "You want to be an advocate."*
>
> **Coach's Comments**

In essence, capitalism is the only economic system that is compatible with individual freedom. In every other form of economy, a person is, in one way or another, a slave to the non-entity known as the "public good." In the anti-capitalist society of *Atlas Shrugged*, the Hank Reardens and the Dagny Taggarts of the world are constantly at the mercy of the government's whims and fancies because, whenever it deems that the "public good" is threatened, the government can justify any action towards them. Points one and two of Directive 10-289—where workers must stay where they work and businesses must stay in operation—clearly illustrate how an anti-capitalist economy can literally enslave its people "in the name of general welfare."

For the complete text of David Press's winning essay, visit the Coach's Locker Room at ScholarshipCoach.com (Keyword: ARANDESS).

CONTACT INFORMATION

Keyword
ARANDESS

Submissions for all three contests are accepted via e-mail.

General Inquiries:
E-mail: contests@aynrand.org
Website: www.aynrand.org/contests

Anthem Submissions:

Anthem Essay Contest, Dept. W
The Ayn Rand Institute
PO Box 6099
Inglewood, CA 90312

E-mail: anthemessay@aynrand.org

The Fountainhead Submissions:

The Fountainhead Essay Contest, Dept. W
The Ayn Rand Institute
PO Box 6004
Inglewood, CA 90312

E-mail: tf-essay@aynrand.org

Atlas Shrugged Submissions:

Atlas Shrugged Essay Contest, Dept. W
The Ayn Rand Institute
4640 Admiralty Way, Suite 406
Marina del Rey, CA 90292

E-mail: atlasessay@aynrand.org

RELATED AWARD PROGRAMS

For more information on a Related Award Program, enter the associated keyword in the "Enter a Keyword" box located in the Coach's Locker Room section of ScholarshipCoach.com

■ Jane Austen Society of North America Essay Contest

Designed to encourage students to read novels by British writer Jane Austen (such as *Pride and Prejudice, Sense and Sensibility,* and *Emma*), this essay contest asks students to answer questions based on her works. In North America, high school, undergraduate, and graduate students compete in their respective divisions to receive one of three $500 cash prizes. Each applicant submits a 1,200- to 2,000-word essay chosen from a number of topics provided by the society. Additional societies around the world sponsor Jane Austen–themed contests as well. Entries are due in early May.

Keyword
JANEAUST

■ Signet Classic Student Scholarship Essay Contest

High school juniors and seniors compete for five $1,000 scholarships awarded on the basis of a two- to three-page essay about a literary work selected by editors at the Signet Classic publishing imprint. Contest officials annually choose one classic novel from a group of over 300. Such novels have included *The Red Badge of Courage* and *Pride and Prejudice.* Essays are due in mid-April.

Keyword
SIGNCLAS

Barry M. Goldwater Scholarship Program

In the *Goldfinger* spy movie, James Bond saves the day with his secret agent skills. In the Goldwater Scholarship Program, *you* can save $7,500 in tuition with your not-so-secret scholarship savvy.

The Barry M. Goldwater Scholarships are named after the former U.S. senator and Republican presidential candidate from Arizona. The purpose of the awards is to encourage outstanding students to pursue careers in engineering, the natural sciences, or mathematics.

Each college may nominate four students for these prestigious awards: Students must be sophomores or juniors majoring in such fields as chemistry, biology, physics, computer science, and geology. The nomination process for this competition depends on the particular college you attend. Applicants must be ranked in the top 25 percent of their class, have at least a B average, and plan to continue with graduate study.

Every year, approximately 300 entrants in the competition—students with impressive nomination forms, letters of recommendation, biographical and educational information, and essay responses—will each be awarded up to $7,500 in scholarship money. The actual amount of the scholarship award is based on each student's

TARGET RECIPIENT

■ Undergraduate sophomores and juniors

ENTRY REQUIREMENTS

Nomination | Academic Info | Short Answer | Essay

Recommendation | Activities & Credentials | Interview

DEADLINE

■ February

	Keyword
SCHOLARSHIP COACH.com	**BARMGOLD**

The average amount awarded to recipients is $6,300.

In general, the students who receive nominations are those who are proactive about seeking them out.

unmet cost of tuition, books, and fees. Sophomore recipients are eligible to receive two years of scholarship assistance, while juniors who apply will be awarded only one year of aid.

Applications are due in early February, and winners are announced in early April.

■ A CLOSER LOOK

The application process begins when the student has secured the nomination of a faculty member at his or her college or university. The four-page nomination form asks for basic biographical information as well as a significant amount of educational information including relevant courses taken, graduation requirements, and a short statement of career goals and future plans. Students are also expected to provide a listing of honors, awards, and scholarships received and a listing of activities (both those associated with the intended career field and other extracurricular activities and employment).

Most of the Goldwater nomination forms can be downloaded and filled out in a text program for a more uniform, professional look.

In addition to stating their career goals, students will be asked to provide a short essay about their professional aspirations and how their education plans and current academic program will help them achieve those objectives. Furthermore, students are asked to highlight an experience that was important in strengthening their motivation for their intended career. They also have the opportunity to provide a statement to the review committee containing any additional information they feel is important to mention (such as ethnic, occupational, and economic family information).

About 1,200 nominations are received yearly.

The final part of each student's application is a 600-word essay describing a proposed research topic that is relevant to the student's field of study. The essay should include four basic parts:

- A description of the problem or issue

- Some idea for research that may have a large impact on the problem or issue

- The part of the research in which the student would be involved

- An explanation of the relevance of the problem or issue to the student as an engineer, scientist, or mathematician

Essays should also have attached illustrations, a bibliography, and references when appropriate.

Additional nomination documents include three evaluation forms, an official transcript, and an institution nomination form. At least one of the evaluation forms must be completed by a faculty member in the student's field of study, and one can be from any other faculty member or individual who is knowledgeable about the applicant's potential. The institution nomination form is the responsibility of each school's faculty representative; it simply calls for a verification of the student's nomination and information about the nominating institution.

The judging panel for the Goldwater program is made up of deans from collegiate institutions around the country, including the Air Force Academy, the Naval Academy, Yale, Ohio State, and Georgia Tech. The initial round of judging is done on a state-by-state basis. Then the top entries from each state are forwarded to the finalist round, with larger states often advancing more nominees. (However, there is no guaranteed number of winners for each state.) In addition, those who don't make the finalist round in the state judging may be designated "at large" candidates: Two additional groups of judges review those candidates, and the strongest applicants among them join the other finalists. All finalists are then scored numerically from one to four, with the top scorers deemed scholarship recipients. The other finalists are named honorable mention winners.

Insider Info

In a recent application year, 157 men and 145 women were selected as Goldwater Scholars.

Insider Info

Although the contest application calls for a minimum B average, it should be noted that the contest winners tend to have higher GPAs, particularly in courses relating to their majors. "It's unusual to see anything lower than about a 3.7 or 3.8," notes Gerald Smith, the president of the Goldwater Scholarship Foundation.

COACH'S ANALYSIS

Filling out the Goldwater application is, quite simply, a balancing act. On one hand, written descriptions of past scientific exploration and future research interests should be sufficiently *general* so that the judges—many of whom will not have specific knowledge about your field—can comprehend what you're saying. On the other hand, to demonstrate competence and a deep understanding of your field, you should include more *specific* information and detailed knowledge.

To achieve this balance in your essay, take a threefold approach. First, start out by introducing your topic in a general way that any reader familiar with science can understand. Once you've communicated the basics, you can delve into a more technical treatment. Be specific in this treatment, but don't get so bogged down in details that readers might get lost. At the conclusion of your essay, try pulling back to take in a big-picture view of what you've just described and proposed.

"I wrote a first draft of the essay and my adviser said, 'You know what, they're not going to understand this,'" says Goldwater Scholar Shannon Boettcher, who won while a sophomore chemistry major at the University of Oregon. "I had to think of creative ways to explain things. I tried to use everyday objects as metaphors for something more complex." Boettcher, for instance, used the metaphor of "water into a sponge" to explain a complex attribute of "polymer conductivity."

Gerald Smith, the foundation president, says that although most judges may not understand the details of a given applicant's scientific research, at least one judge will have the background necessary to grasp the basic premise behind the proposed project.

Keep in mind that the most successful applicants have generally already begun research in the field they want to explore. "It's really important to have a firm grasp on the research you want to propose, and to propose research related to what you have already done," emphasizes Goldwater Scholar Jessica Kirkpatrick of Occidental College. "It shows that you already have detailed knowledge and have taken steps to pursue that knowledge."

Citing and referencing other papers of importance to your proposed research can also add to your scientific credibility.

More specifically, having undertaken prior research demonstrates a certain level of commitment to your field. Try to communicate this sense of commitment to your recommendation writers as well, so that they can highlight it in their letters. Potential alone is not enough; Goldwater judges want *evidence* that you will follow through on the plan you've proposed.

One last bit of practical advice: Because questions on the application form may overlap one another somewhat, try to coordinate your answers so that your most compelling information and credentials are equally distributed among your responses. "Some of the questions are really similar, but you have a limited amount of space," Kirkpatrick notes. "Make sure that you don't repeat yourself."

Jessica Kirkpatrick
Albany, CA
Goldwater Scholar
$7,500

SHORT-ANSWER RESPONSE

Winning
Entry

In response to a question about an activity or experience that has strengthened her interest in a scientific career, Jessica Kirkpatrick described a physics program she founded at Occidental College.

I created an opportunity to practice mentoring while also helping my major department, when I developed a Physics adaptation of the Academic Mastery Program (AMP) which was being utilized in other disciplines. AMP provides an optional workshop as a supplement to introductory classes in which upperclass majors facilitate discussion, problem solving, and experiments among beginning students. After approaching the Physics Department I was able to implement this program during my sophomore year, serve as a facilitator for the past year and a half, and obtain funding so that it is now a permanent offering. The experience of founding Physics AMP has helped me learn a lot about generating funding for projects and about the administrative processes of a college. Facilitating the program has given me insight into what it will be like to mentor a student research group as a professor. Both of these roles involve sharing physics expertise as well as guiding students through the solution of scientific problems. I received great pleasure from helping struggling students understand a topic, and sharing my love and passion for physics. My experience with AMP has intensified my interest in practicing science in a university setting. A Physics Professorship would combine my love for research with my desire to inspire interest in others.

Kirkpatrick says she wishes she had applied as a sophomore, rather than waiting until her junior year, because she could have had two years' worth of scholarship funding.

Coach's Comments

Jessica Kirkpatrick
Albany, CA
Goldwater Scholar
$7,500

SHORT-ANSWER RESPONSE

Winning
Entry

When asked about any additional personal information she wished to share with the Goldwater judging panel, Kirkpatrick chose to discuss her triumph over a learning disability.

I am a member of a minority group which has received recognition only in recent years. When I was a junior in high school I was diagnosed with a learning disability. Although I had achieved greater academic success than other learning disabled students at my school, I could not match the reading and writing speed or skills of my "normal" peers. Towards the end of my junior year I started working with educational therapist David Berg, who helped me appreciate my strengths and understand my different learning style. My confidence and effectiveness improved because of increased self-awareness and I accepted working harder to achieve the same marks as my classmates. As a result my motivation and performance skyrocketed. When I came to Occidental, I did not know whether there would be any other learning-disabled students on campus. I felt alone until I met another successful student who had similar learning issues. We believed that learning disabled students could learn from each other and stay more resolute when given a venue in which to share strategies and ideas. With several other students, I founded The Learning Difference Association (LDA), an organization which promotes awareness of learning disabilities and helps LD students cope with the emotional, academic, and social issues they face. LDA now thrives with approximately 20 members, and was awarded Club and Organization of the Year in 2000 by the Occidental College Student/Alumni Association.

It's generally a good idea to emphasize obstacles you've overcome. Kirkpatrick included this paragraph in her application because she wanted to let the judges know that "there's a big discrepancy between how well I read and how smart I am."

Coach's Comments

CONTACT INFORMATION

Keyword **BARMGOLD**

Goldwater Scholarship Review Committee
2201 North Dodge Street
Iowa City, IA 52243-4030

Phone: (319) 341-2333
E-mail: goldh2o@erols.com
Website: www.act.org/goldwater/

RELATED AWARD PROGRAMS

For more information on a Related Award Program, enter the associated keyword in the "Enter a Keyword" box located in the Coach's Locker Room section of ScholarshipCoach.com

■ National Science Foundation Graduate Research Fellowships

This is a program for undergraduate or graduate students who want to pursue a research-based degree or doctoral degrees in science, math, or engineering. Designed to help students over a three-year period, the 900 fellowships offered provide stipends of up to $21,500 per year, in addition to the annual $10,500 cost-of-education allowance. Electronic and paper applications, composed of biographical information, test scores, recommendations, an outline of a plan of research, and a record of previous research experience, are due in early November.

Keyword **NSCIFGRF**

■ National Defense Science & Engineering Graduate Fellowships

This is a program for undergraduate seniors planning to begin a graduate school program leading to a Ph.D. in science or engineering. Students submit an application form, official transcripts, recommendations, and GRE test scores. Between 100 and 200 NDSEG Fellowships of varying amounts are awarded each year. Applications must arrive at the American Society for Engineering Education offices in early January.

Keyword **NATLDEFS**

Burger King/McLamore Scholarship

Looking for a "whopper" of a scholarship program?
Concerned that you can't "ketchup" with rising tuition?
Don't "relish" the idea of college loans?
"Lettuce" help you!

That's what the friendly folks at the Burger King/McLamore Foundation might have said when they created the Burger King/McLamore Scholarship—a college cash program in which it's actually possible to have too *high* a grade point average.

Based upon the premise that some students aren't at the top of their class because the necessity of part-time work affords them less time to study, this foundation specifically targets students with "mid-range" GPAs—between 2.5 and 3.5 on a 4.0 scale—who work an average of 15 hours every week for at least 40 weeks per year. The only exception to the scholarship program's work requirement rule is if there are mitigating circumstances preventing a student from taking on a part-time job.

Currently, the foundation awards about 1,600 of these $1,000 scholarships annually—with another 400 scholarship awards expected to be added next year. The money is intended for use in a student's first year at a college or vocational school. Scholarship checks are made jointly payable to the winning student and his or her school.

To apply for the scholarship, applicants must also participate in school and community activities, have a school official attest to financial need (although it is not necessary to submit formal financial data), and be

TARGET RECIPIENT

■ High school seniors

ENTRY REQUIREMENTS

Activities & Credentials | Academic Info | Financial Data | Nomination

DEADLINE

■ January

	Keyword
ScholarshipCoach.com	**BURGKSCH**

Money Matters

nominated by a high school in the United States, Canada, or Puerto Rico. Each year, one student per school may apply.

Applications may be obtained from a school counselor and are due in early January. Winning students are notified in late April.

■ A CLOSER LOOK

The designers of this scholarship program specifically set out to recognize those students who must work out of financial necessity—average and moderately above-average students who, they feel, get lower grades than they would if they didn't have to work part-time.

The three-page application form reflects this focus. Applicants must list their work experiences, attach a paycheck stub from their most recent job, and submit a very brief endorsement from an employer who is not a family member. Space is provided on the form, however, for describing special circumstances that prevent a student from gaining employment. Possible circumstances listed on the form include:

- ■ The need to provide care for elderly or sick relatives or for siblings
- ■ Participation in school activities that require daily participation
- ■ The need to assist with family-owned businesses
- ■ Physical disability
- ■ Transportation difficulties

Instead of having students submit data about their family's financial situation (program administrators note that commonly used financial data can sometimes be misleading), the program leaves it up to a high school official to certify that an applicant needs help in paying for higher education. On the application form, a school official is asked to indicate whether a student has a modest family income, receives a free or reduced lunch, has an unemployed parent, has more than one family member in college, or has some other reason for needing financial assistance to attend college.

Entrants must also describe their goals and aspirations, list school and community activities, submit an official transcript, and obtain a very brief nomination statement from a school official (*not* a separate recommendation letter, however).

Citizens' Scholarship Foundation of America (CSFA)—a Minnesota-based organization that administers numerous scholarship programs—conducts the judging and selects recipients for this scholarship. In this judging process, the proximity of a student's school or home residence to a Burger King restaurant has a substantial impact on the final award recipients, because particular restaurants earmark awards for students at local schools or from nearby neighborhoods. The Burger King Corporation itself currently awards more than 530 scholarships to students located near company-owned restaurants, while Burger King franchisees provide more than 800 scholarships to students in areas near franchisee-owned eateries. Not all Burger King restaurants participate in the scholarship program, but more are being added on an ongoing basis.

How can you determine if your local Burger King participates? In addition to asking your college counselor, Bentonne Snay, executive director of the Burger King/McLamore Foundation, advises checking with the manager of your local Burger King. If your local restaurant doesn't already participate in the scholarship program, Snay suggests encouraging them to begin participation by contacting the national foundation.

What if you don't live near a participating Burger King restaurant? You can still be awarded one of the 267 foundation-sponsored scholarships. One such award is specifically earmarked for each of the 267 major Burger King regions.

COACH'S ANALYSIS

Because the program was designed to honor Burger King Corporation co-founder James McLamore, an entrepreneur who worked his way through preparatory school and college, it's no surprise that students with significant work experience have the best chance of winning. Keep in mind, however, that the underlying philosophy of the program is to reward not just work, but *work undertaken out of financial necessity*.

As a result, your application should clearly communicate that your part-time work was done out of true financial need, not out of your desire to own a shiny red sports car. A great place to stress this point is in your statement of goals and aspirations. In addition to summarizing your educational plans, career objectives, and future goals, discuss how you have already taken action steps toward attaining these goals through your part-time employment and work experience. If you have been working to save money for college, be sure to mention this, too. Including such a statement illustrates that you have already seized the initiative in paying for your education and demonstrates that you are someone determined to do whatever it takes to make that education possible.

"A lot of people work because their parents make them," says Burger King winner Alexandria Bagaria of Chesterland, Ohio. Because her dream was to attend a school in another part of the country (she now attends the University of Colorado at Boulder), she tried to emphasize that she was someone who "needed to work to pay for college" and was taking steps to make that dream a reality.

To help illustrate the quality of your work experiences, don't limit the description of your jobs to the names of your employers and the positions you have held. Application rules permit you to attach additional sheets, which enables you to add more descriptive information.

Craft your job description to highlight any special responsibilities you have had, any admirable qualities you have exhibited (such as work ethic, leadership, initiative, or entrepreneurship), and any recognition that you have received (such as winning an "Employee of the Month" award). Remind your employer to back up such information in the small space for employer comments included on the form.

Insider Info

In addition to this core emphasis on work experiences, the judging methodology rewards those who have also managed to find space in their day to participate in extracurricular activities and community service. "The more work experience you have, the better you will do," notes Barb Webber, the CSFA administrator who manages the program. "But we're also looking for well-rounded students."

To put your school and community activities in the best possible light, think strategically about how you assemble your activities list. The spot of highest visibility in such a list is at the very top. Since application judges review piles of submissions, there is no guarantee that they will thoroughly read *all* of your meticulously crafted listings. They will, however, read the items that appear *first*.

Because of this, you should rank your activities in order of importance, with the top of the list reserved for activities you definitely want the judges to notice. These are the activities that you have initiated or founded, or in which you have held a position of responsibility or have made a special contribution. If you spend a substantial number of hours per week on an activity, be sure to note it—especially since the program's judging methodology takes notice of the demands on a student's time. Just as you should do on your list of work experiences, add some description to each listed activity to illustrate the most compelling aspects of each endeavor.

STATMENT OF GOALS AND ASPIRATIONS

Winning
Entry

In this short statement, Alexandra Bagaria describes some of her school- and work-related activities, and how such endeavors move her toward her goals.

I am 18 years old with a very busy life. If I am not at one of my two jobs I am at softball, and if I am not at softball I am still at school helping out with one of my myriad activities. Hard work, determination, pride, and focus are

four characteristics that describe my work ethic and me.

For example, during high school I had the opportunity to be involved and be a leader in the kindness-promoting group Project Love, which has brought me satisfaction and the most joy. This group has brought me to the realization that being nice matters; it makes a big difference. I know what it is like to not be at the top of the overbearing food chain in high school, which is why promoting kindness among my fellow students has been a priority on my list.

Another priority is my dream to go away to college. Growing up in Chesterland, Ohio, I have lived a sheltered life, both culturally and educationally. I look forward to the future with my eyes wide open and head higher to broaden my horizons at a big university. This scholarship would be a step along the way to making my dream a reality. I have completed many of the other steps needed to reach my destination, including the effort to receive above average grades in my classes, the time devoted to student council, the teaching PSR, and the ability to be leader on the sport field for volleyball, basketball, and softball. One of my final steps: I am working to be financially able to move away to college. I currently work at a party center/restaurant and a fitness center, which is why this scholarship would be most beneficial to me. I know I have what it takes to take charge of myself and my life to be where I want to be in the future.

> Bagaria says that in this essay she was "trying to get across the fact that I had worked at this for a long time." Going away to college, she says, "wasn't a last-minute decision. It meant something to me."
>
> Coach's Comments

CONTACT INFORMATION

Keyword **BURGKSCH**

Burger King Scholars Program—US
Scholarship Management Services, CSFA
1505 Riverview Road
Saint Peter, MN 56082

Fax: (507) 931-9168
E-mail: bk@csfa.org
Websites: www.burgerking.com/bkscholars
www.bkscholars.csfa.org

RELATED AWARD PROGRAM

For more information on a Related Award Program, enter the associated keyword in the "Enter a Keyword" box located in the Coach's Locker Room section of ScholarshipCoach.com

■ McDonald's Arching into Education Scholarships

Building on the theme of fast-food-sponsored scholarships, McDonald's offers awards for minority students in the Tri-State area (New York, New Jersey, Connecticut). Eligible students can apply for awards from four separate programs: the African American Heritage Scholarships, the GospelFest Music Scholarships (for music majors), BMOA Scholarships (considering financial need, leadership, and work experience), and Tri-State Scholarships (offered in conjunction with United Negro College Fund schools). Within these programs, large numbers of awards are allocated and amounts vary. All applications are due in late April.

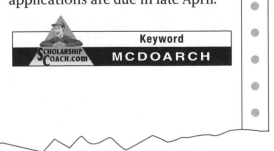

Keyword **M C D O A R C H**

Coca-Cola Scholars Program

When 250 high school seniors gather in Atlanta each year, it's no great mystery what carbonated beverage is served at mealtimes. With close to $2 million of award money to dispense each year, the Coca-Cola Scholars Foundation can help quench the thirst of a diverse group of students needing college cash.

To apply to the Coca-Cola Scholars program, applicants first complete an electronic "bubble" form available through the website. Questions on the form solicit an applicant's GPA and class rank, school and community activities, and past employment. Based on this form, the foundation selects between 1,500 and 2,000 students as semifinalists and sends these students a more detailed application to complete—one that requires a more comprehensive listing of activities and family information, as well as two recommendations, a school transcript, and a student essay.

The foundation awards 50 scholarships of $20,000 each, plus 200 scholarships of $4,000 each. In addition, the foundation administers a $20,000 award for study at Emory University in Atlanta for those interested in attending that institution.

Based on these written applications, 250 students are selected as finalists and invited to attend a Scholars Weekend in Atlanta, with all travel and accommodation costs covered by the program. During the weekend, students participate in a packed activity schedule—including a group community service activity—and also undergo

TARGET RECIPIENT

- High school seniors

ENTRY REQUIREMENTS

| Academic Info | Short Answer | Activities & Credentials |
| Recommendation | Interview | |

DEADLINES

- Preliminary: October
- Semifinalist: February

| | Keyword |
| SCHOLARSHIP COACH.com | **COCASCHO** |

Money Matters

Added Bonus

Home-schoolers may also apply to the Coca-Cola Scholars program. Such students should contact the foundation for specific instructions.

individual interviews with final-round judges. The 50 "national" winners are then selected from the group; the remaining students receive the 200 "regional" scholarship awards.

Preliminary applications are due in late October; for those who qualify for the next round, semifinalist applications are due in mid-January.

A Closer Look

To apply for the scholarship, students must access the Coca-Cola Scholars Foundation website (www.cocacolascholars.org) and answer a series of questions. The first section asks for academic information, including grade point average, class rank, class size, and type of school. The second section presents a listing of seven different school activities—including student council, school yearbook, literary publication, and National Honor Society. (Unfortunately, there's no mention of the MTV Couch Potato Council or the National Mall Shoppers Society.) For each of the seven activities, applicants must indicate whether they have participated, the specific grades in which they have participated, and any leadership positions held. Students must also calculate the total number of clubs in which they participated during high school (and list two sample clubs), calculate the total number of awards they have received, and then describe their athletic participation.

Section three of the application highlights participation in community organizations and volunteer service, while section four examines the applicant's employment activities (focusing on average number of hours worked). The final section includes blanks for basic biographical information, such as name, address, and social security number.

The foundation uses a point-based mathematical formula to convert each submitted application into a numerical score—with scoring performed by a computer rather than by individual judges. The 1,500 to 2,000 semifinalists, those with the highest scores, are notified in mid-December that they have advanced to the next round of competition.

Once students have advanced to the semifinalist round, they must complete a much more detailed written application. Application materials feature a biographical questionnaire that includes a listing of school activities, employment experiences, and volunteer work. Students also provide four short-answer responses that, in recent years, have addressed the following topics:

If you don't select The Scholarship Scouting Report, I won't hold it against you!

- What is the most stimulating book or article you have read in the last six months?

- What qualities distinguish you as a leader, and how have you demonstrated those qualities?

- Select your favorite service activity and describe why it is important to your community and to you.

- Describe how your family has influenced your development.

Semifinalists must also submit materials from school officials and written recommendations. First, a school official fills out a form that asks questions about key characteristics of the school (including size, curriculum features, and graduation requirements) and includes blanks for the student's GPA, class rank, and standardized test scores. In addition, the school official must attach the student's high school transcript. Students must also submit two letters of recommendation—one completed by a member of the school faculty and another from an employer or an individual who can comment on the student's community service record.

Finally, semifinalists complete an essay of 750 words or less that should "demonstrate style, depth, and breadth of knowledge and individuality." Although the essay question does change from time to time, in recent years it has been: "What—or who—motivates or inspires you to achieve?" Semifinalist materials must be submitted by mid-January, and the 250 finalists are notified in late February.

To evaluate semifinalist applications, Coca-Cola convenes the Program Review Committee—a panel of 27 professionals who have experience in academic fields (such as college deans, admissions counselors, and teachers). These professionals gather together for an intense weekend of application reading and finalist selection. According to foundation officials, each committee member is given an evaluation sheet with suggested scoring guidelines, but members are given considerable discretion to follow their own individual judging methodology. In general, finalists are selected according to "commitment, character, and personal motivation," as exhibited through participation and leadership in school and community activities—particularly volunteer service. Judges are encouraged to select a diverse group of students with a wide range of ethnic backgrounds, economic circumstances, and interests.

In April, finalists attend the Scholars Weekend in Atlanta—with all 250 students who attend guaranteed at least a $4,000 scholarship. A 27-member National Selection Committee (different judges than the ones who determined the finalists) oversees the judging process during the weekend. Selection committee members have included representatives from schools such as Emory University, Stanford University, and Louisiana State University; government officials such as the mayor of Charlotte, North Carolina; a former Miss America; and individuals from minority-focused institutions such as the United Negro College Fund, the American Indian Graduate Center, and the Japanese American Cultural Community Center.

To determine the 50 national scholars who receive $20,000 awards, each student undergoes a 20-minute

Insider Info

Students are required to attend the Scholars Weekend in order to receive any scholarship funds.

Coach's tip: For this interview, do not *discuss your love of Pepsi!*

interview with a panel of three selection committee members. Although the topics of the interviews depend on the particular committee members participating, students are often asked questions based on information provided in their semifinalist applications.

After returning home, finalists are informed by mail whether they have been designated a national or regional scholar.

◼ COACH'S ANALYSIS

The Coca-Cola Scholars Program places substantial emphasis on making sure each year's class of winners "represents a diverse cross-section of young people." In a recent application year, 46 percent of scholarship recipients were minorities, 64 percent were female, and 89 percent attended a public high school. If you are a member of an ethnic minority group (or have worked on projects promoting multiculturalism), have a medical disability, or are from an economically disadvantaged area, you should highlight those facts in your Coca-Cola application—such factors do play a prominent role in the judging. (Of course, many past Coca-Cola Scholars don't fall into any of these groups.)

As you make your way through each phase of the application process, learn from the successes and mistakes of past applicants. First, when tackling the initial electronic "bubble" form, be aware that every item you list on that form translates into a different point-value by an elaborate computer algorithm. According to contest administrators, responses typed in on the electronic form in sentence form play a very *minimal* role in initial judging.

To do your best on this form, you need to sit down and think of *every* possible activity, award, or credential that could apply to the given question. When you think you've thought of everything, sit down and rack your brain some more! You should also ask parents, siblings, and anyone else who knows you well to look over your list to see if you've forgotten anything. How important is this? Program officials told one recent Coca-Cola Scholar that they had to examine each applicant's computer-generated score all the way out to the *eighth decimal place* to separate out the semifinalists! "Think of every little thing that you have done," advises Arthur Abrams, a Coca-Cola Scholar from Washington, D.C. "That's what I did, and it got me through the first round. One or two extra activities can make a difference." If certain credentials could apply to multiple categories on the electronic form (you're not permitted to list them more than once), try to spread them out in a strategic way so that you have something to enter for as many different application questions as possible.

Once you've been named a semifinalist (congrats to you!), your application strategy should shift to take advantage of the semifinalist application format. In particular, when answering the four short-answer questions, by all means take into account the very small space you have to make your case. Although the general scholarship application principle of *making your answer intensely personal* most definitely applies, you have to achieve this in a modified organizational format: Instead of crafting a drawn-out introduction, make your opening sentence more of a thesis statement that declares the main point of your response. Don't overload your response with too many major points, and definitely don't turn it into a glorified list of accomplishments. Prioritize your potential points, stick to one or two of the most important, and make sure that you develop them adequately with a specific example or anecdote. You won't have space for an actual conclusion, but try to end on a poignant thought that supports or extends your main idea.

"I would let all my thoughts spill out on a rough draft sheet, then condense it to a new sheet of paper, then condense it again until it fit on the form," notes Alfonso

Morales, Jr., a Coca-Cola Scholar from Houston, Texas. "I tried to focus on the high impact material. You want to make it sound like you could go on and on about the topic if you only had more space. Come up with a last sentence that keeps the reader wanting to know more."

After advancing to the finalist round (way to go!), get ready for your interview in Atlanta by reviewing your semifinalist application several times and preparing what you would say about each activity, award, credential, or item listed. Although the substance of every interview depends on the interests of individual judges, numerous Coca-Cola Scholars have commented that during their interview, they were actually surprised to be asked specific questions about what they had considered to be very minor parts of their application. "Almost everything we talked about came from the smaller questions and random elements of the [semifinalist] application," relates Debra Siegel, a Coca-Cola Scholar from New York City. During Siegel's 20-minute interview, they spent about 10 minutes discussing her choice of a stimulating book (*Tuesdays with Morrie* by Mitch Albom), five minutes on the work she had done at a local paper, and the remaining five minutes on "a few random clubs" off her activity list. "They never asked about the main essay, and touched on quite minor things," she recounts.

As you prepare for each item, don't just review in your mind what your position was and how many hours per week you spent on it. Instead, try to think of one story or example that you could tell that really captures the essence of the activity or credential—an anecdote that also communicates to judges the desirable personal qualities you hope they'll notice about you. And above all, when it comes time for your interview, be enthusiastic, smile, and have fun. No matter how formal the interview situation, your Coca-Cola interviewers are just people—not carbonated beverages. They like to have fun, and they would much rather have enjoyable interview experiences than boring ones.

Insider Info

Since you'll be able to read short bios of the National Selection Committee before you travel to Atlanta, consider ahead of time the types of things each member would likely be interested in. (You can even find out more about those individuals by using online search engines.)

ESSAY SUBMISSION

Winning
Entry

In this winning essay, Alexandra Hartman describes her involvement with children and how a touching experience with one special child continues to inspire her as she pursues her own dreams.

Over the last few years the level of responsibility that has marked my interaction with younger children has steadily increased. Assuming the responsibility of being a safety on the bus, a babysitter, an assistant swim coach, a lifeguard, camp counselor, and classroom teacher have all enriched my life with an awareness of how each child, no matter how different they all are, have one very important thing in common, the need to be loved, cared for, and protected. Through my work with a variety of children from various life situations, I have also come to know that many children have this very essential need left unmet. I have seen their hungry little eyes search for someone to affirm their worth and celebrate their specialness. If anything has inspired me to achieve, it is when these little eyes have rested on me as that person. Because of the active role I play in so many children's lives, I have found that along with the burden of always having to be a good role model for these children, a tremendous reward is attached, an inspiration to try and do and be my best even when I sometimes didn't feel like it. Please understand that children are twice as loving as they are lovable so it wasn't fear that I wouldn't measure up to their image of me that inspired me to achieve but the idea that I wanted to be worthy of the affection and admiration they hung around my neck, hug by hug. Because of my involvement with children, I further feel inspired to try and help to overcome the limited opportunities or abilities of some of these children who may be sick, poor, underfed, abused, or neglected and help them come to know and experience the love, joy, care, and protection that they deserve. I am constantly inspired and amazed at how loving, trusting, and forgiving these children are towards all adults, even those who have failed them. Their resilient compassion continually inspires me to overcome my own anger and resentment over my life's little disappointments and setbacks that pale in comparison to their life situations.

Perhaps one of my greatest sources of inspiration came in the form of an eight-year-old little boy, Brian. Brian was comical as he was curious, mostly ears, wanted to be a fireman or the President depending on the time of day. I met Brian while volunteering at a special summer camp for children infected and/or affected with HIV/AIDS. Brian was both. Having lost both his parents to the disease, Brian was now struggling himself to manage the ravages of the disease. Here was a little boy who had grown used to being shunned by the world while living in medical foster care, who for this week was offered a glimpse of being normal and living without the stigma of his condition. His frail little body was as weak as his dreams were strong, so I often carried him around camp, piggyback style. All the while, he would be singing camp songs or whispering secrets in my ears. During that week of campfires, arts and crafts, water sports, and talent shows, I would often catch his eyes fixed on me, and the way he looked at me rocked my soul and stole my heart. An outstretched hand, an empty lap, a voice telling a story through the darkness at bedtime, a smile when he won, a hug when he lost, I really hadn't given him very much to deserve the kind of unconditional love he offered me in return. Brian made me aware and thankful for so many things in life (not to mention life itself) that I had taken for granted. I, so privileged by my healthy body and mind, was humbled by the strength and wisdom of this child. Brian changed me forever and continues to inspire me to live life to the fullest and to share the best of who I am with others. He left footprints on my heart that led me to places that I never could have gone without him.

> *During her 20-minute finalist interview in Atlanta, the judges asked Hartman specifically about Brian. She spent about one-third of the interview talking about why she was so inspired by him.*
>
> Coach's Comments

SHORT-ANSWER RESPONSES

Winning Entry

In the Coca-Cola semifinalist application, students were asked to discuss the most stimulating book or article they had read in the past six months. Four winners responded as follows:

Androni Henry
Grand Rapids, MI
National Winner
$20,000

Discussing the often argued but never resolved conflict of technology versus experience and wisdom, Marlo Morgan's "Mutant Message Down Under" is the story of an American woman's personal transformation after living and interacting in a Nomadic Aboriginal tribe in the outback of

Australia. Ms. Morgan's descriptive explanation of the value of simple truths, faith, and universal oneness in modern society spurred me to address the issue with my peers in order to gain a deeper understanding of our society and the interactions taking place in it. Although the book's spiritual odyssey is fictional, its message should reverberate throughout society . . . in order to impact the world, we must experience it, not watch it.

Brad Jerson
Stony Brook, NY
National Winner
$20,000

Recently, while accompanying my mom to an oncology appointment, I read a magazine article that will remain with me for a long time. "Mommy, Make Me Better" is an inspiring story of a family's battle with their three-year-old son's diagnosis and treatment for Ewing's sarcoma, a rare form of cancer. Gabriel's mother, who candidly shares her feelings and emotions through this heart-wrenching story, tells the details of their initial discovery, rigorous testing, grueling chemotherapy, and surgery. The devastation of Gabriel's baldness, along with the amputation of his finger, brought frightening stares from other people. Having to wear a feeding tube for six months drew even more comments from strangers. I was so upset when I read that a mother would not let her son sit next to Gabriel on a ride at an amusement park because she thought "he might be contagious." After reading this article, I realized that if this world were a perfect place, the words "child" and "cancer" would never appear in the same sentence. But the unfortunate reality is that each day, young innocents, like Gabriel, who have only begun to live their lives, suddenly begin to find their world torn apart by this unforgiving disease.

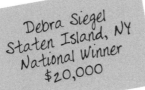
Meagan Seitz-Smith
Lebanon, CT
National Winner
$20,000

A new way of thinking, challenging reality, opening up your mind: these are a few results of reading "Out of the Silent Planet" by C.S. Lewis. This is easily one of the most stimulating books I have ever enjoyed. Not merely a science fiction fantasy, this story of a man explor-ing existence beyond earth, at first against his will, helped me gain a more open perspective of the universe, and even life on our own planet. It picks apart the basis for racism and prejudice of humans against those of their own species, and of those that they consider to be inferior. My mind is now strengthened with the ability to inquire beyond what seems to be reality, and make discoveries of my own.

Debra Siegel
Staten Island, NY
National Winner
$20,000

Tuesdays with Morrie by Mitch Albom is one of the most intensely moving books I have ever read. Though not yet a classic, this work presents themes and ideas in such a way to make the subject matter universal to readers of all ages. While it may be a true account of the months prior to the death of Professor Morrie Schwartz, the book focuses on the importance of living life to its fullest. After reading this brief but enlightening book, I felt empowered, enlivened, and ready to face any challenges the world could throw at me. Mitch Albom wrote a fantastic piece of literature that embodies the spirit of the *carpe diem* mentality. With a gentle, **see**mingly simple writing style, and a powerful execution, Albom's book inspired me to look at the finer details of life and to never take even the smallest bit of happiness for granted.

CONTACT INFORMATION

Keyword
COCASCHO

Coca-Cola Scholar Foundation, Inc.
P.O. Box 442
Atlanta, GA 30301-0442

Phone: (800) 306-2653
E-mail: scholars@na.ko.com
Website: www.coca-colascholars.org

RELATED AWARD PROGRAMS

For more information on a Related Award Program, enter the associated keyword in the "Enter a Keyword" box located in the Coach's Locker Room section of ScholarshipCoach.com

■ Coca-Cola Two-Year Colleges Scholarship Program

Also sponsored by the Coca-Cola Scholars Foundation, this program awards 400 students with $1,000 scholarships at institutions offering two-year degrees. Emphasis is on diversity and community service. Requirements include a minimum GPA of 2.5, completion of at least 100 hours of community service within the previous year, and enrollment in the next term at a two-year institution. Nominations are due in late May.

Keyword
COKE2YRC

■ Gates Millennium Scholars

With a similar focus on recognizing minority students, the Gates Millennium Scholars Foundation awards scholarships to high school seniors who have Native American, Asian-American, African-American, and Hispanic-American ancestry. This program seeks to recognize students who are gifted academically but do not have the financial resources to attend college. Qualified students may be nominated by a school administrator and will then be evaluated based on community service activities, leadership potential, academic excellence, and financial need. Award amounts will vary. The deadline is in early February.

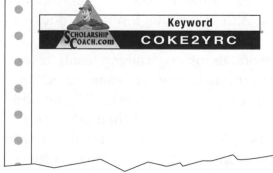

Keyword
GATESMIL

Collegiate Inventors Competition

TARGET RECIPIENT

- Undergraduate and graduate students

ENTRY REQUIREMENTS

Project   Essay   Supporting Materials

DEADLINE

- June

**Keyword
COLINVCO**

Money Matters   Added Bonus

It's faster than a speeding cook . . . able to leap stuck lids with a single twist . . . and more powerful than a frazzled adult struggling with a childproof cap. It's the "Twistmaster"—a nifty device that netted its inventors $20,000 from the Collegiate Inventors Competition.

In order to participate in this annual competition sponsored by the National Inventors Hall of Fame, current undergraduate and graduate students—under the guidance of a project adviser—must submit original, working, and documented scientific innovations. Students may enter as individuals or as a team of up to four students. At least one member of the team must be a full-time student; the others may attend school part-time.

To enter, individual students or student teams are expected to submit an essay of 1,500 words or less describing key characteristics of their invention. There is no limit to how many inventions a student may submit, but each entrant may win only once during a particular contest year. Students may enter projects that they either have or have not yet patented, and project advisers must verify the originality of the project. Entrants must have also done a thorough literature and patent search to ensure that the invention does not infringe on someone else's patent.

Up to six individuals or six student teams receive $20,000 cash prizes (unfortunately, team members must split the prize), with project advisers receiving an additional $10,000 in cash. Winners and their advisers also receive an all-expense-paid trip to the National Inventors Hall of Fame in Akron, Ohio—where they attend a special award ceremony and have the opportunity to meet leading scientists and inventors. In past years, winners have also been awarded $2,000 gift certificates to a well-known computer products website.

All of these materials must be submitted by the early-June contest deadline. Finalists are notified in September, and winners are contacted in November.

A CLOSER LOOK

Projects may include inventions that are completely original, or ones that improve upon an existing idea in a substantial way. To participate in this contest, students must prepare a short, but detailed, overview of a scientific or technological invention they either are still pursuing or have completed. The required 1,500-word essay must describe:

- The invention itself

- The problem the invention is meant to address

- The benefits of the invention (economic, environmental, and societal)

- How the idea improves upon existing technology

- The roles the adviser and student(s) played in the process

Entrants can send in slides, illustrations, photos, videos, or other data (showing that the invention, design, or idea is workable) if they feel the invention needs to be explained further.

In addition to the documented patent search (which will not count toward the 1,500-word essay limit), entrants must submit a letter from their adviser (500 words or less, written on official letterhead) outlining the significance of the invention or idea, the student's special characteristics, and the student's role in the invention process. The release form, signed by students and advisers, must accompany the entire package.

Judging for the Collegiate Inventors Competition is divided into two phases. For phase one, about 40 judges review the submitted inventions and applications. Most of the judges are from the private sector—including industry professionals, doctors from the Cleveland Clinic, and retirees from NASA. Three separate judges review each application; each of them has some expertise in the field they are reviewing.

At this initial phase of the contest, each judge evaluates each application on a 100-point scale. Half of an applicant's total score is derived from the actual number of points received. To adjust for differences in judging standards, the other half of the applicant's score comes from the relative ranking of the applicant compared to others reviewed by the same judge.

About 25 inventions make it to phase two of the judging process. During the second phase, nine judges spend a weekend reviewing the materials of all 25 finalists. In recent years, the phase two judging panel has included the inventor of the electron microscope, the director of technology acquisition at Procter & Gamble, the chief science officer at Hewlett-Packard, the executive director of research at Corning, a representative from the U.S. Patent & Trademark Office, and the president of the National Biomedical Research Foundation.

DePuy says he would spend about one hour reviewing each application.

According to Ray DePuy, the program coordinator, judging is a process of elimination—in which weaker inventions are eliminated one by one until the winners remain. As a former phase one judge, DePuy would first look at the basic information, reading the essays and explanations once through. Then he would go back and look at the pictures and diagrams to get a more complete understanding. If anything remained unclear, he would re-read the written materials. Then he would fill out the written scoring sheet.

Traditionally, about two-thirds of the applications have been from graduate students, with the remaining one-third from undergraduates. More than three-fourths of the winning inventors in recent years have been graduate-level students (usually doctoral candidates or post-docs).

■ COACH'S ANALYSIS

Contrary to what some students expect, in recent years the Collegiate Inventors Competition has become less of a traditional "invention" competition—as in the invention of a *physical* device—and more of a competition rooted in advanced laboratory-based scientific research. Traditional physical devices are still represented in the winner's circle (such as the aforementioned "Twistmaster"), but greater numbers of winning inventions in recent competitions have been derived from Ph.D. dissertation work—systems and processes in myriad fields.

If you are a student planning to enter a traditional physical device—let's say the latest and greatest armchair that will revolutionize "sitting" as we know it (who knew that your years spent as a "couch potato" would pay off!)—you should emphasize the underlying science or engineering work behind your invention. This strategy makes logical sense in a competition in which you will go head-to-head with laboratory research that may have been under way for many years.

If you have been pursuing extensive scientific research, then you have two main challenges. First, you need to frame your work as an *invention,* rather than merely research, by highlighting the creativity, ingenuity, and originality of what you have done. To do this, many past winners have found it helpful to focus their application on one particular element of their research. "In my case, the application happens to be a 70 percent share of

Dhaval Doshi (shown right with his adviser, Jeffrey Brinker) won for his work on "optically-adjustable nanostructures." Doshi is a fifth-year materials science Ph.D. candidate at the University of New Mexico.

my Ph.D. research," relates Collegiate Inventor winner Dhaval Doshi. "For some winners it was just a 10 or 15 percent share because they happened to stumble upon a novel phenomenon which they investigated further."

Second, a particularly challenging task for research-minded students is shifting into a business frame of mind and evaluating their work from the perspective of its economic impact. This is important not only because the judging criteria emphasize it, but also because the judges for this contest naturally think in such terms, since they are all from the private sector (rather than being bow-tie-wearing, pocket protec- tor–toting university professors). "A lot of researchers are lousy busi- nessmen," notes DePuy. "The judges get to evaluate them from an economic perspective."

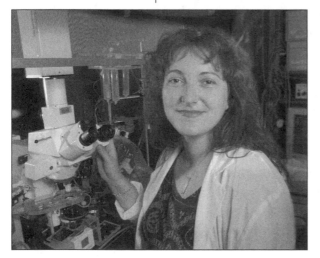

Dana Perkins, originally from Romania, won for her research titled "Gene Therapy of Alzheimer's Disease Using Herpes Virus Vector."

Many applicants, for instance, will never have done a patent search before applying to the program. "You need to have strong science behind what you are putting on paper, but you also must think in economic terms," explains Collegiate Inven- tor winner Dana Perkins of the University of Maryland.

"Thinking about the marketability . . . that was the jump I had to do."

One aspect of doing this means thinking about how your invention could be applied beyond the near term. "You need to put a different spin on what you've done and brainstorm ways the invention could be used," Doshi advises. "When you are doing your normal work, your horizon is about two to five years. . . . When you are writing the application, you have to think 'what will I be able to do in five years after working to advance the science?'"

Likewise, Daniel Fletcher of Stanford University says that you have to approach this contest differently than you would for a science fair or a scholarship program like the Intel Science Talent Search. "In those other settings people are much more interested in seeing how you went through the scientific process," he notes. "In this competition how you arrive at the idea is less important." Fletcher suggests placing special emphasis on the novelty of your idea and the ultimate impact it could have.

Because judges have to get through a large volume of paperwork per application—and all are busy industry professionals—boost your chances by being direct and concise. View your submission as an elongated and technically explicit memo, rather than a condensed dissertation or thesis. According to DePuy, long-winded explanations are immediate turn-offs for program judges: "Don't add a lot of extraneous materials that are only vaguely related to your invention. Some people submit materials that are several inches think. The winners' materials are usually a quarter of an inch thick. Be brief and to the point."

To further advance your cause, make sure that your adviser recognizes the importance of his or her letter in the judging process and is prepared to emphasize the uniqueness and independence of your work. According to DePuy, many people with worthwhile inventions are ruled out in the judging process because their projects seem more adviser-driven than student-driven. "The adviser

Insider Info

letter on behalf of the student really gives you a good idea," DePuy explains. "Sometimes it looks like the adviser is really running things and is just using the student as slave labor."

Dhaval Doshi
Albuquerque, NM
Award Winner
$20,000

OPTICALLY-ADJUSTABLE NANOSTRUCTURES

Winning Entry

In this essay excerpt, Dhaval Doshi describes the potential economic, environmental, and societal benefits of his invention.

Economic Benefits:

As described above, each of the modes of patterning are of relevance for one or more technological areas. Correspondingly we anticipate there to be broad economic benefits specific to these technologies. More generally, we view our invention as enabling our multi-billion dollar photolithography infrastructure to be used to define the structure and function of materials on the nanoscale and therefore to be useful to developing new capabilities of U.S. industry in the burgeoning area of *Nano-Technology*. Ultimately, the self-assembly approaches we have developed may provide an alternative to lithography as means to fabricate materials at the 10-nanometer length scale. This is significant as, according to Moore's 1st and 2nd Laws, the cost of photolithography-based Fab to achieve 10-nm feature sizes would exceed 1 trillion dollars.

Environmental Benefits:

The greatest potential environmental benefit of the invention stems from the optical adjustability of the pore size with sub-nanometer resolution. Our recent work demonstrated the fabrication of self-assembled nanoporous films as supported gas separation membranes (molecular filters) with the highest combination of carbon dioxide/methane selectivity and carbon dioxide flux yet reported. These membranes are of great immediate interest for the efficient purification of natural gas—enabling utilization of our low purity gas reserves.

In general, the development of membrane-based purification processes as opposed to energy intensive cryogenic and distillation processes could save enormous amounts of energy in the chemical and petrochemical industries where the majority of the energy budget is devoted to purification.

At the awards ceremony in Akron, Doshi was able to meet physicist James Hillier, the father of the modern electron microscope. "I use the electron microscope every day," says Doshi, "and I actually got to meet him!"

Furthermore, the ability to optically tune the pore size may enable the development of efficient air separation membranes, *i.e.* those capable of separating air into oxygen and nitrogen (which differ in molecular diameter by less than 0.02-nanometers). Air separation is the Holy Grail of membrane science. It could be used for enhanced combustion *i.e.* combustion using oxygen rather than air. This is both more efficient and avoids the generation of NO_x.

Societal Benefits:

We envision two major societal benefits. First, air separation membranes would provide a low cost, portable source of oxygen. No longer would people suffering from respiratory illnesses be forced to drag around oxygen bottles—instead they could use air as the oxygen source, greatly improving their quality of life. Second, the tunable porosity and surface chemistry of these materials will allow the fabrication of highly specific chemical sensors for detection of chemical weapons, biological weapons, and explosives *via* molecular recognition. The tunable optical properties will allow us to integrate these sensing elements with diffraction gratings and waveguides needed for optical output.

To read more from Dhaval Doshi's winning entry, visit the Coach's Locker Room at ScholarshipCoach.com (Keyword: COLINVCO).

CONTACT INFORMATION

Keyword
COLINVCO

The Collegiate Inventors Competition
c/o The National Inventors Hall of Fame
221 S. Broadway Street
Akron, OH 44308-1505

Phone: (330) 849-6887
Website: www.invent.org/collegiate/

RELATED AWARD PROGRAMS

For more information on a Related Award Program, enter the associated keyword in the "Enter a Keyword" box located in the Coach's Locker Room section of ScholarshipCoach.com

■ Hertz Foundation Fellowships

Undergraduate seniors and graduate students interested in, and working toward, attaining a Ph.D. in the applied physical sciences (such as astronomy, physics, applied mathematics, chemical engineering, physics, and biology) may apply for these fellowships. Hertz Fellowships may be used at one of more than 30 schools, including Harvard, Stanford, Cornell, Purdue, Northwestern, and many other distinguished institutions. Each stipend is valued at $25,000 for a nine-month academic year and is renewable for up to five years (contingent upon demonstrated progress). Applications are due in early November.

	Keyword
SCHOLARSHIP COACH.com	HERFOUND

■ FIRST Robotics Competition

Student teams from Canada, Brazil, the United Kingdom, and most U.S. states gather at the FIRST Robotics Competition to solve engineering design problems in a creative and competitive environment. Participants are eligible for a variety of scholarships, many of which are school- or membership-specific. Awards amounts range from $2,000 to full-tuition scholarships. Competitions are first conducted on the regional level (deadlines vary according to region), and the national competition is held in early April.

	Keyword
SCHOLARSHIP COACH.com	FIRSTROB

Discover Card Tribute Awards

Mention the words "credit card" and "college student" together in the same sentence, and many a bill-paying parent may run for cover. But if we're talking about the Discover Card Tribute Awards, those same parents may instead make a mad dash for the program's application form.

Based on the philosophy that not every student's achievements can be measured in grade points alone, this highly regarded program offers high school juniors the chance to compete for big-time scholarship awards. The program doesn't require a GPA or class rank in the stratosphere: While the program does specify that applicants have a minimum 2.75 GPA for their freshman and sophomore years (junior-year grades aren't considered), a student's actual GPA or overall academic record is not a judging consideration once this minimum bar has been met. (Put another way, whether you have a 2.8 or 3.9 GPA won't make a difference.)

To apply, students submit recommendation letters, a "criteria statement" comprised of three short essay responses (primarily on topics related to extracurricular activities and personal achievements), a separate "goals paragraph," and a school transcript demonstrating that the student has met the minimum GPA requirement.

At least 450 applicants, nine in each state, will be awarded $2,500. The top nine entrants overall are designated national winners and each receives $25,000. Scholarship monies may be used for any type of education or training beyond high school, including certification

TARGET RECIPIENT

■ High school juniors

ENTRY REQUIREMENTS

| Essay | Recommendation | Short Answer | Academic Info |

DEADLINE

■ January

| | Keyword |
| ScholarshipCoach.com | DISCTRIB |

Money
$
Matters

Added Bonus

or license, trade or technical school, or two- or four-year colleges and universities. After advancing through state and national judging levels, winners are invited to attend (all expenses paid) an award ceremony in Chicago, Illinois.

Applications must be received by early January, and winning students will be notified by the end of May.

A CLOSER LOOK

If students choose to write about community service, a verification statement (signed by project supervisors) is also required.

Applicants are required to write a criteria statement on three of the following four topics: *special talents, leadership, community service,* and *obstacles overcome.* The entire criteria statement must be written in paragraph form (rather than submitted as a list) and be less than two pages in length. Students are instructed to convey to judges a sense of *past* accomplishments related to the each judging criterion, and each section should appear under a separate heading. As for the goals paragraph, it should be no more than 200 words (sorry, you can't submit a ten-page-long paragraph) and should outline the student's future aspirations with special emphasis on educational and career objectives.

Applicants must also include with their materials three recommendations written by adults (over age 21) who are *not* family members. (A recommendation doesn't quite carry the same weight when it is from the people who once changed your diapers.) Recommendation writers should use specific examples based on firsthand knowledge to support statements made by the student in the criteria statement. Furthermore, recommendation letters are required to be not longer than two pages and must include an original signature. Tell your recommendation writers to delete any mention of your GPA: Entrants are instructed *not* to include their actual grade point average anywhere in the application except in their official transcripts.

The official transcript must be signed and sealed by a school official.

Before state-level judging begins, submitted applications are sorted into three groups based on each student's specified career goal. The three career groups are defined as follows:

▌ Arts and Humanities

▌ Science, Business, and Technology

▌ Trade and Technical

Once a student has been assigned to one of these three categories, he or she is judged against others in that group. State judges, selected from educational, business, and governmental groups, weigh each judging criterion, as well as the goals paragraph, on an equal basis. In each state, a total of nine scholarships are available—with a quota of three per career category.

In some states with large numbers of applicants, additional prizes may be made available.

Top winners from each state then advance to the national judging round. At the national level, "blue-ribbon" judges include celebrity entertainers, athletes, politicians, journalists, as well as past Discover Card Tribute Award winners. The same judging methodology that is used on the national level is used on the state level.

▌ COACH'S ANALYSIS

Students entering the Discover Card Tribute Awards must answer the quintessential question that has faced mankind since the beginning of time: Which three of the four judging criteria should I choose?

To help you make this decision, focus on the "obstacles overcome" category. That's because an analysis of past Discover Card winners reveals that a large percentage of past recipients have overcome major medical obstacles. (In one recent year, five of the nine national winners had faced major health challenges.) So, to determine whether you should choose the "obstacles overcome" judging category, ask yourself whether an obstacle you have faced has truly had a major impact on virtually every aspect of your life. If it has, then you should select this judging category. If it hasn't, you're probably better off with the other three.

Once you've determined the three judging categories that you're going to address directly, the savvy scholarship applicant—that's you—knows that students can't just sweep their fourth category under the judging rug. After all, *you will be directly compared to other students who will have addressed this fourth judging category*. Because of this, you should try *indirectly* to work in a discussion of this fourth area into either your criteria statement or goals paragraph, or in one of your letters of recommendation. You may even want to work in a discussion of your "unique endeavors"—a fifth judging category that was part of the application in prior years, but has since been eliminated. Rather than create a separate header for unique endeavors, just allude to such examples and credentials in other areas of your criteria statement.

"Since you could only choose three out of four categories, for me it was a toss-up between community service and leadership," relates Josh Sundquist, a national Discover Card Tribute Award winner from Harrisonburg, Virginia. "I chose community service because I felt that I had more unique things to differentiate myself with for community service and I knew that my journalism teacher would talk about my leadership, enabling me to actually address the leadership criteria."

Once you've tackled the criteria statement, you've got to stare down another age-old question: *What do I want to do with my life?* To write this goals paragraph, try to demonstrate four main points. First, you want to show *why* you're interested in a particular career; judges want to know what is motivating you along the path you've outlined. Next, you want to demonstrate that you've taken

This doesn't mean discussing your unique ability to tie the stem of a cherry using only your tongue! In my own winning Discover Card application, I discussed an apprenticeship I served with a local filmmaker.

the time to consider *how* you're going to reach this career goal—including any action steps you've already taken toward the career and any educational milestones just around the bend. Judges want to see that you understand what's involved and are willing to do what it takes to accomplish your objectives. Third, you want to illustrate your potential to excel in the field, which often involves showing that you have already begun to exhibit the skills and abilities necessary to succeed in this specific area.

"If you have no idea what you want to do, pick something," suggests national Discover Card winner Ariel Overstreet, who grew up in Big Timber, Montana. "The judges like to know what [career] you're thinking about, and whether or not you're going to change your mind ten times. They understand that as a junior in high school you don't necessarily have everything figured out."

Insider Info

Keep in mind that on both the state and national levels, three separate awards are given for each of the three career divisions. So if you can't decide whether to focus your goals paragraph on one career goal or another, choose the one that places you in a career division that seems to give you the best strategic chance to win. (This will likely be the career division that is best related to your past activities and credentials.)

Need special worksheets, forms, and other tools that help you obtain quality recommendation letters? See the third book of my scholarship trilogy, Scholarship Seeker's Toolbox.

Finally, because the judging procedure places heavy emphasis on letters of recommendation, make sure that your recommendation writers fully understand the judging criteria for the program, and what elements of your record you need them to focus on. "I was afraid all of my letters would emphasize my one obstacle," emphasizes Audrey Nelson, a national Discover Card winner from Cody, Nebraska, who overcame a brain tumor. "When I asked them to do a recommendation letter, I gave them a piece of paper that specifically said what I needed their support on."

Joshua Sundquist
Harrisonburg, VA
National Winner
$25,000

CRITERIA STATEMENT: OBSTACLES OVERCOME

Winning
Entry

In the text below, Joshua Sundquist relates how determination, perseverance, and a positive attitude helped carry him through health-related challenges.

I will never forget waking up from my second biopsy at the University of Virginia Medical Center. I will always remember those first few moments in the recovery room. Several nurses gathered around to take a chest X ray. Then my parents entered and leaned over me. They told me that I had cancer. I started crying. I thought cancer meant death, and that my life would end after only nine years.

Doctors told me that I had a rare form of bone cancer, Ewing's Sarcoma, in my left leg. I was given a 50/50 chance to live. They put me on an exhausting chemotherapy cycle that would stretch over twelve months. Every three weeks, I would go into the hospital for three to five days to receive another chemotherapy treatment.

After three months of this schedule, the tumor in my leg still covered my entire femur and was beginning to spread into the muscle. The decision was made to amputate my leg at hip. I remember that I knew that I would have a harder time the rest of my life, but I also knew that this was the best chance I had to live the rest of my life.

Doctors told me that I'd spend three weeks recovering in the hospital after the amputation. But if I learned anything from having cancer, I learned that life is too short to waste looking back, making excuses, or feeling sorry for myself. By the third day after surgery, I was running laps around the children's floor at the hospital. They released me after five days.

After the amputation, I spent nine more months on chemotherapy. During that year, I spent almost 100 days in the hospital. I felt sick and tired all the time. But in those 365 days, there wasn't one day when I didn't think about

In this essay, Sundquist does a good job of interchanging long and short sentences. This gives the essay a nice tempo and keeps the reader interested.

Coach's Comments

the day when I would be cancer free. That goal of becoming healthy and normal, of having hair and energy, was the one thing that kept me going. It's why I'm still here six years later.

In the months following my amputation, I slowly returned to athletics. I've learned to ski, bike, swim, and play soccer with one leg. This year I made the ski team at Massanutten, my local ski resort. Although it's challenging to be the only one on the team with a disability, racing against able-bodied competitors is the best way to stay sharp for the national disabled races I will be competing in later this season.

I cannot discuss my challenges without thanking God and my family. With God's help, my family has gotten through not only my cancer, but the more recent cancer of my mother. In 1998, she was diagnosed with lymphoma (this is not at all connected with my cancer). After six months of chemotherapy, she was declared in remission, and we continue to pray that she will remain healthy.

Audrey Nelson
Cody, NE
National Winner
$25,000

Winning Entry

CRITERIA STATEMENT: COMMUNITY SERVICE

In this excerpt, Discover Card winner Audrey Nelson discusses her community service involvement, in particular the friendship and comfort she offered a neighbor recovering from a brain tumor.

The most meaningful community service I provide is comforting and just becoming friends with a woman who is also recovering from a brain tumor. I was introduced to Geniece, who is 42 years old, by a former neighbor. Claudia

(my neighbor) knew I would be willing to counsel Geniece through this life-threatening, life-changing ordeal we have both shared. I now have her phone number, and we email each other frequently. Together, we discuss many of our similar difficulties and frustrations, realizing that life does go on and understanding that the setbacks of life only serve to build character. We have also discovered that this event is molding us into stronger, more compassionate people. It makes my heart feel pleasant knowing that I am alleviating a woman's fears as well as helping her to get her confidence back on that difficult road she has to travel. In fact, right now I am compiling a video of myself so Geniece will be able to watch it, hopefully providing her with some encouragement and motivation to move on with her life.

I participate in many other community service activities within my isolated agricultural community. Due to the size of our school and its staffing, I have been the student aide in the science department for the last two years, assisting in grading papers and recording them, photocopying worksheets and exams, or, realistically, doing anything that needs to be done. Last year, I volunteered as the Jr. High Assistant Coach, teaching girls how to play basketball during their hour of P.E., and also during as many of the practices as I could attend.

To read more from Audrey Nelson's winning application, visit the Coach's Locker Room at ScholarshipCoach.com (Keyword: DISCTRIB).

CONTACT INFORMATION

Keyword
DISCTRIB

The Discover Card Tribute Award Program
c/o AASA
P.O. Box 9338
Arlington, VA 22219

E-mail: tributeaward@aasa.org
Website: www.aasa.org/discover.htm

RELATED AWARD PROGRAMS

For more information on a Related Award Program, enter the associated keyword in the "Enter a Keyword" box located in the Coach's Locker Room section of ScholarshipCoach.com

■ **Amateur Athletic Union Youth Excel Program**

Also recognizing students who have faced life-changing obstacles (such as blindness, cancer, and other significant illnesses, disabilities, or hardships), this program salutes those high school seniors who have overcome such challenges to become successful in sports and academics. Students submit information about athletics, academics, and community involvement, as well as an essay about the obstacles they have overcome. Prizes include three awards of $3,000, $1,500, and $500. Applications are due in early January.

Keyword
AAUEXCEL

■ **Horatio Alger Association Scholarships**

With a similar focus on extracurricular activities and triumphing over adversity, this association awards scholarships to high school seniors who have been involved in community and school activities, have a GPA of at least 2.0, and can demonstrate financial need. Awards are allocated for 100 students at $10,000 each, and 200 more are given $1,000. State awards are also offered. Application deadlines are generally in late October and December.

Keyword
HORALGER

DuPont Challenge

Picture this: You're walking across your grandmother's living room, sipping an ice-cold glass of grape juice. Before you know it, you've tripped over your own feet and have spilled your favorite fruity beverage on your grandmother's new Berber carpet. Make that *white* Berber carpet.

But don't despair! Grandma has DuPont Stainmaster carpeting, and what's more, you're about to stumble upon an opportunity that will help leave your college bank account stain-free. It's called the DuPont Challenge, and it's an essay competition that encourages students in grades 7 through 12 to analyze pressing technological or scientific issues.

To apply, students must attend school in the United States, U.S. territories, or Canada, and submit essays of 700 to 1,000 words about a technological or scientific theory, development, or event that intrigues them. Entrants are grouped into two separate divisions: one for 7th- through 9th-graders (junior division) and another for those in grades 10 through 12 (senior division).

One first-place winner from each division is presented with $1,500, plus an all-expense-paid trip for the winner, a sponsoring teacher, and a parent to Space Center Houston. Two second-place winners are awarded

TARGET RECIPIENT

■ Grades 7–12

ENTRY REQUIREMENTS

Essay

DEADLINE

■ January

Keyword
DUPCHALG

Money
Matters

Added
Bonus

$750 each, and two third-place winners each receive $500. Forty-eight students from each division are given additional $50 prizes.

Applicants for both divisions must submit their essays by late January.

▮ A Closer Look

Students may choose any area of scientific study to investigate in fields such as geology, math, astronomy, medicine, computer science, physics, archaeology, and the natural sciences. Past winners have discussed theories, scientific developments, technological developments, or events.

Applicants must incorporate a variety of research materials, discuss the effect their subject has had on humankind, and employ proper writing techniques. Each essay must include a bibliography of all sources consulted for the project, including sources not directly quoted. Any source quotes should be attributed in the text itself, rather than in endnotes or footnotes.

Astronaut Rex Walheim (center) congratulates first-place winner Nancy Huang (right) and her sponsoring science teacher, Greg Ring (left), during the festivities at Space Center Houston.

In addition to the 700- to 1,000-word essay length requirement, students should also be aware of the strict rules regarding the presentation of entries. Entrants frequently include diagrams and illustrations with their essays (this isn't permitted), include their name on the essay itself (don't do this, either), and forget to assign a title to their essay (think of something catchy).

Beware that any entry that does not conform to the official rules will be disqualified before the judges see it, as will essays whose entry forms are not signed by both a teacher and student. The good news about having to deal with such strict requirements is that they tend to eliminate a lot of the competition.

As for judging protocol, the program utilizes four distinct rounds of judging—with 25 middle- and high-school science and English teachers evaluating the essays. During the preliminary round, judges look to see if the writing level of each essay meets a minimum standard. Once essays have cleared this initial screening, the focus shifts: During the intermediate and semifinalist rounds, essays are grouped into a series of batches and the ones with the highest levels of scientific research and analysis advance. In the final round, judges rank each remaining essay numerically, considering both content and writing style, to determine the winners.

During the course of this process, the judges, in particular, look for evidence of four key qualities in submitted essays.

First, they look to see that you have chosen a subject that is appropriate to the contest. Winning essays tend to be written on what judges deem to be "important" topics, such as the functioning of the human brain, the eradication of smallpox, and the effect of mercury on the human body. So if you're planning on researching the true identity of the meat-like substance in the cafeteria "beef stew," you might want to reconsider.

Second, the judges examine whether you have carefully considered how your chosen topic affects you and

Even though the guidelines are available to everybody, in contests of this type a significant percentage of the entries are disqualified because the strict instructions have not been followed.

Insider Info

Look for information about your topic in books, magazines, scholarly journals, and newspapers. If you want to find some basic information about your topic in the encyclopedia, take a look at the sources listed at the end of the encyclopedia article.

mankind in general. If you have decided to write about a technological development, what are the universal applications and benefits of the new technology? Or has the development somehow made life more difficult for a significant portion of the population? If, for example, you have elected to write about a theory, how would proving or disproving the theory affect you and the general population?

Third, judges want evidence that you have used a wide variety of materials when researching your topic. Getting friendly with your encyclopedia is not *nearly* enough for this competition. The judges expect in-depth analysis of the topic on your part, and this is not possible without solid background research.

Lastly, judges expect that your essay should be free of spelling or grammatical errors, and should be well organized, clearly written, and easily understandable. Teachers, in fact, are encouraged to help proofread for basic spelling, grammar, and syntax errors.

■ COACH'S ANALYSIS

For most students, the challenging part of the DuPont Challenge lies in the fact that their essay submissions must simultaneously have elements of both complexity and simplicity: You must explain very complex, technical subjects in simple, easy-to-understand ways. To achieve this, you'll find it helpful to have strong reference materials to draw upon, and to engage in a methodical process of honing your writing.

To find the right reference materials for your subject, your first stop should probably be your science teacher. Ask your teacher to suggest some books or scientific journals that might prove useful to you. If your teacher isn't particularly helpful, try other science teachers at your school. Also try your local librarian, and while you're at the library, peruse magazines such as *Scientific American*.

The Internet can also be a good starting point, but make sure any online sources you reference are reliable and trustworthy.

If you live in a college town, contacting a local professor in the field of your intended topic can make the process of finding such materials much easier. Spending the time to find quality reference materials is key, because locating the right book or journal article can help you better understand the topic and better communicate your understanding to the judges. The shortest path to making this essay much more difficult than it needs to be is to be too timid to ask others for help.

Because a hallmark of DuPont Challenge winners is their ability to thoroughly survey an entire scientific field in a relatively small amount of space, the manner in which you hone and refine your essay is one of the most critical aspects of the essay writing process. Before revising an essay, try to distance yourself somewhat from the material. If possible, take a day or two off from working on the essay and allow the material to simmer in the back of your mind. When revising your own work, get in the habit of reading your essay out loud—or have someone else read your essay out loud to you. Reading aloud gives your ears a chance to catch what your eyes miss. If something is awkwardly phrased or out of place, you'll hear it right away. (Incidentally, this is good advice for revising all of your essays.)

Ask science teachers and other students in your science class to read your essay and provide you with feedback on its strengths and weaknesses.

After analyzing numerous winning essays from the DuPont Challenge, I've noticed that most essays, regardless of topic, skillfully address five key areas of the given subject matter. So as you hone your essay, pay special attention to make sure that you have:

- Traced the historical development of scientific knowledge on your subject and have shown how current knowledge builds upon earlier research.

- Summarized the key issues now facing modern-day scientists and have described any differences of opinion or areas of contention in the field.

- Included technical language appropriate to the field, but have also explained this jargon in a way that everyone can understand.

■ Discussed the scientific or technological unknowns surrounding your subject matter and outlined the biggest obstacles standing in the way of further scientific breakthroughs.

■ Forecasted where relevant scientific knowledge is headed, and hypothesized about the type of advancements that may occur in the near or more distant future.

Insider Info

In addition, look for ways to make the opening sentences of your essay interesting and memorable. "There is something that stands out about the papers that win," says program coordinator Gail Rudd. "They have a little twist that makes them unique, such as an interesting story at the beginning." Rudd notes, for instance, that one standout essay exploring Global Positioning Systems (GPS) opened with an account of a stolen painting—and how it was located with a computer chip. In general, as you hone your essay, seek to find creative ways to catch—and keep—the judges' attention.

Ravi Randhava
Evanston, IL
First Place
Junior Division
$1,500

THE MYSTERY OF HUMAN MEMORY

Winning

Entry

In this excerpt from his winning essay, Ravi Randhava explores the science behind how the brain stores memory.

Do you remember what you ate for breakfast today? How did your brain recall that information? Memory is the ability to remember something that has

been learned or experienced. It is a vital part of the learning process that allows people to store new information and use it to build on concepts they have already learned.

Although scientists have come up with over 40 different names for different types of memory, they still don't understand exactly what happens when the brain stores memories. Neuroscientists divide memory into two major categories: declarative and procedural. These divisions are based on content and kind of information.

Declarative and *procedural* are terms originally developed in the 1970s by computer scientists working to simulate the brain. Procedural memory includes our memories of learned skills. It is a process of knowing how to do something, such as riding a bike. Procedural memory seems to be stored in the brain's cerebellum.

Conversely, declarative, or explicit, memory is sometimes described as a process of knowing "that." It includes both episodic and semantic memories. Episodic memories are of past episodes from our personal lives, and semantic memories include stored general knowledge. All declarative memories are stored in the cortex, a complex part of the brain scientists are only beginning to understand.

Short-term and *long-term* are other simple descriptions of memory, based on staying power and size. Short-term memory, which is very limited in size, can hold a fact or image as long as you actively think about it. Before information even reaches short-term memory, it passes through sensory memory, which holds it for only an instant. Some information from short-term memory enters long-term memory, where it is permanently stored, and can be recalled after many years. Long-term memory includes a huge amount of information, which enters as a result of either repetition or intense emotion.

While there is still a lot to learn about memory and the brain, scientists know that storing new memories involves both chemical changes in the nerve cells in the brain and changes in their physical structure. These changes occur in a tiny section of the brain called the hippocampus. The hippocampus sits on the inner part of each temporal lobe. Studies of people whose memory has been damaged have convinced scientists that the brain's medial temporal lobe and hippocampus are key in transforming short-term memories into permanent ones, and also that permanent memories are stored in another, unknown part of the brain. The hippocampus is part of the larger cerebral cortex, which contains about 70 percent of our brain cells.

Although human memory is often compared to that of computers, it doesn't really work like any known system. The brain has multiple memory systems, each playing a different role while working together at the same time. For example, when you're riding a bicycle, the memory of how to operate the bike comes from one set of neurons, while the memory of the route to your destination comes from another.

Notice how Randhava's bicycle example communicates a complex scientific idea in an easy to understand way.

For the complete text of Ravi Randhava's winning essay, visit the Coach's Locker Room at ScholarshipCoach.com (Keyword: DUPCHALG).

Nancy Huang
South Pasadena, CA
First Place
Senior Division
$1,500

Winning
Entry

Morphometrics:
The Study of Shapes Helps to Solve Medical Enigmas

In this essay excerpt, Nancy Huang investigates the potential impact of mathematical shape theory on the treatment of disease.

> *I was being watched and followed by this World War II character who demanded I get a job in construction and shape up. Tibetan Buddhists were reading my mind because I had caused Mount St. Helen's Eruption earlier that year. They were training me to become a great Buddhist saint, which required a life of abject poverty and isolation.*
>
> —Ian Chovil, a recovering schizophrenic

Schizophrenia seems to come from out of nowhere to devastate minds. After decades of research to understand and treat schizophrenia, mathematics itself may hold the key to the disease's hiding place.

Morphometrics, an innovative method of analyzing shapes, may enable doctors to tell what changes occur in the brains of schizophrenics before they lose contact with reality. The field also provides clues to the development of fetal alcohol syndrome and Alzheimer's disease and is improving the ability of brain surgeons to map out the routes they will take to perform operations.

The world's first professor of morphometrics, Fred Bookstein, was inspired to apply math to medicine after his nephew suffered a psychotic episode. The principle behind morphometrics originated in the sixteenth century in the work of artist Albrecht Durer. Durer laid out gridlines over the faces in his portraits. By moving the lines while maintaining the features in the same position relative to the grid, Durer transformed the face any way he wanted.

In order to generate caricatures of himself, Bookstein attached a grid to 13 landmarks on a

Program coordinator Gail Rudd notes that Huang's opening quote from a recovering schizophrenic helped make her essay stand out.

Coach's Comments

scanned picture. He moved a few of the landmark points around, thus focusing the grid to warp and bend as if a thin metal plate were attached to it. Engineers have used such "thin-plate splines" for years, but it was Bookstein who realized that these composite images are a perfect way to represent changes in "shape space," and to detect shape differences. Shape is an elusive concept, yet modern science requires precise descriptions of shapes. "Morphometrics gives you a language for talking about shapes," says Jim Rohlf of the State University of New York.

Prodded by his nephew's misfortune, Bookstein studied brain scans of 14 schizophrenics and 14 non-schizophrenic volunteers. He labeled 13 landmark points on each of the brains, converted the points into shapes, and averaged them. When he compared images of the shapes of normal brains with those of the schizophrenics, he detected an obvious difference. In the schizophrenics, the corpus callosum, the central conduit for all communications between the two sides of the brain's cortex, seemed swollen. "To the extent that this pattern is correct, it would permit me to figure out who's going to get it before they have their first psychotic breaks," said Bookstein. By early detection, doctors can try prescribing medication in advance or counsel the patients to avoid alcohol and addictive drugs, which can complicate the disease.

* * *

French mathematician Henri Poincare said, "He [the mathematician] studies mathematics because he delights in it, and he delights in it because it is beautiful." Shape theory in Bookstein's hands is mathematics made flesh: It not only sheds light on mental illness, it may change a doctor's diagnosis or his decision on where to cut a brain.

Bookstein is an outsider who dared to think "outside the box" and to take on problems that most experts considered unsolvable. As Isaac Asimov said, "There is a single light of science, and to brighten it anywhere is to brighten it everywhere."

For the complete text of Nancy Huang's winning essay, visit the Coach's Locker Room at ScholarshipCoach.com (Keyword: DUPCHALG).

CONTACT INFORMATION

Keyword
DUPCHALG

The DuPont Challenge
c/o General Learning Communications
900 Skokie Boulevard, Suite 200
Northbrook, IL 60062-4028

Phone: (847) 205-3000
Website: www.glcomm.com/dupont

RELATED AWARD PROGRAMS

For more information on a Related Award Program, enter the associated keyword in the "Enter a Keyword" box located in the Coach's Locker Room section of ScholarshipCoach.com

■ **American Fire Sprinkler Association Scholarship Contest**

High school seniors interested in writing about the science and technology of firefighting may submit essays of 700 to 1,000 words written on a topic relating to the use, benefits, or history of automatic fire sprinklers. A recommendation and bibliography are also required. Creativity and the use of original sources are rewarded with national scholarships of $3,000, $2,000, and $1,000, as well as regional awards of $1,000. Applications must be submitted by early December.

■ **Computer Professionals for Social Responsibility Essay Contest**

Undergraduate and graduate students are invited to write essays on topics related to the social implications of contemporary information technology. Suggested topics include computers and the environment, computers and the law, women in computing, and privacy. Essays should be no more than 2,500 words long and may include graphics. Awards range from $100 to $500. Entries must be endorsed by a faculty member and may be submitted in either December or May.

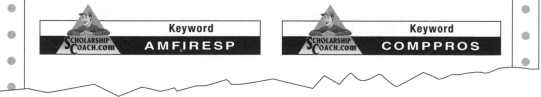

Keyword
AMFIRESP

Keyword
COMPPROS

Elie Wiesel Prize in Ethics

Here's the scenario: You come home from college during winter break and while making eye contact with a cute member of the opposite sex, you ram the family car into a telephone pole. The question is, do you:

A. Pretend that the two-foot-long dent in the front of the car doesn't exist.

B. Swear that the dent was there before you drove the car.

C. Blame it on your seven-year old baby sister.

D. Quickly gather your things and head back to school.

The answer, my scholarship-seeking friends, is none of the above. What you should do is fess up to your crime and then begin work on a 3,500-word essay for the Elie Wiesel Prize in Ethics competition.

The Elie Wiesel Prize—named after the famed author, Holocaust survivor, and Nobel Peace Prize winner—is open to undergraduate juniors and seniors (in the United States and Canada) who submit a 3,000- to 4,000-word essay on a student-selected topic that addresses a pressing ethical issue of personal importance. Each essay submission should use the student's personal choices and life experiences to illustrate the topic, question, or dilemma chosen.

TARGET RECIPIENT

■ Undergraduate juniors and seniors

ENTRY REQUIREMENTS

Essay

DEADLINE

■ December

Keyword
ELIEPRIZ

The mission of the Elie Wiesel Foundation for Humanity, the contest sponsor, is to "advance the cause of human rights by creating forums for the discussion and resolution of urgent ethical issues."

Money Matters

A panel of judges awards five monetary prizes, with the first-prize winner receiving $5,000. Second and third prizes of $2,500 and $1,500 are also awarded, along with two honorable mention awards of $500 each.

All entries must be postmarked by the early December deadline.

A Closer Look

Each year, Elie Wiesel himself selects the three suggested essay topics, all of which deal with broad ethical questions. Recent suggested essay topics have included:

- What issue concerns you most and what concrete proposals would you make to deal with it?

- Reflect on the most profound moral dilemma you have encountered and what it has taught you about ethics.

However, students may submit essays on a topic of their own choosing, as long as the essay deals with ethical issues in some way. "It's okay to write about anything you want as long as it deals with the theme of the contest," states Program Coordinator Annika Wadenius. "Reading the past winning essays really gives you a good idea of the variety of topics that can work."

Furthermore, the rules stipulate that the essay may be written from a wide variety of perspectives, and may be "biographical, historical, literary, philosophical, psychological, sociological, or theological" in nature. Many students have submitted essays adapted from term papers they had already written for college courses.

To ensure anonymous judging, no identifying references (such as an applicant's name or school) should be included on the title page or within the manuscript itself.

Applicants for this award have commonly been English, philosophy, political science, and history majors, with English and philosophy majors the most prevalent.

Entrants are also required to have professors endorse their essays. Endorsing professors must sign a faculty sponsor form, where they acknowledge that the submitted essay is intelligent and thought-provoking. Recommendation letters are not required.

Each year, the same group of professors from around the country—known as the Reader's Committee—perform preliminary judging duties. Although these professors specialize in a wide variety of academic fields, all have ties to the foundation's work or to Elie Wiesel himself. A team of two professors reads each essay, discussing the essay's merits in person or over the phone.

According to Wadenius, students aren't disqualified for exceeding the 3,000- to 4,000-word limit by a small amount. "The reader's committee is not super strict about word limits or things like that. They want a good essay to go on to the next round." What the Reader's Committee does look for is well-thought-out essays that exhibit a depth of feeling and grapple with a moral dilemma. Furthermore, they look for originality and imagination, intensity and unity, and eloquence in writing style.

Rather than award points to each essay, the judges look to see if the essays meet the general standards of the contest. Although there is no quota on the number of essays that will move on to the next phase of judging, through this process about 40 to 50 essays are chosen as semifinalists. Once the semifinalists have been identified, all members of the Reader's Committee read each semifinalist essay. Then each pair of judges selects their top 10 to 15 essays, and subsequently ranks them on a numerical scale from favorite to least favorite.

After the rankings of all the judges are compared, the top 10 to 15 essays overall advance to the final round, at which Elie Wiesel and his wife, Marian, personally select the winners.

Insider Info

"I swore never to be silent whenever and wherever human beings endure suffering and humiliation. We must always take sides. Neutrality helps the oppressor, never the victim."

–Elie Wiesel

■ Coach's Analysis

I'm sure you've realized by now that 3,000 to 4,000 words does *not* a short essay make. If you approach this task smartly, however, writing an essay of this length doesn't have to be on the same fun level as having your wisdom teeth pulled by your burly next-door neighbor.

To choose an appropriate topic for your essay, the most important thing is that you are passionate about the topic. Passion is a quality that quickly surfaces in most of the past winning entries. If you feel strongly about what you're writing, you'll be able to delve into the ethical issues in a deeper way that can't help but bubble up to the surface. In most cases, the tone with which you approach the topic should be academic (after all, the judges are professors), but your tone should also strive to capture an individual spirit, belief system, and personal point of view sometimes missing in academic writing. Elie Wiesel's own celebrated written works are good examples of the power of penetrating, personal, and passionate writing.

Some past applicants have actively sought to choose a topic directly related to the Holocaust, an approach that has both advantages and disadvantages. On the plus side, the judges for this contest will undoubtedly be interested in the topic; on the minus side, they are generally such experts in the field that it may be difficult to compose an essay that captivates them with an original idea or approach. If you are interested in ethical issues raised by the Holocaust, perhaps the safest strategy is to write about other historical events, world crises, societal problems, or issues and then show how your topic does, in fact, relate to the questions raised and lessons we've learned from the horrors of the Holocaust.

I strongly recommend incorporating the essay as part of a class writing assignment. This works especially well for term papers. For many of your classes, no matter what the academic discipline, you will have plenty of

For more advice on choosing scholarship essay topics, see my special guide, Scholarship Essay Boot Camp (for more info visit ScholarshipCoach.com).

leeway to choose the specific topic for your paper. By selecting a topic related to ethics—something easily done in virtually every field of study—you make it eligible for the Elie Wiesel prize. If you have to write a paper anyway, why not write it in such a way that you become eligible for more college cash?

Even more important than the time savings are the many benefits that accrue from this classroom approach. You'll be able to tap the brains of professors and teaching assistants affiliated with the class; the insights you gain will make your eventual submission exponentially better.

"The criteria for the Wiesel competition already fit a paper I had written to a remarkable degree," says Matthew Mendlham, a second-place winner in the contest. "I got two or three professors to look over my essay and offer suggestions of both style and content."

Because strong Elie Wiesel submissions involve substantive research into the available literature on a particular topic, ask these instructors to direct you to resources and reference materials that you probably wouldn't find elsewhere on your own. "Talk to professors, older students in your major whom you respect, and other thoughtful and like-minded people," suggests Mendlham. "Find out what sorts of periodicals and media they find to be the most reliable and insightful."

The comments you receive from your professors have an additional benefit: Since professors from around the country serve as Elie Wiesel judges (Elie Wiesel himself is a professor at Boston University in the religion and philosophy department), you'll be able to get a "trial" judging round from individuals who come from a similar perspective as your eventual essay evaluators. Taking into account their comments, you'll be able to shore up your essay's weak spots.

If you're especially ambitious, seek out other professors on campus (other than just your own instructors) who have insights on the ethical issue you choose. Find out when they have office hours and ask them plenty of questions.

WHAT TOPICS HAVE WINNERS WRITTEN ABOUT?

Past winners in the Elie Wiesel program have tackled a wide variety of ethical questions and topics in their winning submissions. Here are a few of the approaches winning students have taken when competing for this prestigious prize:

▪ First-place winner James Long (College of William and Mary) focused on how we have become desensitized to the horrors of genocide in his passionate essay, "Deaths in Paradise: Genocide and the Limits of Imagination in Rwanda." According to Long, by dealing with atrocities on a general, collective level instead of on an individual basis, we fail to fully comprehend and address the suffering inflicted on its victims.

▪ Matthew Mendham (Taylor University) earned a second-place prize for his essay entitled "Replication and Repugnance: Leon Kass on Human Cloning." To tackle this complex topic, Mendham examined Kass' writings on the subject and used them to make a case against permitting human cloning—arguing that not only would cloning endanger human dignity, but few benefits would be sacrificed if cloning were banned.

▪ Laura Overland (University of Missouri) addresses the issue of informed consent in her first-place composition entitled "Their Lives in Our Hands: Fulfilling Our Ethical Obligations to the Terminally Ill Enrolling in Research Studies." To do this, Overland relates the moving story of Anne, a woman with terminal cancer who enrolls in a clinical research study of a new experimental treatment, only to be horribly disappointed at the outcome and health side effects. Overland argues that many terminally ill patients are not given enough information to make truly informed decisions about whether or not to participate in medical research.

▌ In his second-place essay entitled "The South African Truth and Reconciliation Commission and the Case of Stephen Biko," Jason Costa (Emory University) relates a serious dilemma faced by the new government in post-apartheid South Africa: bring criminals to justice, or expose as much truth as possible. Costa outlines the downside of the commission's policies, using the Biko case as an example of when it does not work—when justice may outweigh the need for truth without consequences.

CONTACT INFORMATION

Keyword
ELIEPRIZ

The Elie Wiesel Prize in Ethics
The Elie Wiesel Foundation for Humanity
529 Fifth Avenue, Suite 1802
New York, NY 10017

Phone: (212) 490-7777
Fax: (212) 490-6006
E-mail: info@eliewieselfoundation.org
Website: www.eliewieselfoundation.org

RELATED AWARD PROGRAMS

For more information on a Related Award Program, enter the associated keyword in the "Enter a Keyword" box located in the Coach's Locker Room section of ScholarshipCoach.com

■ Olive W. Garvey Fellowship Program

College undergraduate and graduate students under age 36 (in any country) submit an essay of 3,000 words or less to the Independent Institute, answering a question about economic and personal liberty. Past topics have included "Does the new economy require a free economy?" Awards range from $1,000 to $2,500. Because the contest is offered only every other year, the deadline for applications is in May of odd-numbered years.

Keyword
OLIVFELL

■ Acton Institute Essay Competition

High school, undergraduate, and graduate students interested in religious themes submit a 1,750- to 2,500-word essay dealing with a provided quotation from an essay by Lord Acton (such as his "Essay on Irish Education"). First-, second-, and third-place winners are given $2,000, $1,000, and $500 respectively. Entries are due in mid-November.

Keyword
ACTONESS

■ Woodrow Wilson National Fellowship Foundation

This program is for graduate students expecting to earn a Ph.D. within two years. Applicants are expected to demonstrate an interest in pursuing research into religious or ethical values. Any major field of study and any specific topics are welcomed as long as they relate to broad questions in religion or ethics. About 35 fellowships of $16,000 are awarded each year. Dissertation proposals are due in early December.

Keyword

WOODWILS

Elks Most Valuable Student Competition

How many times have you driven right by your local Elks building without realizing that the Elks would be a great source of college funds? Would it surprise you to learn that the many Elks lodges (there are over 2,000 of them) spread throughout America's cities and towns offer an impressive amount of financial aid to college-bound high school seniors in their communities?

The Benevolent & Protective Order of the Elks of the USA are the benefactors behind the Elks Most Valuable Student Competition—a scholarship program that couples merit-based judging criteria with demonstrated financial need.

The program is geared toward high school seniors who can put together an impressive application packet consisting of a list of activities and honors, glowing recommendation letters, test scores, a transcript, and a statement of professional goals. Entrants must also submit a parental statement outlining family financial data and explaining why their son or daughter needs monetary aid for higher education.

The top six students selected nationally, three males and three females, divide up $240,000 in scholarship money: The first-place winner of each gender receives $60,000; second-place winners receive $40,000, and third-place winners claim $20,000 in college cash. Furthermore, 494 additional students from around the country are each awarded $4,000 in prizes, payable over four years of schooling. In addition to these national awards (totaling over $2.2 million!), there are also numerous awards at local or regional levels—scholarships worth hundreds, or even thousands, of dollars.

TARGET RECIPIENT

- High school seniors

ENTRY REQUIREMENTS

Activities & Credentials

Essay

Financial Data

Academic Info

Short Answer

Recommendation

DEADLINE

- January

Keyword
ELKMVSTU

Money
$
Matters

Local lodges process entries in early January before sending them on to state and national competitions. National winners receive word in mid-May.

A Closer Look

The application itself is composed of numerous components. First, students must submit SAT or ACT scores, as well as an official high school transcript. Second, students must complete a series of lists, including ones for extracurricular activities (divided according to number of years of participation), leadership positions held, awards and honors, and employment and community service. Students may also attach additional exhibits of their choosing that showcase their achievements in school, service, and extracurricular activities.

In addition, applicants must write an essay of not more than 350 words that describes the "role leadership has played in high school accomplishments, determining career aspirations, achieving these life goals, and preparing for college." Each applicant must also obtain two letters of recommendation—one from a high school teacher and another from someone not affiliated with his or her school.

Program rules specify that the completed application, including attached documents, must not exceed 20 pages.

The program evaluates financial need by requiring applicants to complete a one-page financial analysis worksheet. The worksheet includes questions regarding the family's taxable income, number of dependent children in college, home equity, miscellaneous assets, and the student's personal financial resources. Parents must also include a statement of 200 words or less summarizing the family's financial obligations and resources. Parents may exceed this word limit if explaining extenuating circumstances involving a noncustodial parent or medical expenses.

To standardize the judging methodology, local, district, and state judges follow a judging manual put together by the national foundation. At the national level, all three judges review each of the 500 national finalist applications. The scores of all three judges are averaged together and the students with the highest average point totals win the largest scholarship awards.

The manual stipulates that applications are judged on a 1,000-point scale according to three basic criteria: *scholarship* (450 points), *leadership* (350 points), and *financial need* (200 points). Frank Saurman, retired dean of admissions and financial aid at Syracuse University who helped redesign the Elks scoring system, says that strict formulas, combined with some judging discretion, are used to score each application.

Insider Info

To award points for scholarship, Saurman says, judges primarily look at standardized test scores (either SAT or ACT). Although the actual point scale may be redefined from time to time, typically a 1,600 on the SATs is worth a perfect 450 points in the scoring system, while a 1,000 SAT score is worth 200 points. Judges also have the discretion to bump up overall scholarship scores for good grades in challenging courses and a strong class ranking.

To score the leadership category, judges follow an elaborate system of awarding points for specific leadership positions held in particular types of activities. To do this, Saurman says, judges employ a four-tier system. Tier one activities are worth the most points, and tier four activities are worth the fewest. Tier one activities include being president of the student body or editor of the school newspaper. Common tier two activities include being captain of the football team or first chair in band or orchestra. Tier three activities might include being president of a club or organization or second chair in band or orchestra. Finally, tier four leadership activities generally involve being an officer of any club or organization.

Complex formulas, including a system of bonus points, are used to score students whose multiple activities fall into different scoring tiers. Judges also factor in a student's awards and honors, employment, and community service participation in a similar manner. Through this process, each judge may adjust scores and point awards based on his impression of the student's essay, letters of recommendation, and additional materials.

For the financial need category, a mathematical formula, not unlike ones used by college financial aid offices, is used to evaluate an applicant's family income and assets. Lower income and asset levels result in higher scores. A family that has more children currently in college—thus increasing the tuition burden on the family—would also be awarded more points. Judges retain the discretion to adjust point awards for extenuating circumstances or unique considerations described in the parental statement.

▌ COACH'S ANALYSIS

To win one of the top six national prizes (ranging from $20,000 to $60,000), you need to score high in all three major judging areas—scholarship, leadership, and financial need. If your scores aren't high in one area, however, you can still take home significant college cash: According to the judges, high scores in two out of the three categories is often enough to advance from your state level and claim one of the 494 awards of $4,000 each. For this reason, even if your financial need (as calculated by your family's income and assets) is likely to be much less than other applicants, you should still apply for the award.

To make sure that you get the highest scores possible in all three judging areas, let's tackle each of them one by one. For scholarship, because the bulk of the points depend upon SAT or ACT scores, consider retaking these standardized tests (and studying extra for them) if your scores are not as high as you would like. (Since you only need to submit one set of either SAT or ACT scores, you'll

Insider Info

be able to send in your best results.) Using the current Elks methodology, if you boosted your overall SAT score from 1,000 to 1,200, it would raise your point allocation in the Elks competition from 200 to 380 points. Likewise, boosting your SAT scores from 1,200 to 1,400 would cause your awarded points to jump from 380 to 425.

Because judges can further bump up your scholarship point total based on your success in classes of high difficulty, make sure that any honors, advanced placement (AP), or International Baccalaureate (IB) classes are clearly indicated on your transcript. Talk to the registrar or another school official (perhaps the principal) about including the official course guide description of such classes (which emphasizes the rigorous nature of the coursework) on an addendum sheet attached as part of the official school transcript. If your school is known for its challenging curriculum and high percentage of college-bound students, try to have this information included as well.

To maximize your points in the leadership area, put the greatest emphasis on formal, school-affiliated activities in which you have held an official leadership position. Because the judging methodology awards the greatest number of points to traditional activities that can be found in schools across the nation, place such activities at the top of your lists and attach additional exhibits that support your efforts in these areas. Once you've done this, you should then highlight your community service endeavors, as judges frequently use their own discretion to boost point totals for excellence in these areas. "The [Elks] scholarship itself is meant to be a community outreach program," remarks first-place national winner Mark Longstreth of Columbus, Ohio. "If community outreach was important enough to them [the Elks organization] to create the scholarship program, I figured it's something they would value in applications submitted to them."

To increase your score in the financial need category, invest time with your parents in crafting a really

Looking like a political pro, Elks national winner Mark Longstreth (right) meets Dennis Hastert (left), speaker of the U.S. House of Representatives. While a freshman at Georgetown University, Longstreth toured Capitol Hill with Elks President Dwayne Runmey (center) and met leading politicians.

strong statement that summarizes your family's obligations and resources. If your raw financial data doesn't reflect your *true* need, this is your time to explain. When you do this, be sure to include the fact that you and your parents are not just relying on the Elks organization to fund your education, but have taken many steps *as a family* to address the financial considerations of a college education. National judge Jim Tilton, who also serves as the executive director of student financial services at Columbia University, explains that the judges like to see that "the student and family have already made efforts" to work for and save college funds.

Keep one additional point in mind: For this program, it's probably wise *not* to emphasize your likelihood of receiving large amounts of financial aid or scholarships from colleges or private sources. According to Tina Vu, a past Elks winner who later interned in the scholarship division at the Elks national headquarters, highlighting substantial outside aid can lessen your chances of winning: "Sometimes the judges knew that students would get financial aid from somewhere else and seemed not as interested in giving a [Elks] scholarship."

STATEMENT OF FUTURE GOALS

Winning
Entry

Mark Longstreth illustrates in the text below that a personal commitment to leadership can impact all areas of a young person's life.

A quarterback's charismatic enthusiasm, focus, and leadership can lead a down-spirited football team to a game-winning touchdown drive. The quarterback's leadership directly affects and is a crucial component to what both he and the team achieve. I exude, exemplify, and apply the many aspects that leading entails every day. Similar to the quarterback's guidance of his team, my leadership results in the achievements that have been merited throughout my life and the lives of those I affect; leadership plays a gargantuan role in the possibilities for success that lie ahead in my bright future.

Leading includes exemplifying the ideal. As a three-season captain in both cross country and track, I have encountered this aspect often. By working both hard and focused in cross country, I have influenced my teammates to work in the same manner. This entire team work ethic merited not only my individual state meet berth, but also the only three regional qualifying teams in the history of my high school's boys' cross country program.

Leadership includes both the ambition to break precedent, leading the way to higher levels of success, and the discipline to execute a goal into reality. I have chosen to take a different path than the five family members in front of me in terms of college selection and even the option of college itself. I aspire to educate myself in an excellent liberal-arts institution, forming a solid and wide base from which I can expand into the business world, and eventually become a major force in business. The discipline required to drive my whole self toward the success of my goals will enable me to realize these goals.

> *In his application, Longstreth used a technique employed by many savvy scholarship applicants: If he didn't have space to talk about an important credential in his essay, he would ask his recommendation writers to highlight these areas.*
>
> Coach's Comments

To lead is also to initiate, or spark. I am the sole motivating force behind my preparation for college. I diligently work at my studies during high school every day, in every subject, so that I have the highest

advantage upon entering college. I am also taking the initiative by not only applying to selective schools where I feel I could prosper,
but also in applying for financial aid and scholarships so that I can gather the resources needed to attend my school of choice.

The many aspects of leading that I epitomize daily are the forces that compel myself and those around me to achieve, aspire, and elevate ourselves to higher levels of success. I have specifically exploited these leadership qualities for my successful preparation for my next level of education—college. Just as leadership provides the means for the success of a quarterback and his team, leadership has already made possible and in the future will be the key tool for accomplishing any task, challenge, or endeavor that I have pursued or will pursue in the promising years that lie ahead.

CONTACT INFORMATION

Keyword
ELKMVSTU

Applications should be submitted to local Elks chapters for preliminary judging.

MVS Competition
Elks National Foundation
2750 N. Lakeview Ave
Chicago, IL 60614-1889

Phone: (773) 755-4700
Website: www.elks.org

RELATED AWARD PROGRAMS

For more information on a Related Award Program, enter the associated keyword in the "Enter a Keyword" box located in the Coach's Locker Room section of ScholarshipCoach.com

■ Elks Americanism Essay Contest

Also sponsored by the national Elks organization, this program is for students in grades 5 through 8 who submit a short, patriotic essay. Entrants compete in two age divisions for prizes ranging from $200 to $500. Entries should be submitted to local lodges by the late March deadline.

Keyword: ELKAMESS

■ Jaycees Scholarships

The United States Junior Chamber (also known as the Jaycees), another service-oriented organization with local chapters, sponsors The Jaycee War Memorial Fund. The fund awards scholarships to high school seniors and college undergraduates and graduate students who show leadership qualities, academic potential, and financial need. Awards of $1,000 are allocated for 25 student winners. Application forms are available directly from the Jaycees for $5. Applications may be requested until the beginning of February.

Keyword: JAYCSHO

■ Olin L. Livesey Scholarship Fund

High school seniors are eligible to receive awards from the Olin L. Livesey fund (named after a wealthy benefactor) if they are exceptional in areas of scholarship, leadership, school and community participation, and potential to succeed. Like the Elks Most Valuable Student Scholarship, financial need is a judging criterion. Students submit activity lists, recommendations from teachers and community leaders, transcripts, and test scores. Awards range from $250 to $10,000 (according to monetary need). Preliminary and secondary applications are due between October and June.

Keyword: OLINFUND

Felix Morley
Journalism Competition

"Do not ever, under any circumstances, tell the government you own a dog." When Jason Brooks penned the newspaper article containing this thought-provoking sentence, little did he know that it would help him bring home a first-prize award of $2,500 and some journalistic prestige along the way.

Named after the Pulitzer Prize–winning journalist and editor of the *Washington Post*, the Felix Morley Journalism Competition is intended for either full-time students under age 25 in high school, college, or graduate school, or working journalists under age 26 who have an interest in writing about the classical liberal tradition. Sponsored by the Institute for Humane Studies (IHS), the contest is open to writers who wish to submit articles, essays, op-ed pieces, reviews, and editorials that have been printed in a student newspaper, professional publication, or other periodical. Students should send in three to five pieces that deal with such classical liberal subjects as:

TARGET RECIPIENT

- High school students
- Undergraduates
- Graduate students
- Journalists under age 26

ENTRY REQUIREMENTS

Writing
Sample

DEADLINE

- November

| | Keyword |
| SCHOLARSHIPCoach.com | FMORCOMP |

- The protection of individual rights through private property, rule of law, and contracts

- Free trade, free migration, and peace

- Voluntarism in human relations

- Noninterventionist foreign policy

In addition, applicants must submit a résumé (listing academic and

professional experience, academic honors and awards, extracurricular activities, and publications) plus provide a brief description of writing interests and career goals.

Money Matters

Cash prizes in the amounts of $2,500, $1,000, and $750 are awarded to the first- through third-place winners, and a limited number of runners-up receive $250 each. Applicants should submit their writing samples in late November.

▮ A Closer Look

Traditionally, the vast majority of applicants have been current college students or graduate students, followed by a much smaller number of college graduates who are still under the age of 26. The fewest applicants have been high school students. The competition, however, does *not* have a quota of awards set aside for each age group.

Of the three to five articles that are to be included in an application, at least two of them must explore classical liberal principles such as the ones mentioned above. Other submitted articles should indicate the applicant's range and quality of writing. Entrants are not permitted to submit articles written several years ago: Each article must have been published no earlier than July in the year preceding the deadline date.

Insider Info

The program's methodology evaluates applicants according to a standard of achievement appropriate for their age and experience. "Our judging paradigm is to compare students to their peers," relates Dan Alban, a program director and judge for the competition. "We compare high school entrants to a standard for high school students." For instance, a recent entrant who was a freshman in college did not write at a level near that of older applicants, but won nonetheless. "We were impressed with his ability compared to other freshmen in college," Alban said.

Judging is divided into three phases. In the first phase, four to six members of the IHS staff divide up the submitted applications and review them to make sure that the articles are on topic and are well written. Overall, about 30 to 40 applications have traditionally advanced to the next round of judging.

In the second round of judging, distinguished journalists and writers review each submitted application—with two or three judges reviewing each submission. The judging panel includes journalists and writers from the *Wall Street Journal,* the *National Journal, Forbes, Reader's Digest,* and the Cato Institute, among others.

Second-round judges evaluate the articles according to three equally weighted judging categories. The first category, *writing ability,* is judged on four subcategories: (1) basic competence, (2) style, (3) use of facts, and (4) effective argumentation.

The second category, *classical liberal interest and understanding,* is divided into three subcategories: (1) demonstrated appreciation of markets and private property, (2) demonstrated appreciation of classical liberal principles beyond free markets, and (3) sophistication of understanding and exposition in chosen classical liberal subject areas.

Finally, the *potential for development* category takes into account the applicant's demonstrated writing ability, stated writing interests and career goals, and his or her likelihood of growth as a writer.

For each of these subcategories, as well as the umbrella category as a whole, applicants are rated as either exceptional (top 2 percent), very good (top 10 percent), good (top 33 percent), fair (middle 33 percent), or poor (bottom 33 percent). Judges may also write comments next to their ratings.

The scores from the judges are totaled and averaged for each of the categories and subcategories; the top 12 to 15 scoring applications advance to the third and final round of judging. In this round, a past program director, a distinguished print journalist, and Alban (as current program director) review each finalist's application carefully. "We read all of the submitted articles in detail," explains Alban. "We look for a variety of publications, a variety of topics, and a variety of writing styles."

▌ COACH'S ANALYSIS

With its libertarian bent, the Institute for Humane Studies is an organization founded on a belief in smaller, less intrusive government and greater rights to individuals. The fundamental challenge for an applicant in the Felix Morley competition is to demonstrate (through submitted articles) a deep exploration of these classical liberal principles while also showcasing a wide range of writing styles and skills.

If possible, I strongly suggest submitting the maximum-allowed five articles. Submitting this number of articles provides you with a greater ability to demonstrate the range and depth of your understanding and skills. Because judges are looking for evidence of appreciation of different classical liberal principles, I recommend submitting two articles about *economic* liberties (such as free markets and private property), and two articles about *civil* liberties (such as First Amendment rights and free migration). Ideally, your fifth submitted article should demonstrate the range of your writing ability by tackling an entirely different topic, perhaps in an entirely different writing style. Within these guidelines, try to include as much variety as you can: The quickest path to boring your judges is submitting articles that are all about the same fundamental issue.

Because the judges are busy and may spend varying degrees of time reviewing your articles, definitely submit your material with your best articles featured first.

When choosing articles to submit, make sure that your articles truly highlight classical liberal principles; don't reference them very briefly or only in the abstract. Judges comment that many applicants make the mistake of sending in articles that are only in small part related to liberty or else merely highlight *related* concepts—such as patriotism and democracy—but not liberty itself. Classical liberal principles must make up a *substantial* portion of your articles: After reading the first few paragraphs of an article, a judge should be able to tell what type of classical liberal principle you are exploring.

If you haven't written enough articles that meet these subject guidelines, try to work such topics into your upcoming journalistic endeavors. Spend a little extra time seeking out article topics that are a good fit for the contest, and resist the temptation to submit what you happen to have on hand. "I submitted my articles as soon as the contest was open, but I would recommend waiting until close to the deadline," offers Bishop Grewell, a 25-year-old honorable mention winner in the competition. "In the intervening months between sending my submission and the deadline, I wrote at least one piece that I would rather have submitted. You never know what could change in a month or two, and it is best to take the flexibility offered by the deadline."

In addition, to demonstrate your original approach, always try to find creative ways to tackle classical liberal topics. First-place winner Jason Brooks, for instance, highlighted the intrusiveness of absurd government ordinances by writing a humorous news article on a Toronto, Canada, law that forbids residents from owning certain types of spiders. While many program applicants are skilled writers, the ones who rise to the top tend to do so by the fresh approach embodied in the diverse articles they submit.

Winning

Entry

WHAT TYPES OF ARTICLES
HAVE WINNERS SUBMITTED?

Although the Institute for Humane Studies represents some very serious and intellectual subjects, this does not mean students need to be stuffy when choosing articles for the competition. Jason Brooks, a first-place $2,500 winner, submitted articles published in the *Toronto Star* and the *Ottawa Citizen* that were written in an entertaining, informative style but that still directly addressed classical liberal principles. The majority of Brooks's submissions, like the article about spiders mentioned previously, outlined the absurdity of laws passed by city governments and their interference in private affairs:

■ In one news article, Brooks relates the story of a woman who neglected to license her dog because he was dying. Rather than being allowed to pay a fine, the woman was taken to court by the city government, where she had to prove beyond a doubt that her dog was dead and buried.

■ In an editorial piece, Brooks discusses a city law that prohibits homeowners from cutting down a tree more than 6 inches in diameter without first obtaining a permit—even if they planted it themselves. According to the law, if a neighbor objects to the removal of the tree, the permit is denied.

■ In another article, Brooks describes a self-guided city tour he took using a route-map outlined by the city government. Among other things, the impracticable map listed sights that hadn't yet been built, exhibits that had never been finished, and locations where on-site employees had no idea what he was talking about.

■ Finally, Brooks interviewed a lawyer who flaunts parking laws by parking in spaces that are not quite covered by city regulations. According to Brooks, this parking rebel drives to work, the theater, and restaurants, parking in these undesignated and easily exploitable spaces.

CONTACT INFORMATION

Keyword
FMORCOMP

Institute for Humane Studies
3301 N. Fairfax Drive, Suite 440
Arlington, VA 22201-4432

Phone: (703) 993-4880 or (800) 697-8799
Fax: (703) 993-4890
E-mail: ihs@gmu.edu
Website: www.theihs.org

RELATED AWARD PROGRAMS

For more information on a Related Award Program, enter the associated keyword in the "Enter a Keyword" box located in the Coach's Locker Room section of ScholarshipCoach.com

■ Hearst Journalism Awards Program

Established in the 1960s and sponsored by the William Randolph Hearst Foundation (named after the newspaper and magazine magnate), this program targets undergraduate students enrolled in journalism programs at participating schools. Competitive categories include print (feature, sports, and editorial writing), photojournalism (black-and-white photos of actual events), and broadcast news (audio- or videotapes of any eligible broadcast). Award amounts range from $500 to $5,000. Deadlines vary by competition.

■ Humane Studies Fellowships

This separate program, also sponsored by the Institute for Humane Studies, is for undergraduate juniors and seniors, plus graduate and professional students, who are proposing a course of study relating to the advancement of a free society—in particular, free market economies. Applicants submit test scores, transcripts, recommendations, a $25 application fee, and an essay outlining their proposed field of study. The Institute grants 80 awards of up to $4,500, with individual award amounts varying. Applications are due in late December.

Keyword	Keyword
HEARJOUR	**HUMASTUD**

Glamour's Top Ten College Women

What do you get when you cross a famous newsstand publication with a national scholarship competition? If you're guessing the *National Enquirer* "Abducted by Aliens" Award, you're wrong: We're talking about *Glamour* magazine's Top Ten College Women competition—a program that once gave an award to that diva of dining and decorating, Martha Stewart, then a student at Barnard College.

Of course, back when Martha won, the program sought to recognize the "best-dressed college girls." Changing with the times, the program now recognizes women who have "made substantial contributions to their communities, expanded their academic knowledge, and who have demonstrated a desire to make their mark in the world."

To apply for the award, an entrant must be a female in her junior year of college. Applicants submit an official school transcript, a listing of extracurricular activities, a 500- to 700-word essay, one or more recommendation letters, and any other relevant items that can help judges get to know the applicant (such as videotapes, newspaper articles, and work samples). Each one of the ten women selected will be awarded $1,000 and a trip to New York City.

In order to compete, all documentation must be submitted by late January. Winners are notified by early June.

TARGET RECIPIENT

- Undergraduate junior women

ENTRY REQUIREMENTS

Essay | Activities & Credentials | Recommendation | Academic Info

DEADLINE

- January

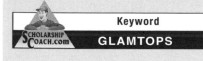

| | Keyword |
| ScholarshipCoach.com | **GLAMTOPS** |

Money Matters | Added Bonus

▌A CLOSER LOOK

The topic for the application essay is straightforward: Entrants discuss their most meaningful achievements and their relation to future goals. In addition to the essay, the heart of the application process is the submission of a list that describes, by year, the applicant's campus and community participation. In developing this list, applicants are instructed to describe their specific contributions and responsibilities for each activity.

As for the awards and honors list, it can include scholarships received since entering college, honor societies joined in college, athletic awards, or honors received for campus or community activities. Applicants are also encouraged to submit any additional materials that expand upon the information provided in their applications and illustrate a commitment to their future plans.

Insider Info

The reader's services department of *Glamour*, the office responsible for responding to reader mail, first screens all submitted applications. Three preliminary judges, headed up by the reader's services editor, review and judge all of the submitted applications on the basis of academic excellence, involvement in campus and community activities, and leadership experience. Rather than using a quantitative scoring system, the judges employ a process of elimination—placing uncompetitive applications in a discard pile until the field is narrowed down to 20 to 30 finalists. These finalists are then interviewed over the phone for about ten minutes. Based on each interview and the application materials, the judges write a one- to three-paragraph summary of each applicant, including any new information from the interview that was not included in the written application.

Once this stage of the judging is complete, all of the finalists are forwarded to the executive editor and managing editor of *Glamour*, who carefully review the materials of each finalist, including her interview summary, and reach a consensus on ten proposed winners.

■ COACH'S ANALYSIS

To understand the judges' point of view, you need to think like the editor of a women's magazine. When *Glamour* editors are putting together the annual feature on the contest winners, they want to select a group of talented and inspiring female college juniors who show a full range of interests and achievements. This becomes evident when you look at the short, descriptive tagline given to each winner in a recent magazine feature story. Next to their names and photographs, winners were categorized as a "People's M.D.-to-Be," "Passionate Politico," "Math and Music Maestro," "Military Heroine," "World-Poverty Crusader," and "Reproductive-Rights Defender."

Insider Info

"We really want to represent the world at large and show that these women are from different backgrounds, races, schools, and have very different interests," says Executive Editor Kristin van Ogtrop. "Many of our finalists wanted to be doctors. Out of ten winners, we're not going to have five of them doctors."

So your mission, should you choose to accept it, is to develop a theme in your application that illustrates your unique interests and the distinctiveness of your future plans and career objectives. The more distinctive and specific you can make these goals—and the more you can describe how you will contribute to society through this career path—the better your odds of appealing to judges who look for, van Ogtrop notes, "a real and proven drive to help other people." So don't just write in your essay or on your application that you want to be lawyer, social worker, or scientist. Go one step further by describing a specific project, endeavor, or venture you'd like to pursue

Because Glamour *is obviously a women's magazine, it makes sense to feature any work you've done on women's issues.*

in that capacity that is bold, innovative, and will contribute to society in some way. Spotlight those aspects of your record and goals that others with similar career interests are unlikely to include.

Because the *Glamour* application allows you to submit additional supplementary materials of your choosing, seize this opportunity to support your goals, interests, and credentials with strong evidence of your ability. Many past winners have substantially strengthened their applications by including newspaper clippings, writing samples, artwork portfolios, performance videotapes, in-depth descriptions of key activities, extra letters of recommendation, and other examples of their work. If you have additional letters of recommendation that add strong support to your credentials, definitely include those as well. (If the extra recommendation letters aren't that great, it's generally better *not* to include them.)

If there are articles in the school newspaper written about you or about an activity you participate in, they are great to include, too.

Glamour winner Tami Bui of the University of California, Irvine, emphasized her work on Asian-American issues by including articles she had written in an Asian news magazine on campus, pictures of herself in leadership roles, and pamphlets and brochures from major campus organizations that highlighted her contributions. "They can't tell the magnitude of the project or program just from the name," Bui said. "The brochures helped them to understand."

Jenny Carrier, a *Glamour* winner from the University of Minnesota, Minneapolis, included as supplementary material pictures from her White House internship, a newspaper clipping announcing her selection to work in the office of her U.S. Senator, two extra recommendation letters, and two term papers she wrote describing her views on pressing legal and public policy issues. This comprehensive exhibit reinforced her desire for a future career in law and politics. "It helps to submit extra materials so that they get a better, more complete picture of who you are," Carrier explains. "Including the [term] papers helped me bolster my career goals and provide evidence that I do care about these issues and am not just making it up for the application."

The key is not to overload the judges with extraneous material, but rather to focus your supplementary materials on highlighting one or two areas that you most want the judges to notice. Imagine that the magazine's editors are writing a feature story on you and your promising future: What would you want them to be sure to include? What do you think their readers would want to know?

Once a student has made the finalist round, she will typically be notified by phone and will be asked to participate in a quick phone interview. Rather than doing the interview on the spot, it's usually best to set up an appointment so that you'll have some time to prepare. Jenny Carrier, for instance, notes that although her interview was successful, if she could do it all over again she would say that she was busy at the moment, "so that I could have had a résumé in front of me and thought a little bit about my answers."

Because a major focus of the telephone interview is learning anything new about you that has happened since your application was submitted, prepare some timely new information about yourself and your latest projects. Remember, the editors who select the winners will be reading a summary of the interview, rather than hearing your actual responses. Make an effort to include plenty of juicy tidbits that will stand out when passed along in written form.

ESSAY SUBMISSION

Winning
Entry

In the essay excerpt below, Jenny Carrier describes how her participation in activities, internships, and jobs related to politics and law has helped her prepare for her future career.

At the White House Office of Legislative Affairs, I was able to continue monitoring the activities of Capitol Hill; however, my perspective changed to that of the interests of the President. My time spent in Washington, D.C., was the most fascinating ten weeks of my life because I was given important duties that were integral to the smooth functioning of the White House. While I was interning at the White House, a staff member in my office had to leave for a month and a half due to a personal emergency, and I was subsequently asked to take over his tasks. Thus, I performed duties such as assisting in drafting responses from the President to Congress concerning legislation and issues of national security, helping manage correspondence from Members of Congress to the President, and acting as a White House liaison in helping to promote the President's legislative agenda. In addition to these responsibilities, the Office of Legislative Affairs decided that since I handled these new duties well, I was allowed to be the sole worker in the Congressional Correspondence Department for the week of the Democratic National Convention. During this week I answered all the questions that came in from Members of Congress and figured out the tasks that needed to be done—all on my own. This was definitely a learning experience because as an intern I was used to being told what to do and to complete somewhat menial tasks; however, this internship gave me the opportunity to be a leader in a capacity that I had never experienced before.

Another meaningful experience has been working for over two years as a legal-administrative assistant at Legal Assistance to Minnesota Prisoners, a law clinic at the University of Minnesota Law School. My office provides free representation to indigent prisoners with legal problems. I have been able to balance my schoolwork and activities with working approximately thirty-five to forty hours a week between my two jobs. This in itself has been a major achievement because without this income, I would not be able to attend college, as I fund my education and living expenses on my own. My job as a legal-administrative assistant is also an achievement because I work in the area of law that I would like to enter into—defense of indigent citizens.

> *Always keep a personal inventory of each task you complete for a given job, internship, or activity. This will come in handy when composing credential-oriented essays such as this one.*

Finally, balancing school and my jobs with campus activities has been my most challenging achievement thus far in college. I have successfully narrowed down my interests into organizations that I can contribute effectively to and still have time for my scholastic work. I am a student senator, member of various student organizations, and have held leadership roles in most of them, including being the Vice President of College Democrats at the University of Minnesota. It has been important to me to help shape the direction that my University is heading toward and to enhance the overall happiness of the student body; thus, participating in campus organizations has been the outlet through which I can achieve those goals.

My scholastic background, internships, job experience, and campus activities have combined to help prepare me for a career as a public servant. I hope to one day use the leadership experience gained in these activities to be an effective and influential voice for those that do not often get heard.

To read more from Jenny Carrier's winning entry, visit the Coach's Locker Room at ScholarshipCoach.com (Keyword: GLAMTOPS).

CONTACT INFORMATION

Keyword **GLAMTOPS**

Glamour's Top Ten College Women Competition
4 Times Square
New York, NY 10036

Phone: (800) 244-GLAM
Fax: (212) 286-6922
E-mail: hcw@glamour.com
Websites: www.condenast.com and http://us.glamour.com

RELATED AWARD PROGRAMS

For more information on a Related Award Program, enter the associated keyword in the "Enter a Keyword" box located in the Coach's Locker Room section of ScholarshipCoach.com

■ Calgon "Take Me Away to College" Scholarship

Undergraduate women who submit two short essays on topics relating to goals and success compete for seven scholarships of $2,500 each. The essays, which are judged on their creativity, expression, and grammar, are due in the fall.

Keyword
CALTAKME

■ Soroptimist Programs

The Soroptimist organization offers various awards to young and mature women pursuing higher education. The Violet Richardson Award is for students ages 14 to 17 who have participated in community volunteer activities. The Women's Opportunity Awards Program recognizes women in need of additional education to further their careers while serving as the primary financial supporters for their families. Women's Opportunity applicants are eligible for awards ranging from $3,000 to $10,000. Because local clubs select Richardson winners, amounts and deadlines vary. Applications for the Women's Opportunity Awards are due in local clubs by mid-December.

Keyword
SOROPPRO

■ Talbots Women's Scholarship Fund

This program targets women who have earned a high school diploma or GED *at least* ten years ago and who are returning to college to pursue an education. The 55 winners are awarded between $1,000 and $10,000 each. Application materials include a recommendation, an essay (on a topic such as "What achieving a degree means to me"), and a list of work experience and activities. The deadline is in early March.

Keyword
TALBFUND

Guideposts' Young Writers Contest

When Scott Schneider decided to help tutor students at his high school, he didn't realize that the experience would have a profound impact on his life. In fact, not only did the inspirational learning experience affect him on a personal level, but by writing about it he was able to win $10,000 for college through *Guideposts'* Young Writers Contest—a competition sponsored by *Guideposts* magazine, a religious, interfaith publication.

High school junior and seniors, or students in equivalent programs outside the United States, enter this competition by submitting their stories about a personal inspirational experience. Submitted manuscripts must be less than 1,200 words.

The top ten entries in the contest each year are awarded $10,000, $8,000, $6,000, $4,000, $3,000, or one of five $1,000 awards. Ten more winners in the contest will receive prizes in the form of gift certificates for college supplies. Winning entries may be published in *Guideposts* magazine—further adding to one's credentials as a published writer.

Entries must be submitted by the late-November deadline. Winners are notified prior to the June issue of *Guideposts*.

TARGET RECIPIENT

■ High school juniors and seniors

ENTRY REQUIREMENTS

Writing Sample

DEADLINE

■ November

Keyword
GUIDEWRI

ScholarshipCoach.com

Money $ Matters

▮ A Closer Look

Contest administrators expect students to think about an experience they have had that changed their life in some way, big or small, and to write an inspiring story about the event. Each entry must be under 1,200 words, previously unpublished, and typed double-spaced. The stories must be true but should not simply be a list of important events or good deeds performed.

According to Katherine Slattery, a contributing editor to *Guideposts* magazine, the judging initially focuses on the quality of the work rather than on content. "The first thing I think we're looking for is literary merit . . . our goal is to nurture future writers," she says. Once this first criterion has been met, judges look for an "experience where the young person gains an insight, learns a lesson, is changed. A wonderful experience can happen in any sort of venue."

As you might expect, editors at the magazine are the ones who conduct the contest judging. Each judge selects the manuscripts he or she thinks should be advanced, and the top 30 to 40 entries are read by a five-editor panel that makes the final award determinations.

Insider Info

Slattery also advises making your entry appropriate to your age and experience, because that is the standard by which it will be judged.

▮ Coach's Analysis

One of the great things about the *Guideposts* competition is that you can leverage past or future school writing assignments. Leveraging schoolwork will not only save you time, but will also generate substantial feedback from your teacher because it's part of a class assignment. This feedback can help you hone and improve your work, thereby making it substantially better for the *Guideposts* competition.

Third-place winner Carey Olson of Ellensburg, Washington, for instance, originally wrote her story for an

English class assignment. The assignment was to write about a place of special meaning, and Olson chose to describe a dilapidated church in rural South Dakota that she had visited each summer of her childhood. To see how she adapted her writing for the *Guideposts* contest, let's first examine a brief excerpt from her initial English class version:

> The tones that I can hear within the dying piano ring harmoniously through the church, filling it with life. That life fills me somehow in a way I can't really understand. I don't go to church because I haven't yet found one that I personally believe to be true, though I hope to someday. However, that's not what this is about. There's just something in that church that is mine—an unexplainable feeling that confirms there's something beyond the comprehension and mind power of mankind.

Characterizing her initial version as "more scientific" in tone, Olson said she tried to give her account a more spiritual feel when preparing the story for submission to *Guideposts*. After input from her parents, she edited the passage to "aim it more at the new audience":

Winning
Entry

> The tones that I can hear within the dying piano rang harmoniously through the church, filling it with life. That life fills me somehow in a way I can't really understand. If there's Truth in any church, it's in that one for me. The only proof I need is in the sound of the piano. There's something in that church that is mine—an unexplainable feeling that confirms there's something beyond the comprehension and mind power of mankind.

The piece evolved still further when the magazine selected Olson as one of its top three winners and decided to publish it. This is because editors at *Guideposts*, not Olson herself, edited the piece for publication.

As you can see in the third version of the same excerpt, such magazine editing changes were *not* insignificant:

The tones of the dying piano ring through the space, filling it with life. That life fills me in a way I can't really understand, an unexplainable feeling that brings me closer to God.

It is interesting that the edited version includes a direct reference to God, which wasn't in the submitted version—a reference that makes the published version even more in sync with the religious nature of the magazine.

This suggests that, in general, as you create your narrative, you should approach it as if you are a freelance writer hired by *Guideposts* to compose their cover story: Find a subject that is appropriate for a young person to write about (no narratives about your impending "midlife crisis"), and craft your narrative in such a way as to mesh well with the underlying tone of the magazine.

"Write about something that you have a lot of passion about, something that really means something to you," advises fourth-place winner Leah D'Emilio. "For this contest, they are looking for essays that other people can relate to. . . . To make it fit *Guideposts,* I tried to tie in God and religion more directly."

Also keep in mind that although it is helpful to look at entries published in the magazine—the top three winning entries are published in the June issue each year—the versions of the entries that appear in the magazine are never the same as the material submitted by the winning students. Typically, the published versions will sound much more polished, refined, and poignant than the originally submitted versions, as editors have honed the piece for a professional publication. So use the published pieces as examples of what works, but don't assume that your submission has to be at that level to win a top award.

WHAT HAVE PAST WINNERS WRITTEN ABOUT?

Winners in the *Guideposts* contest have written on a wide range of topics. To jog your thinking, here's a sampler of winning story concepts.

- First-place winner Andrew Bonner of Durham, North Carolina, wrote about the night his father was mugged and brutally beaten by two attackers—to the point that his father lost consciousness. In the aftermath of the harrowing incident, Bonner felt an appreciation of God's love, bringing good out of evil.

- Second-place winner Rose Weill, a resident of McLean, Virginia, and a member of her school's outdoor adventuring club, described the challenge of learning to rock climb. Although the climb feels impossible at times, she draws strength from her faith and trust in God—conquering the rock cliff in the process.

- First-place winner Scott Schneider of Norfolk, Nebraska, wrote about his experience volunteering as an aide in his school's special education program. Although the experience tested his patience at first, he grew to enjoy his time as a tutor and gained perspective on the obstacles he faced in his own life—learning to appreciate the blessings that he had previously taken for granted.

▌ Second-place winner Kimberly Ann Shope of Flower Mound, Texas, told readers about her friend, Trey, a mentally handicapped man who helped her recover after undergoing emergency surgery for a badly broken and twisted leg and ankle. Although she had once taught Trey to "dust off and try again" after he fell while learning to ride a bicycle, Trey reminded her of the power of those words as she rehabilitated from her own injury.

**CONTACT
INFORMATION**

Keyword

GUIDEWRI

Young Writers Contest
Guideposts
16 East 34th Street
New York, NY 10016

Phone: (845) 225-3681
Website: www.guideposts.com/young_writers_contest.asp

RELATED AWARD PROGRAMS

For more information on a Related Award Program, enter the associated keyword in the "Enter a Keyword" box located in the Coach's Locker Room section of ScholarshipCoach.com

■ Amy Writing Awards

This is a writing competition for both students and nonstudents who have had a religious article published in a secular publication. The article must have quoted the Bible directly and must have dealt with a significant social topic, such as divorce, political morality, religion, family life, or addiction to drugs or alcohol. Each entrant may submit up to ten articles. There are over a dozen awards, ranging from $1,000 to $10,000. Entries are due by the end of January.

■ Baker's Plays

High school students interested in writing a story about any topic dealing with "the high school experience" are eligible for the competition. There are no requirements regarding length or specific subject, but it must be feasible to produce the story as a play on the high school stage. Religious themes are encouraged but not required. Prizes are $100, $250, and $500 awards. Entries are due in January.

Keyword: AMYWRITE

Keyword: BAKEPLAY

Holocaust Remembrance Project

TARGET RECIPIENT

■ High school students

ENTRY REQUIREMENTS

Essay

DEADLINE

■ April

Keyword
SCHOLARSHIP
COACH.coam
HOLREMEM

Money

$

Matters

Added

Bonus

The Holocaust Remembrance Project, sponsored by the Holland and Knight Charitable Foundation and the U.S. Holocaust Memorial Museum in Washington, D.C., was designed to commemorate the struggles endured by millions of persecuted people and to remind us that state-sanctioned genocide must *never* be repeated.

High school students (under age 19) submit essays of 1,200 words or less that analyze the lessons of the Holocaust and address the idea that humankind shall never again accept terrorism or genocide as public policy.

The best entries are awarded 10 top-tier prizes, ranging from $1,000 to $5,000. These 10 winners also receive a five-day all-expense-paid trip to Washington, D.C., to visit the U.S. Holocaust Memorial Museum, as well as other historic sites and tourist attractions. Other students are given cash awards, including 10 awards of $300 each, and 10 prizes of $100 each.

Entries must arrive at the contest administrator's office postmarked by the designated date in late April. Prize winners receive word by mid-June, with final award announcements made at a banquet in late July.

■ A Closer Look

Each contest year, different questions about the Holocaust are posed in the official application literature. Students are expected to focus on one of these questions or on a combination of them. Past questions have included:

■ How do the lessons of the Holocaust relate to your understanding of the concept of diversity in society today?

■ How do these lessons relate to the concept of world citizenship?

■ What has your study of the Holocaust taught you about the devaluation of human life and the consequences of embracing such inhumanity?

Actual essays may focus on a specific event or person during the Holocaust but should still deal with one or more of these central questions.

Each essay submitted should include a title page with the student's name, contact information, essay title, and essay word count. A bibliography must also be included. All pages should be numbered, with the entrant's name only appearing on the title page. Students are expected to use a variety of sources when preparing to write the essay, including books, tapes, videos, and personal interviews.

A bibliography is not required if students use common knowledge and public record. However, if specific sources are used, documentation of sources must be included.

Although the judging process for the essay competition may change slightly from year to year, there is usually a preliminary screening process for applications. Thomas Holcombe, the program coordinator, reviews all entries, checking to make sure the basic guidelines have been followed. In the past, entries have been disqualified for a variety of reasons (such as entries written as fictional stories or poems), but Holcombe says he doesn't usually penalize for formatting mistakes.

After the initial screening process, each entry is distributed to three different judges. Holland and Knight employees, who make up the judging panel, read the essays, assigning them scores of 1 to 20 and advancing the top 200 to 300 submissions overall. A new panel of ten judges—made up of teachers, college professors, Holocaust survivors, as well as Holland and Knight employees—reads the top essays and determines which students will receive prizes.

▌ COACH'S ANALYSIS

A behind-the-scenes analysis of the official instructions given to program judges (immediately before they score the essays) reveals what it takes to win this competition. According to these instructions, a paper receiving a perfect score of 20 (on the 1 to 20 scale) should have the following:

▌ A cogent thesis statement (a clear statement of your main idea) followed by three or more specific examples from the Holocaust

▌ Specific language that powerfully communicates the horror of the Holocaust

▌ Evidence of substantial research

▌ Visceral or personal understanding of the effects of the Holocaust on contemporary life

Judges are instructed to score papers in the 17 to 19 point range if they accomplish most of what is described above but do not feature strong diction, vocabulary, sentence variety, or tone, as expected of top papers. Essays that receive 14 to 16 points lack emotional power and include one example that is noticeably lacking sufficient supporting evidence. Those essays that receive scores in the 11 to 13 point range not only lack a strong thesis and specific examples but also fail to effectively connect the Holocaust to the present—or else focus on the present at the expense of documenting the past.

Based on these instructions and other interviews with scholarship personnel affiliated with the program, I've come up with a checklist of seven common mistakes to avoid when entering this scholarship essay contest:

1. Do not imply your thesis. State the main idea of your essay directly in one or two sentences near the beginning of your essay, so that the judges will be able to quickly decipher what you are writing about.

2. Do not use fewer than three major examples from the Holocaust. To make sure the judges note all three of your examples, your essay should be, at minimum, five paragraphs long—consisting of an introductory paragraph, the three example paragraphs, and a concluding paragraph.

3. Do not make broad, sweeping statements about the Holocaust without backing them up with specific facts. Be sure to highlight specific factual information about actual events that occurred during the Holocaust. (You could include statistics, for instance.)

4. Do not describe the Holocaust as if you were writing a dictionary entry. Your description should convey a heartfelt and personal sense of the utterly horrific nature of the Holocaust.

5. Do not make only passing references to the effects of the Holocaust on contemporary society. Make sure that each paragraph of your essay constantly reinforces how the lessons of the Holocaust have

enormous implications on the actions we take as individuals and as a society in the future. Be specific in explaining precisely how and why this is so.

6. Do not submit an essay without a substantial bibliography. To demonstrate that you did your homework, include a minimum of five suitable bibliographic citations.

7. Do not use nonspecific language such as "thing" and "everybody." Judges are specifically told to look out for this type of language (and they may deduct points accordingly). If you do find yourself using these words, replace them.

If you can avoid these seven big mistakes, you'll be well ahead of most other students going for this essay prize.

Kelli Murphy
Gulf Breeze, FL
Award Winner
$500

ESSAY SUBMISSION

In the essay excerpt below, Kelli Murphy examines the factors that caused the Holocaust and how such factors can be prevented in the future.

The Holocaust. Simple words that bring to mind the suffering and death of eleven million people at the hands of the Nazis. These words also remind us that future genocide must be stopped. Learning about the major factors that caused the Holocaust in Germany—anti-Semitism, dictatorship, lack of resistance both internally and internationally—can prevent future Holocausts. The factors that enabled the Holocaust and measures that will prevent their emergence should be examined.

The first enabling factor that helped to start the Holocaust was prejudice. In this case, the prejudice is called anti-Semitism. Most Germans in the 1930s were anti-Semitic and used the theory of Social Darwinism to their advantage, stating that their race, called the Aryans, were superior, while the Jews were a race that "'lived off' the other races and weakened them." Therefore, to destroy all Jews was to preserve Germany and to not do so was unpatriotic and treacherous. The solution to the problem of anti-Semitism, or prejudice, is education. The belief that everyone is equal must be instilled in children at home for it to really take effect.

> When composing an essay such as this, Murphy advises forcing yourself to just sit down and write. "At first glance it seems daunting and you don't want to do it," she says, "but once you get started it's not so bad."
>
> Coach's Comments

The emergence of a dictator is the second factor in the cause of the Holocaust. With the majority of Germany's population anti-Semitic, a person could easily become a dictator; one such dictator-to-be was Adolf Hitler. Hitler used the Germans' anti-Semitism to his advantage by blaming all of Germany's problems on Jews, stating that it "was part of a worldwide Jewish conspiracy." The German people, swayed by Hitler's speeches which seemed all too true to Germany's non-Jewish citizens, elected him Chancellor of Germany on January 30, 1933. It wasn't long before Hitler was a dictator, and the democratic Germany was gone. In the military, all German soldiers were required to "render unconditional obedience to Adolf Hilter." Now that Hitler was a dictator, his ideas were rarely challenged; any opponents of the Nazi regime were killed. This would effectively stop any form of resistance in Germany, allowing Hitler to continue unhindered. The solution to the problem with a dictator is a strong, democratic government. While Germany did have a democracy, it was too easily corrupted. A capable, democratic government that used the system of checks and balances would have been an effective force blocking Hitler's rise to power and eventual dictatorship.

For the complete text of Kelli Murphy's winning essay, visit the Coach's Locker Room at ScholarshipCoach.com (Keyword: HOLREMEM).

Winning Entry

Megan Landfried
Greenville, PA
Award Winner
$500

THE CONSEQUENCES OF
THE DRIVE FOR A PERFECT RACE

In this essay excerpt, Megan Landfried conveys her emotional reaction to the horrors of the Holocaust and highlights her strong, personal feelings during a recent trip to Germany and Italy.

Throughout my life, I have never had any problem saying I was of German ancestry. I did not realize, while I was growing up, what my relatives had done to the rest of this world. As I have matured and become educated about World War II, however, I have become almost embarrassed to admit that I am of German heritage. I am extremely grateful that during high school I have not been discriminated against like some minorities have been.

World War II is one of the biggest atrocities in our history. This conflict involved every part of our world during the years 1939 to 1945. To completely understand the great loss inflicted by the Nazis, and to entirely understand why this war should be remembered, one must understand that Hitler's view of Europe was clearly one without Jews. He believed in a perfect race. Anyone who was different from him and his followers was to be killed.

*   *   *

It must be remembered that the execution of innocent people was not a side effect of the war but one of the primary goals of the Nazis. It was a well-planned effort by Hitler to dispose of every trace of the Jewish religion in Europe. No other group has ever been condemned to die as the Jews had been. In Hitler's mind, Jews were the most important enemy, the cause of all of Germany's economic problems. He stopped at nothing to make them pay for causing these "problems." Hitler diverted trains essential to the war effort to load people on and carry them to their deaths at the nearest concentration camp.

Recently, my grandfather and I traveled to Italy and Germany. We visited Foggia, Italy, the city in which he was stationed during the war. This was my grandfather's third trip to Europe, but the first time he had revisited Foggia. He told me that as much as he did not want to go back and relive what had happened over the three years he had been there, it was important for him not to forget and for me to learn so I would be able to pass on the information to my generation and those to come. We continued to travel to Germany. One of our stops was Dachau, a concentration camp outside of Munich. Although this camp was not large like Auschwitz, it was still very disturbing. The atmosphere made me nauseous and ashamed. The feelings I had haunt me to this day. When I asked my grandfather what was the most frustrating part of the war he replied, "50 years ago I fought to stop hate, and today I still see it every day, on the news and in every aspect of our lives. It frustrates me that so many of my friends and family died for a cause that means nothing anymore." Still, fifty years later, hatred haunts our world. Even now people are discriminated against because they are of a different race, religion, or social lifestyle.

Landfried wrote the initial draft of this essay for her English class. She had originally written it as a straightforward description of her trip to Germany and Italy, but she modified it for the contest by focusing on the Holocaust.

For the complete text of Megan Landfried's winning essay, visit the Coach's Locker Room at ScholarshipCoach.com (Keyword: HOLREMEM).

CONTACT INFORMATION

Keyword
HOLREMEM

Holland & Knight Charitable Foundation, Inc.
400 N. Ashley Drive, Suite 2050
Tampa, FL 33602

Phone: (866) 452-2737
E-mail: tholcomb@hklaw.com
Website: http://holocaust.hklaw.com/

RELATED AWARD PROGRAMS

For more information on a Related Award Program, enter the associated keyword in the "Enter a Keyword" box located in the Coach's Locker Room section of ScholarshipCoach.com

■ Jay Shalmoni Memorial Holocaust Art & Writing Contest

Students in grades 9 through 12 in any of the 50 states may apply for these awards. Applicants are expected to interview a Holocaust survivor and write an essay or create art (in artistic or documentary form) based on the interview. Entries should be creative, tasteful, and sensitive. Students may contact the Los Angeles Museum of the Holocaust to be put in touch with a survivor. All entries are due in mid-March.

Keyword
JSHALMON

■ National Foundation for Jewish Culture Awards

Grants offered by this foundation recognize Ph.D. students pursuing research, publication, and teaching in the field of Jewish studies. To qualify, students must have met all requirements for doctorate studies, except for the writing of a dissertation. Applicants are also expected to have enough proficiency in Hebrew or Yiddish to pursue their chosen career. Awards amounts and the number of fellows vary each year. Applications are due by early January.

Keyword
NATLFJCU

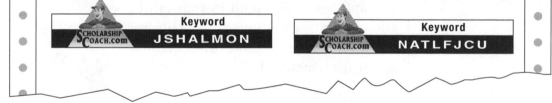

Intel Science Talent Search

You enjoy learning about science in your spare time. You get good grades in science-related classes. You have a curious fondness for Bunsen burners.

Perhaps, then, you're a natural candidate for a scholarship from the Intel Science Talent Search—a program sponsored by the computer chip manufacturer that seeks out the brightest scientific minds in American high schools and "increases these students' opportunities for scientific and intellectual exploration through scholarship awards." Put another way, the program stuffs serious cash in the pockets of some math- and science-savvy high school seniors on their way to brilliant careers in technological fields. (In fact, five past recipients have actually gone on to win Nobel prizes.) To apply, students must be either high school seniors attending school in the United States or U.S. territories or U.S. students studying abroad.

The core component of the application is a 5- to 20-page report that summarizes the student's work on an original scientific research project. Entrants must also send in transcripts, adviser verification forms, short-answer question responses, and other standard application materials.

TARGET RECIPIENT

- High school seniors

ENTRY REQUIREMENTS

Project | Short Answer | Academic Info | Interview

DEADLINE

- November

| Keyword |
| INSCITAL |

SCHOLARSHIP COACH.com

With a history of more than 60 years, this program is one of the oldest of its kind. It was previously called the Westinghouse Science Talent Search (when it was sponsored by the Westinghouse Electric Company).

Money
Matters

Added
Bonus

The overall first-place winner of the Intel Science Talent Search receives a whopping $100,000 scholarship prize. There are also second and third prizes of $75,000 and $50,000, three $25,000 awards, and four additional scholarships at $20,000 each. Additionally, 30 students are given $5,000 for their higher education and 300 semifinalists are awarded $1,000 each.

The top 40 applicants overall, named finalists, receive an all-expense-paid trip to Washington D.C. (typically in March), where they participate in interviews with program judges and exhibit their projects at the National Academy of Sciences. The 40 finalists also receive laptop computers.

All application materials, including research reports, are due in late November.

▮ A Closer Look

This application for the Intel Science Talent Search is not one that a student can fill out the night before. The most daunting task, of course, is completing the research report that details the student's original scientific research, including data and key findings. The report should include a title page, a 75-word summary of the project, and a 5- to 20-page main document. The report should demonstrate that proper scientific procedure has been followed, and that the student has adhered to commonly accepted research guidelines. There is no limitation on the length of time the student has pursued the research, but each project must be his or her own work.

If students have worked on a project involving live, nonhuman vertebrates, an exception form must be completed, and any projects involving human subjects will require an Institutional Review Board (IRB) approval form.

Additional materials must be submitted along with this research report. Students must provide an overview of any extracurricular activities and awards and honors received during high school, and answer questions about their hobbies, summer activities, and future goals. In addition, each student is asked to provide the name and address of a person who has had the most influence in his or her scientific development and to write a short paragraph explaining the choice.

In the second part of the application form, entrants write short essays about their activities and are instructed to discuss their scientific attitude, curiosity, inventiveness, initiative, and work habits. Students are expected to provide specific examples that will help judges evaluate each applicant's promise as a scientist, engineer, or mathematician.

Two additional forms must be completed by the research project supervisor and by an adviser or teacher who can answer questions such as:

▌ What are the student's strengths in areas such as peer relationships, outside activities, and family life?

▌ To what extent is the research the work of the student?

Every application must also include an official high school transcript (in a sealed envelope) and the secondary school record form, which must be filled out by a school official and signed by the student's principal. For certain types of research projects, students are expected to fill out various supplemental forms in addition to the standard application form. Detailed guidelines are provided for formatting and assembling the application materials and research report.

Insider Info

Those who review entries for the Intel Science Talent Search are divided into two groups: evaluators and judges. For the first-round screening of research projects, 200 evaluators, each of whom holds a Ph.D., perform the honors. Evaluators are frequently affiliated with such governmental organizations as the National Institutes of Health (NIH), the National Science Foundation (NSF), and the National Institute of Standards and Technology (NIST), as well as D.C.-area universities.

To score each research paper, the evaluators form teams of three, in which all members have expertise in the same branch of science. Applicant research papers that match a team's area of expertise are then submitted to the team for evaluation. Each evaluator on the team generally scores the paper individually and if scores vary between team members by more than one point, they debate the merits of the paper until a consensus is reached.

The entire focus of these evaluators is on the research paper itself: Although they may look at the student's transcript and short-answer responses, this is *not* an explicit part of the first-round evaluation process. The entire evaluation process is conducted within a five-day period.

Insider Info

After this process is complete, the top 360 papers (as scored by the evaluators) are submitted to the judges—a board of ten distinguished scientists from a variety of disciplines. In recent years, Dr. Andrew Yeager, a professor of Medicine and Pediatrics at the University of Pittsburgh Medical Center and Cancer Institute, has chaired this judging panel. Unlike the evaluators, all ten judges work together as a group during the entire judging process.

First, the judges go through each application to verify that it meets program standards: Through this elimination process, the 360 applications are whittled down to 300 semifinalists. The judges then proceed to choose the top 40 research projects. All ten judges openly debate and discuss the research projects, typically from the perspective of their scientific disciplines—with a scientist who has specific expertise in a subject area often taking the lead.

Semifinalists are usually announced in January of each year.

According to Ann Korando, who helps administer the program, judges examine a student's short-answer responses and school transcript for two basic purposes. First, they examine these materials to validate and verify that the submitted paper is, in fact, the student's own research. Second, if a student's research is good but not so clearly exceptional as to automatically make him or her a finalist, other factors play a larger role. "If the student's research is not so clearly outstanding," Korando explains, "they look to other evidence." To get through this volume of applications takes the judges about six full days.

Once students have demonstrated their ability to conduct meaningful scientific research on a particular topic, the program shifts its emphasis. "Their research project, and what they do to support that research, is what actually gets them to Washington, D.C.," states Korando. "Once they're one of the 40 finalists, then their general knowledge of science is a large part of their grade." A student's level of scientific knowledge is evaluated primarily through an intensive interview—one that probes areas outside a student's research expertise. "If you are knowledgeable in chemistry," said Korando, "the questions will focus on other fields."

Each student's ability to demonstrate scientific reasoning—and essentially to "think out loud"—determines his or her score. "The judges will ask you some questions that *they* don't even know the answer to . . ." continues Korando, "They want to see how quickly you think on your feet."

One former program judge was known for asking students the following question: "If you were a fish in outer space and swallowed an ice cube, how does that relate to a refrigerator?"

Coach's Analysis

If you're new to the Intel Science Talent Search, there are two things you should know. First, be aware that the types of science research projects that do well in this program take time to complete. Your research project might take anywhere from a couple of months to several years. Second, you should know that almost all winners get substantial help with their research projects from mentors— at least one seasoned scientist, but sometimes several. This just isn't something for which you lock yourself in your room and tackle it alone.

If you tallied recent semifinalists and finalists in the program, you'd notice that students from New York consistently dominate the competition. Why should this be the case? Is it something in the water they drink in the Empire State? It's actually because there are programs in New York that nurture science-minded students, provide them with science mentors as early as freshman year, and help them prepare to enter projects in the Intel Science Talent Search competition!

Your challenge, therefore, is partly of a practical nature: Don't wait for a mentor to find you; it's up to you to find a mentor. There are several places to look in your community. In addition to asking for recommendations from your science teacher, contact college professors, research scientists, and other science practitioners in your area. Retired scientists and science instructors may be especially helpful as mentors; they have a huge amount of information stored up from a lifetime of work yet probably have fewer demands on their time. To find such individuals, target membership associations in your state for retired scientists and science teachers.

To learn additional ways to cultivate your scientific interest or talent, see my special guide, I Love My Bunsen Burner *(for more info, visit ScholarshipCoach.com).*

If you live in a more rural area, try to utilize the unique resources around you. Intel fourth-place national winner Carol Anne Fassbinder of Elgin, Iowa, came up with a biology project based on her family's honeybee colonies in northeast Iowa. After researching and testing compounds that can prevent parasitic mites from destroying bee colonies, she discovered that one compound, in particular, offers the best honeybee protection. (With Fassbinder's family in the business, you can bet she had access to plenty of expert advice.) Another past Intel winner located the e-mail address of a Nobel Prize–winning scientist, boldly e-mailed him, and was thrilled to discover that the distinguished gentleman agreed to mentor her online.

It's also worthwhile to look for summer programs and other opportunities to perform scientific research or work in a laboratory setting. One of the most prominent of these programs in the nation is the Research Science Institute, co-sponsored by the Center for Excellence in

There is no cost to students for tuition, room, and board. The only expense is for transportation to and from the program.

Education and the Massachusetts Institute of Technology (MIT). Each summer, 70 high school students (you apply as a high school junior) gather on the MIT campus to participate in six intensive weeks of science exploration and individual scientific research led by top experts in the field. It's no accident that in recent years students who have participated in the Research Science Institute have regularly won first place in the Intel Science Talent Search competition.

Once you're ready to begin preparing the Intel application materials (at last!), be aware that compared to other science competitions, the Intel program seeks to identify promising future scientists rather than focusing solely on the quality of a student's research project. As a result, in later phases of the Intel competition, greater emphasis is placed on an applicant's overall potential to contribute to science. For this reason, as you complete the written application and answer the short essay questions, you should define the qualities of the ideal research scientist and then try to emphasize your personal qualities that match this definition. According to Intel second-place winner Nathaniel Craig of Sacramento, California, such qualities include creativity, insight, flexibility, incisiveness, and cautious ambition. "Be acutely aware of what it is about you that makes you a talented researcher," advises Craig. "Pay careful and honest attention to the parts of you inclined to the process of scientific thought."

Of particular importance is to demonstrate your love of and commitment to scientific inquiry. "The big thing about Intel," Craig comments, "is that it is all about an individual's passion for doing research."

A SURVEY OF
WINNING RESEARCH

Finalists for the Intel Science Talent Search are chosen from ten scientific disciplines. Let's look at a winning student from each area of study to get a feel for the great variety of research projects that make the grade:

Behavioral and Social Sciences

To study the factors affecting academic cheating by students, Johanna Beth Waldman (Roslyn Heights, NY) created and distributed four question-naires to students attending a summer program at UCLA. As a result of her sur-vey, Waldman was able to determine that while half of the students participat-ing in the study disapproved of cheating, over 90 percent confessed to cheating in some matter—generally for reasons of goal orientation or academic pressure.

Biochemistry

A two-year study of the molecular structure of the human leukocyte antigen in pregnant mothers landed Michael Chiu (Belmont, MA) a spot in the finals. After reviewing the results of the molecular composition in vivo and in vitro, Chiu's studies helped illustrate how a fetus avoids detection by a mother's immune cells (which would normally reject a foreign growth), allowing her to carry the fetus to term. The research he has done may help in the field of problem pregnancies.

Botany

One day Sarah Kessans (Pekin, IN) noticed that the areas under red oak trees yield very little plant life. She experimented with the natural herbicide by soaking sawdust from red oak trees in water for seven days. She then spread the resulting liquid over a section of crops and weeds, and compared the results to the growth of plants in another control group. As a result of her experiment, Kessans discovered that weeds in the treated section did not fare as well as those in the nontreated plot. The new herbicide could have far-reaching effects as an environmentally friendly way to treat crops and a cost-effective solution for farmers.

Chemistry

Parimalram Madduri (McLean, VA) has pursued a project that may have far-reaching effects in the fields of chemistry, planetary science, and high-pressure physics. His research into nitrous oxide resulted in a discovery of a quartz-like phase of the chemical that had not been reported before. Madduri's discovery may bring into existence an entirely new field of study.

Computer Sciences

The ability to *break* secret codes has played a large part in military history and various governmental operations, but the ability to *create* codes is also necessary in order to keep electronic communications private and anonymous. Alan Dunn (Silver Spring, MD) discovered a way to shorten the time needed to encrypt information for electronic distribution. Dunn discovered that two of his strategies caused a 200 to 400 percent increase in the speed of the algorithms he tested.

Engineering

Hans Lee (Monterey, CA) developed an algorithm to estimate a vehicle's lateral acceleration, compare it to the measured lateral acceleration, and then calculate whether a vehicle is out of a driver's control. He also designed and built a "differential torque control system" that can improve how a car handles when the wheels can't get traction. To conduct his experiments, Lee used a go-cart and computer modeling; he was able to demonstrate

a 45 percent decrease in skidding when his system was employed.

Environmental Science

Rishi Vasudeva's (Roswell, GA) project involved a three-year study into possible alternatives for modern disposable diapers. Vasudeva advanced beyond previous hypotheses, showing how proteins used in the food industry could be better adapted for use as biodegradable, waterproof outer shells of diapers. He has now begun experimenting with a biopolymer made from corn protein, which he hopes to improve by adding "plasticizers," allowing diapers to decompose in sewage treatment plants.

Mathematics

The everyday vocabulary of Abdur Sabar (Ballwin, MO) is peppered with such words and phrases as "Laguerre polynomials," "Meixner polynomials," and "combinatorics." This is because Sabar has been investigating the properties of various polynomials. While studying the pattern of

resulting coefficients, he was able to build upon earlier results concerning the positive nature of these coefficients. (If this research doesn't make too much sense to you, don't worry—you're not alone!)

Medicine and Health

Glaucoma, a vision disorder causing blindness through pressure buildup in the inner eye, became the focus of Melissa Radecki's (Lake Oswego, OR) four-year research efforts. Using facilities at Oregon Health Sciences University, she researched the biochemical phenomena

called "stretch"—a process that can help regulate inner-eye pressure and consequently may be useful in glaucoma treatments.

Physics

As an accomplished violin player, Michael Hasper (Tallahassee, FL) decided to pursue a project related to his instrument of choice. Starting with a motor from a windshield wiper, he created an automatic bowing device and built eleven bridges (devices elevating the strings of a violin) to test which shapes and materials function the best acoustically. He determined that no bridge created the optimal sound for all four strings. Hasper did hypothesize, however, that an ideal bridge could be created from fiberglass and spotted maple, constructed according to the famous Stradivarius design.

**CONTACT
INFORMATION**

Intel Science Talent Search
Science Service
1719 N Street, NW
Washington, DC 20036

E-mail: sciedu@sciserv.org

Website: www.sciserv.org/sts

RELATED AWARD PROGRAMS

*For more information on a Related Award Program, enter the associated keyword in the
"Enter a Keyword" box located in the Coach's Locker Room section of ScholarshipCoach.com*

■ Intel Science and Engineering Fair (ISEF)

Competing high school seniors are expected to participate in local, regional, state, and nationally affiliated fairs. Winning students culled from almost 500 fairs throughout the United States and over 40 other nations go on to compete in the ISEF in 15 different categories (including zoology, physics, microbiology, mathematics, gerontology, computer science, botany, and earth and space sciences). Award amounts vary by category. Finalist awards range from $500 to $3,000; category award winners split the $13,000 to $45,000 total for each category; pinnacle awards are up to $50,000 each. The grand prize winner receives a trip to the Nobel Prize ceremonies in addition to a monetary award.

■ Junior Science Humanities Symposium

This program features regional competitions whereby nominated high school seniors submit papers outlining research in any scientific field. The extensive guidelines require careful study for proper presentation of a project. More than 60 students receive awards ranging from $2,000 to $16,000. Deadlines vary by region.

■ **Siemens Westinghouse Science & Technology Competition**

This competitive program is for high school seniors who can submit an individual or team project that contributes to society and enhances the knowledge base of a particular discipline. Awards range from $1,000 to $100,000 for either teams or individual entrants. Projects must be submitted in early October.

Keyword

SIEMWEST

Morris K. Udall Scholarship

A pristine stream ripples through a lush conifer forest . . . tumbling breakers pound against the rocky Pacific shoreline . . . water droplets gently sprinkle a bed of moss at the base of a towering Douglas fir . . . Ah, the matchless beauty of nature. (Think *Deep Thoughts* by Jack Handey!) If you're in the middle of your undergraduate years and want to help protect our beloved environment, then seriously consider applying for a Morris K. Udall Scholarship.

TARGET RECIPIENT

■ Undergraduate sophomores and juniors

ENTRY REQUIREMENTS

Academic Info | Essay | Nomination | Recommendation

DEADLINE

■ February

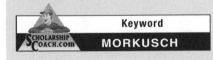

	Keyword
ScholarshipCoach.com	**MORKUSCH**

Named after the congressman who championed environmental causes and the rights of Native Americans and Alaska Natives, the Morris K. Udall Foundation seeks to recognize students who are interested in a wide range of subjects related to the environment. In addition to recognizing students majoring in "environmental-related" disciplines (which is very broadly defined by the foundation), the program also awards scholarships to Native Americans and Alaska Natives for their potential contributions to health care and tribal public policy. The foundation selects 75 to 80 students nationwide to receive scholarships of up to $5,000. Recipients are also invited to attend an orientation weekend held in Tucson, Arizona (usually in August).

Money Matters | Added Bonus

Colleges may nominate undergraduate sophomores and juniors at two- and four-year colleges and universities for the scholarship award. Nominees must then

Applicants must also be U.S. citizens, U.S. nationals, or permanent resident aliens to be eligible.

submit an essay of 600 words or less, have at least a B average, complete a written application, and include three recommendations from people who know them well.

Applications are due in mid-February; the scholars are announced in April.

A CLOSER LOOK

The foundation takes a very inclusive view of "environmental-related" disciplines. Past Morris K. Udall Scholars have majored in a wide range of fields, including:

- Agriculture
- Anthropology
- Biology and other natural sciences
- Cultural studies
- Environmental engineering
- Geography
- History
- Natural resource management
- Political science
- Pre-law
- Public policy
- Sociology

Only about six percent of applications to the Udall program have been from Native American or Alaska Native students.

Likewise, past Native American and Alaska Native applicants have majored in diverse fields related to Native American health care and tribal public policy. Because both environmental and Native American issues can be approached in a multidisciplinary way, the program does not specifically exclude any college major.

The application form for the Udall scholarship features sections on extracurricular activities in high school and college, awards and honors, community and public service activities that illustrate an interest in the environment (or health care and tribal public policy), as well as work experiences. In addition, students must answer short essay questions about their career aspirations and about an activity or experience that has strengthened their commitment to the environment, Native American health care, or tribal public policy. Entrants may also briefly add any personal information they wish to share with the judges.

The applicant's essay, specified to be no more than 600 words, must be about a significant legislative act, public policy statement, or speech made by Congressman Udall that has relevance to the student's career goals and field of interest.

Each college specifies its own nomination procedures. If you want to apply for this scholarship, it's up to you to seek out someone to nominate you.

Each college is permitted to nominate up to six students. Individuals who win a scholarship as college sophomores may reapply as juniors. In addition to completing a new application form and submitting new materials, past scholarship recipients must attach a brief statement describing their activities since receiving the award and describe how an additional year of funding would benefit their studies and career goals.

Recommendation letters must accompany the application form. These letters should be from three individuals who can assess the applicant's "personal characteristics, motivation, and commitment to the environment, Native American health care, or tribal public policy." The foundation encourages applicants to obtain letters of recommendation from faculty in their field of study or from individuals who have supervised their work.

Typically, about 65 percent of Udall scholarship winners have been college juniors and 35 percent have been sophomores.

To determine the amount of the Udall scholarship award, each recipient submits information on the total cost of his or her particular undergraduate institution (tuition, fees, books, and room and board) and deducts from this amount the value of any other scholarships that will be coming in from other philanthropic groups. If a

Students are not required to submit any personal or family financial information (your family's income and assets are not considered).

Scholarship judging for the Udall program occurs in Arizona over a period of two and half days in mid-March.

Insider Info

Because most students apply as environmentalists, rather than as Native American healthcare and tribal public policy activists, I have focused my analysis on the environmental side of the scholarship. However, the strategic principles outlined here do apply to other aspects of the program.

student's resulting cost-of-attendance figure is at least $5,000, he or she will receive a $5,000 scholarship. According to the foundation, more than 90 percent of the Udall Scholars selected each year receive the full $5,000 scholarship award.

Once entrants send in their application materials, all materials are forwarded to a group of ten judges that includes environmental science and political science professors and government officials from organizations such as the Environmental Protection Agency (EPA). The ten judges are divided into teams of two readers, with each team responsible for reviewing a portion of the applications. Meanwhile, two additional judges screen applications specifically from community college students.

Once the applicants have been culled to a group of finalists, all ten judges discuss and debate the merits of each applicant until the 80 scholarship recipients are chosen. There are no quotas of any kind. Unlike other similar scholarship programs for college students, states are not allocated a certain number of winners. Instead, judges are just encouraged to select scholarship winners based on a wide geographic distribution.

▌ COACH'S ANALYSIS

So does your copy of *Earth in the Balance* have more dog-ears in it than Disney's *101 Dalmatians*? But how do you translate this interest in the environment into a persuasive Udall application? Sure, Udall Scholars often list impressive coursework, activities, and work experiences, but for those selected as scholarship winners, such credentials are generally *not* the defining characteristics that set them apart. Instead, successful Morris Udall Scholarship applicants usually communicate three important qualities—fundamental traits that you should try to emulate in your own application.

To start with, Udall Scholars convey an unbridled enthusiasm for the beauty of the environment and a heart-felt passion about the need to protect it. Two-time Udall Scholar Tad Kisaka, for instance, deftly captured this spirit when he described "a raging, white water rafting trip," an "exhilarating hike to the top of Mount Whitney," and how such "raw power and magnificence" makes people realize the environment is worth conserving.

When not scooping up water samples, Udall Scholar Melissa Kenney studies environmental sciences at the University of Virginia.

Second, Udall scholarship winners have usually demonstrated some form of individual initiative in addressing an environmental concern. So be sure to spotlight examples of such initiative in your application; judges are looking for students who take action—*doers,* not talkers. For example, Udall Scholar Melissa Kenney was able to showcase individual initiative by describing a past project:

We applied for and received a grant from the Chesapeake Bay Restoration Fund. Our goals were to help improve the greater watershed and educate the community on how to be stewards of our environment. To help accomplish the goals, I created a brochure for citizens to use that highlighted methods used in the Cooks Creek Restoration Project that could be replicated on their land.

Third, because Morris Udall was a legislator himself, Udall Scholars have traditionally demonstrated in their applications an appreciation for the political considerations involved in enacting environmental legislation. Udall Scholar Jacquelyn Styrna showed how she was working to develop this political savvy in her short-answer responses:

My current intern position at the State Capitol in Lansing, where, under the guidance of James Clift, policy director of the Michigan Environmental Council, I

discuss, analyze, and publicize state environmental legislation, is completely relevant to my future. . . . The knowledge I have acquired while studying the field of Political Science and Environmental Studies has provided me with both a solid and comprehensive understanding of how politics impact environmental quality and how I can involve myself in the process in order to protect and restore nature.

Keep in mind that even though his friends called him Mo, you weren't his best buddy: Refer to him as Congressman Udall in your application.

As you work on completing a rough draft of your application, look for creative ways to highlight these three qualities. It's no coincidence that these same three qualities very much describe Morris Udall and his legislative legacy on behalf of the environment. "What we're trying to do is to award scholarships to students who are like Mo Udall was," explains Christopher Helms, Executive Director of the Morris Udall Foundation. "We want to create a public servant . . . people who understand something about environmental science . . . people who are going to be sophisticated as to the way in which government operates . . . people who we hope will end up in positions that will influence environmental public policy."

Tad Kisaka
Atascadero, CA
Udall Scholar
$5,000

ESSAY SUBMISSION

Winning

Entry

In the text below, Tad Kisaka discusses a resolution introduced by Congressman Udall that recognized the meaningful work of the Outward Bound organization.

For some people it is a raging, white water rafting trip down the Salmon River, for others it is an exhilarating hike to the top of Mount Whitney, but for me it was a weeklong backpacking trip into the Golden Trout Wilderness Area in the Eastern Sierras. All of these experiences can change people's lives by showing them the beauty of the outdoors. Such experiences make people realize that the environment is worth conserving for generations to come so that they too can be taken by the raw power and magnificence of their surrounding environment.

Mr. Udall introduced House Joint Resolution 284, 100th Congress, 1st Session, on May 18, 1987 to commemorate the non-profit Outward Bound organization for its 25th anniversary. The joint resolution designated the week beginning June 21, 1987 as "National Outward Bound Week." Outward Bound has been influential in providing a chance for young people to participate in rigorous outdoor activities and aid in the betterment of the environment. Congressman Udall wanted to make a national week to recognize that Outward Bound is a meaningful organization and deserves credit for bringing young people into the environment to experience it. He recognizes that people who have encountered the greatness of the environment first hand would be more willing to protect and cherish it for years to come.

I am a fishery resources major. I want to become a fish biologist, and manage fish in the wild. Mr. Udall's joint resolution has an impact on my field of interest because young people get exposed to the outdoors and the environment through Outward Bound, and have a reason to care for the environment. The environment is composed of many ecosystems, and the fish have special niches within the ecosystem dependent on many other natural resources. Even though the fish is just one species in a huge web, if it is disturbed, the whole ecosystem can become unhealthy, which in turn makes an unhealthy environment. If the Outward Bound program can get people to see how appealing a healthy environment is, in the long run, all components of the environment, including the fish, are benefited.

This joint resolution is especially applicable to me because, when I realized how extraordinary the environment is, it guided me into a career path where, hopefully, I can present experiences for other people to enjoy. My moment happened in the Golden Trout Wilderness Area. I hooked and landed a huge golden trout and had to decide between releasing the fish or keeping it to eat. I decided to release the fish and return it back to its home waters. I realized that this fish is an important part of the ecosystem and must be preserved for the ecosystem to function properly. Along with providing outdoor experiences for people to enjoy, my job will enable me to apply research and implement laws that protect different species, but more importantly the greater ecosystem.

Notice how Kisaka's account of his trout fishing experience adds to the personal nature of the essay—thereby helping him paint a more complete portrait of himself to judges.

These eye-opening moments have a waterfall effect because now this person can help to conserve the environment by telling a friend, taking action, but most importantly, preserving it for generations to come. Getting splashed in the face with freshwater, seeing the end of the earth from the top of a mountain and catching a beautiful fish from a snowmelt creek are all eye-opening moments showing more people the greatness of our environment.

CONTACT INFORMATION

Keyword **MORKUSCH**

The Morris K. Udall Foundation
Suite 3350, 110 S. Church Ave
Tucson, AZ 85701

Phone: (520) 670-5529
Fax: (520) 670-5530
Website: www.udall.gov

RELATED AWARD PROGRAMS

For more information on a Related Award Program, enter the associated keyword in the "Enter a Keyword" box located in the Coach's Locker Room section of ScholarshipCoach.com

■ Morris K. Udall Ph.D. Fellowships

Students in their last year of writing a dissertation about environmental conflict resolution or environmental public policy may compete for two fellowships of up to $24,000 each. Grad students submit the application, a 500-word autobiography, a résumé, a five-page project outline, transcripts, recommendations, and an institution certification form. At the end of the fellowship, students must submit their completed dissertation to the foundation. Applications are due in early January.

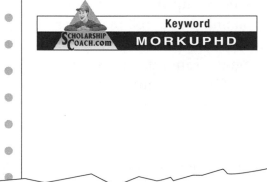

Keyword
MORKUPHD

■ *Backpacker* Magazine's Outdoor Scholarship Program

The magazine offers two different scholarship programs: the Outdoor and Environmental Leadership Award and the Outdoor Writing and Communication Award. College juniors and seniors may apply for the Outdoor and Environmental Leadership Award by writing about their experiences with outdoor leadership activities. They may apply for the Outdoor Writing and Communication Award by submitting previously written materials, along with an article about a current issue. The magazine provides 25 awards of $1,000 each. All materials should be postmarked by the deadline in late March.

Keyword
BACKPMAG

National Alliance for Excellence Scholarships

TARGET RECIPIENT

- High school seniors
- Undergraduates
- Graduate students

ENTRY REQUIREMENTS

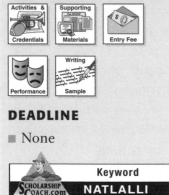

Activities & Credentials

Supporting Materials

Entry Fee

Performance

Writing Sample

DEADLINE

- None

Scholarship Coach.com

Keyword
NATLALLI

The National Alliance for Excellence was founded by Linda Paras, a mother who felt that more assistance should be given to gifted children, such as her own son.

Money
$
Matters

If you could sit down and shoot the breeze with anyone on the planet, who would you choose? Not sure? Well, you better start thinking if you happen to win a special Alex Award from the National Alliance for Excellence (NAE)—an organization that not only awards scholarship money, but also arranges for select winners to receive their prize in a presentation made by the person they would most like to meet.

The NAE scholarship program is open to high school seniors planning to enroll in a college or university and *any* student enrolled in an undergraduate or graduate degree program. Entrants may submit applications for one or more of the four entry divisions: academics, visual arts, performing arts, and technological innovation. Each application must be accompanied by a $5 processing fee.

Entrants are judged solely on the excellence of their work in their field of interest, with the submission requirements varying depending on the chosen field. Monetary awards range from $1,000 to $5,000. Even after an award is received, students may reapply once a year in each category as long as they meet the eligibility requirements.

One unique aspect of this scholarship program is that there is no official application deadline. Instead, the

Jennifer Lindsay receives her Alex Award certificate from actor/comedian Bill Cosby.

program uses rolling admissions: Applications received within a three-month period are aggregated and then batch-processed. In this way, a new awards competition begins every 90 days.

■ A CLOSER LOOK

Although scholarship prizes range from $1,000 to $5,000, the majority of awards tend to be at the $1,000 level. The number of prizes varies from year to year, depending on the amount of available funds. Typically, the National Alliance for Excellence awards approximately 100 to 120 prizes.

The program encourages past winners to reapply year after year: Each year, the past winners compete on equal footing with all of the new applicants. Students may also enter multiple categories during the same judging period. In the history of the program, more than 40 students have won twice and another 20 students have won three times. One repeat winner in the performing arts category, Monica Yunus, won on five separate occasions—accumulating a total of $6,500 in the process.

Yunus is currently in the master's degree program at The Julliard School.

Each applicant must submit two letters of recommendation from individuals of their choosing, in addition to the following supporting materials associated with their respective application category.

ACADEMICS

Applicants submit lists of all awards they have received and of all advanced courses they have taken (such as Advanced Placement or Honors courses). The grades they have received in these classes must also be included. Students applying in this category must have a minimum GPA of 3.7 and standardized test scores of at least 1300 on the SAT or 30 on the ACT.

PERFORMING ARTS

Applicants submit a VHS video (not longer than ten minutes) that includes a monologue or solo performance. Applicants who wish to demonstrate ability in more than one artistic discipline must make a separate video for each. An audio recording may also be included in addition to, but *not* in lieu of, the VHS video.

Not only was Christina Castelli presented her award by composer and former Boston Pops conductor John Williams, but she was also able to audition for him. Castelli hopes to play her violin in a movie scored by Williams. (Imagine *Jaws* theme music here.)

TECHNOLOGICAL INNOVATION

Applicants submit evidence of their expertise appropriate to the type of technological innovation. This may include architectural plans or designs for inventions, mechanisms, and structures. Of special importance is the inclusion of materials that document and evaluate their design solutions.

VISUAL ARTS

Applicants submit 20 examples of their work (slides, photos, and the like), indicating the medium they used and the size of the original work. Those with expertise in filmmaking should include a VHS video (not longer than ten minutes).

Insider Info

Many of the current judges have been past Alex Award presenters.

The number of scholarship winners in any one category depends upon the quality of submissions in that category. In recent years, close to half of the NAE winners have been in the academic category, while the fewest awards have been given in technological innovation.

Once a 90-day application window has been closed, applications are sent out to more than 80 program judges throughout the United States. The specific judges who evaluate any given application depends on the application category. For the academic category, college and university professors serve as judges, while in the technological innovation category, industry experts and patent holders from the private sector are used. For the visual arts and performing arts categories, frequent judges include the former photo director for *Time* (visual arts), a member of the New York Philharmonic (performing arts), and the former musical director for the Broadway production of *Beauty and the Beast* (performing arts).

Each judge rates the applicant on a 10-point scale—

with a score of 9.3 or higher considered exceptional. At this stage, applicants are compared not to one another but rather to a general standard of excellence. An application is typically sent out in sequence to a series of judges—usually five or six—and all must agree that an applicant is indeed exceptional for the applicant to remain eligible for an award.

Judges do not consider any factors other than a student's meritorious achievement in the specific application category. New entries from past winning students are not submitted to judges who have judged these students before.

Applicants that receive exceptional marks from each of the judges become semifinalists and are asked to submit school transcripts and any other background materials that the NAE feels is necessary to get a more complete view of the applicant. Upon doing so, entrants who become finalists are then asked to write a letter to a political leader or media outlet (with copies of the letter sent to the NAE) on a topic dear to the program's creators—the importance of merit-based scholarships. The letter itself factors into the judging process primarily for the academic category, as evidence of the student's writing ability. The finalists in each category are compared directly to one another and compete head-to-head for the available scholarship awards.

The National Alliance for Excellence works to secure other opportunities for its winners. For past winners in the Performing Arts category, for instance, the program has arranged for them to perform at Carnegie Hall.

The aforementioned Alex Award is the highest award the program offers. As part of this award, students select the person they would most like to meet, and the National Alliance for Excellence arranges for that student to receive their award in a presentation made by the individual—with the program covering all travel costs. In recent years, Alex Awards have been presented by comedian Bill Cosby, Supreme Court Justice Sandra Day O'Connor, Academy Award–winning composer John Williams, acclaimed photographer Annie Lebowitz, Senator Edward Kennedy, legendary jazz trumpeter Wynton Marsalis, and several Nobel Prize–winning scientists. If a chosen individual is not available, the

Scholarship winner Lisa Schwartz meets Sandra Day O'Connor (center), the first female justice on the U.S. Supreme Court. National Alliance for Excellence president Linda Paras (right) says that about 90 percent of Alex Award winners' first-choice presenters have agreed to participate.

In many instances, Alex Award winners have been able to secure internships or mentoring relationships with their presenters.

program works to secure the student's second- or third-choice presenter. Of the more than 120 scholarship prizes doled out in a recent year, about 40 percent of them were Alex Awards.

COACH'S ANALYSIS

In preparation for programs like this one, find ways to expand your participation and involvement in your strongest areas. This helps transform your strongest skills into truly standout talents.

To win a scholarship from the National Alliance for Excellence, you need to provide evidence of outstanding ability, notable achievements, and enormous potential in one primary area of expertise. Unlike programs that place a greater emphasis on being well rounded, this program looks for students who excel in *one* core discipline. (The exception to this is in the academic category, in which it is helpful to show excellence in several different academic fields in addition to your area of specialty.)

In preparing their materials for submission, many past applicants have found it useful to leverage past submissions they have prepared for other scholarship programs. Alex Award winner Nat Duca of Boston, Massachusetts, for instance, was able to use a research paper he had submitted to the Intel Science Talent Search (see page 180)

Duca received semifinalist recognition in the Intel Science Talent Search program.

and various science and engineering fairs. Winning in the technological innovation category, Duca notes that because he had been repeatedly revising and improving his research paper, by the time it came to apply for the National Alliance for Excellence program, it was a finely honed work.

Although Valerie Lynch of Orlando, Florida, didn't win a scholarship from the Arts Recognition and Talent Search (see page 48), she took the video she had prepared for it and added new material for her National Alliance for Excellence submission. In revising her video submission, she was able to show her tap dancing skills in a broader range of contexts. "I was able to give them a more complete picture of who I am as a performer and my techniques and abilities," she relates.

In preparing your own submission, consider first applying to other scholarship programs in your area of expertise. Because the National Alliance for Excellence program has very flexible submission requirements, you can bridge multiple applications by first seeking to meet the more rigid requirements of these other programs. Not only does this approach save you time and energy, but it can also foster vast improvements in your submission materials as you refine, edit, and tailor them—submitting your materials as soon as you think they are ready. Due to the NAE's focus on demonstrated excellence, when you apply for this scholarship you'll want to submit a version of your materials that has already been tried and tested—something representative of you at your very best.

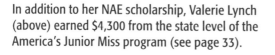

In addition to her NAE scholarship, Valerie Lynch (above) earned $4,300 from the state level of the America's Junior Miss program (see page 33).

For those applying in the academic category, follow the lead of Alex Award winner Ryan Hunter of Marietta, Georgia: In submitting his list of awards, he didn't just do it randomly. Instead, Hunter listed his academic awards first (the academic ones are the most important and relevant to the judging) and divided them into six subcategories—math, science, writing, English, French, and social studies. This helped communicate to the judges all the different areas in which he had achieved some type of academic distinction.

Hunter also included information about the selectivity of an award when it worked to his advantage—for example, he was one of five students in his school to be selected for a special math exam. In general, it's a good idea to include details about the selectivity and significance of an award if it puts the award in a more impressive context. (If practically everyone who can fog a mirror gets the award, however, keep this information to yourself.)

As you brainstorm awards and honors to include in your list, take a broad view of what actually constitutes such recognition. For instance, just being *nominated* for an award, scholarship, or program definitely counts. Even if you didn't win a Barry Goldwater Scholarship (see page 75), for instance, you can mention that your school nominated you as a candidate for that award. Also, if you've been part of a group or organization that received an award or honor, include this information along with an annotation citing your role or position in the group. Remember, the indication of an award or honor is not whether you received a shiny faux-gold trophy or simulated-wood wall plaque.

Joan Hu
College Station, TX
Alex Award Winner
Academics Division
$1,000

Winning Entry

LETTER SUBMISSION

When asked to write a letter to a political leader or media outlet on the importance of recognizing academic excellence, Joan Hu chose to write to Congressman Richard Gephardt. An excerpt from her letter is shown below.

Dear Congressman Gephardt:

I am writing concerning a topic which figures rarely in the legislative discussions of Congress today. This issue has little glamour, no sensationalism, and nothing which would too much concern the present economic or political condition of our nation or the world. Yet it is of great significance: to our nation, our children, and our future. The issue is that of education, and more specifically, the need to honor the best and brightest students in our schools. Excellence in the classroom is so often overlooked or only superficially recognized, in comparison to the laurels, recognition, and pomp heaped upon, for example, professional athletes. We need to reevaluate as a nation precisely what education means to us and to the future of our children, and begin to recognize a heretofore marginalized minority which will very likely define the direction our nation takes in the next century.

Our society prizes highly many nonacademic achievements. Young athletes choose not to attend college or to curtail their education in order to play professionally for enormous salaries; Bill Gates opts to not complete his college degree in order to build a technological empire and become the wealthiest man on earth. Ironically, our children are taught that the success of these cultural icons is tantamount to or even greater than the achievements of those scientists and philosophers who devote their lives to thought and discovery. By the touchstone of material success, athletes and business-men are held in greater esteem by some of our children than the men and women they learn about in school: Nobel Laureates, scientists, poets, artists. It is little wonder that the value of academic achievement has been eroded all the

For the NAE application, Hu submitted recommendations from both her biochemistry professor and her English professor.

Coach's Comments

while in the eyes of our children, for we send them clouded messages about the value of using one's mind to pursue knowledge. When our children see that those who neglected their education in pursuit of material gain are as much or even more rewarded than those who find fulfillment in intellectual pursuits, we are in effect telling them that a lifetime of learning and knowledge is only secondary in importance compared to the materialism of the here and now. More and more children seem to believe that the practical solution to success in our social infrastructure is to put aside their school books in order to pursue dreams of vast fortunes. It becomes little wonder that with this diminution of our educational mores, United States high school seniors continue year after year to score below average on standard measures of aptitude in the math and sciences when compared to the children of other nations.

Now at Harvard Medical School, Hu earned her undergraduate degree from Washington University in St. Louis.

Coach's Comments

We cannot allow this trend to continue. We must and we should reward achievements of the mind as much as we reward the achievements of the material, for we have at stake the fundamental values that define a civilized society: the literacy and intellectual development of the constituency, the possibilities for true progress and growth in the arenas of human knowledge, and the legacy that we leave behind for future generations of mankind. Our choices will determine whether our future is to be a sustained search for knowledge and truth, or whether it is only to be a blind chasing after the materialism of the here and now, which leaves the coffer of human discovery unfilled and the potential of the human mind stunted.

*   *   *

I am writing this letter as a Finalist in the Honored Scholars & Artists Program of the National Alliance for Excellence, an organization which seeks further recognition of academic excellence in youth. The existentialist philosopher Colin Wilson once said that, "The mind has exactly the same power as the hands: not merely to grasp the world, but to change it." I would add one emendation to that statement—that while the hands can mold only what lies before it, the mind is capable of reshaping the entire universe. Indeed, when we reward our children for their academic excellence, we recognize in them not only their present but also their future contributions to the achievements of mankind, and to the progress and development of our small civilization. Their discoveries will open the eyes of our minds to new knowledge and a deeper understanding of the world in which we live, and they will give us the riches of a boundless universe whose depths are still beckoning to be fathomed.

Most sincerely,

Joan Hu

To read more from Joan Hu's letter, visit the Coach's Locker Room at ScholarshipCoach.com (Keyword: NATLALLI).

CONTACT INFORMATION

Keyword **NATLALLI**

National Alliance for Excellence
1070-H Highway 34, Suite #205
Matawan, NJ 07747

Phone: (732) 747-0028
E-mail: info@excellence.org
Website: www.excellence.org

RELATED AWARD PROGRAMS

For more information on a Related Award Program, enter the associated keyword in the "Enter a Keyword" box located in the Coach's Locker Room section of ScholarshipCoach.com

■ Lucent Global Science Scholars Program

This program is for U.S. high school seniors who have distinguished themselves in science and math. Applicants submit two recommendations, a high school transcript, and a 500-word essay about their achievements and interest in math and science, activities, career plans, and reasons why they should be selected. Winners are awarded a $5,000 prize, a trip to Lucent Technologies, and, if available, an internship position at Lucent Technologies or Bell Labs. All preliminary materials should be submitted before the mid-March deadline. Finalist interviews are conducted in May.

■ Robert C. Byrd Scholarships

This federally funded program, named for the distinguished U.S. senator from West Virginia, is intended to honor high school seniors who have demonstrated promise of academic excellence. Various numbers of awards (each worth about $1,500 per year, depending on congressional funding) are offered for each state plus the District of Columbia, Insular Areas, and Puerto Rico. These scholarships are renewable for a total of four years while the recipient is in school working toward a degree. The application process, deadlines, and requirements vary by state.

■ Mensa Scholarships

Founded upon the belief that excellence should be rewarded, local Mensa chapters sponsor awards for high school seniors and undergraduates. Chapter participation varies by location. For most programs, students are required to enter 550-word essays about vocational and academic goals. Entries are due in late January.

National Honor Society Scholarship

TARGET RECIPIENT

■ High school seniors

ENTRY REQUIREMENTS

Nomination

Short Answer

Activities & Credentials

Recommendation

Entry Fee

DEADLINE

■ January

SCHOLARSHIP COACH.com

Keyword

NHSSCHOL

Money
$
Matters

If your school doesn't yet have an NHS chapter, perhaps you can create one.

Founded in 1921, the National Honor Society (NHS) awards membership to students who demonstrate dedication and excellence in four key areas: (1) sleeping, (2) partying, (3) TV-watching, and (4) junk-food consumption. Just kidding. (Don't all rush out to claim your memberships at once!)

Actually, as specified in the National Honor Society constitution, this prestigious organization found at high schools throughout the country seeks to recognize students who exhibit exceptional scholarship, service, character, and leadership.

Each NHS chapter may nominate two seniors for the award, and each nominee must submit academic and extracurricular information, a school transcript, two very brief recommendations, and a short-answer response (less than 300 words) on a topic related to scholarship, service, character, or leadership. Each year, the program awards $1,000 scholarships to 200 deserving students nationwide. A $6 processing fee (typically paid by the high school or NHS chapter) is also required.

Nomination forms must be received at the offices of the National Association of Secondary School Principals (NASSP), creators of the National Honor Society, by the mid-January deadline. Winners are announced in May.

■ A CLOSER LOOK

On the application form, students must submit information about their grades and test scores, extracurricular activities, organizational memberships, awards and honors, community service, and work experience. Space on the four-page application form is very limited; students are not permitted to attach additional sheets and are disqualified if they do so.

Special emphasis is placed on specific extracurricular activities and leadership positions held in those activities: Five key activities are printed directly on the form: (1) National Honor Society, (2) class officer, (3) student council, (4) high school newspaper, and (5) high school yearbook. Students must check the appropriate boxes to indicate any leadership positions held in these activities.

Make sure that you fill out the application form for the current year, not a prior year's form. Because small changes are made to the form each year, students who use an old form are automatically disqualified.

The application form also emphasizes athletic participation (and leadership positions or varsity letters earned in those sports) by establishing a separate list for such participation. The form does not request information on freshman year activities; hence, for each activity, students indicate whether they have participated in grades 10, 11, or 12.

The student essay (of no more than 300 words) is related to a different topic each year. Expect to see questions dealing with different aspects of scholarship, service, character, or leadership. In addition to a high school transcript, brief recommendations by the principal (200 words or less) and a teacher, guidance counselor, or NHS adviser (150 words or less) must also be included.

The National Association of Secondary School Principals (NASSP) forwards all applications to Scholarship Program Administrators, Inc. (SPA), which conducts the initial screening of applicants. To minimize discrepancies between educational systems, students' entries are separated into judging piles based on the students' state of residence and are judged only against other students from their state. To screen the applications, SPA uses a quantitative system, designed by the NASSP, which awards a number of points to each section on the application form—excluding the essay and recommendations, which are not evaluated at this stage in the judging. Once the scores have been totaled, about 1,000 to 1,200 students (the top scorers in each state) advance to the next round of judging.

At this point, a 12-member national selection committee—consisting of educators, educational administrators, and select National Honor Society advisers—makes the final determination of the 200 winners. The committee examines the applications in much greater depth and detail, paying special attention to essays and recommendations; the scores from the prior round of judging do not carry over to this round. Once again, students are compared only against others from their own state and there is no formal system for awarding points. The number of awards per state depends on state population and the number of entries submitted, but every state is guaranteed at least one winner.

▌ COACH'S ANALYSIS

To get by the initial screening round for the National Honor Society Scholarship, you should list as many activities and credentials as you possibly can. According to David Cordts, who helps administer the program, the methodology for this phase of the judging rewards *quantity* more than *quality* because points are awarded for each listed item: The more you list, the more points you get. "Do multiple projects," Cordts advises, "so that you fill out more space on the form."

In other words, do everything in your power to avoid leaving blank spaces. So what do you do if the deadline is fast approaching and you don't have enough activities or

One important organizational element to consider is whether certain endeavors you've undertaken should be logically separated into multiple activities or grouped together as one activity.

credentials to fill up a given list? Try the following strategy: Add a description to each activity on your list, as needed, so that each activity takes up two or more lines. For instance, if one of your listed activities is "Campaign Volunteer," try expanding on it by writing:

Campaign Volunteer
(Coordinator of voter registration drive)

By doing this, you can get rid of extra blanks on the page and expand on your most compelling credentials and achievements. The key idea here is that you *don't* want to add meaningless material just to fill in the blanks. Instead, consider leftover space on the application form as an opportunity to flesh out your existing credentials and make them more persuasive.

If you have more time, a better strategy is actually to expand your participation so that you have more items to include on this and other scholarship applications. Perhaps this means simply joining and participating in that after-school club you've been meaning to check out. . . . Or maybe it means starting your *own* club. (As an added benefit, when you start your own organization, you'll automatically be serving in a leadership capacity!) Seek to participate in endeavors that demonstrate the National Honor Society's four founding principles: scholarship, service, character, and leadership. "If it comes down to two students that are relatively equal," Cordts states, "the judges look to see which one has the most well-rounded approach to all four criteria."

Once you've made the final judging round, your essay and brief recommendations are of extreme importance. Because other parts of the application mainly focus on the *quantity* of activities, credentials, and leadership positions held, the essay and recommendation letters are your main chance to demonstrate the *quality* of your endeavors. Regardless of the particular essay question asked, therefore, you should work into your response

One area frequently left blank is the list of athletic participation. Cordts emphasizes, however, that participating in sports is of the same importance in the judging as other activities.

Insider Info

references to activities, credentials, and experiences in which you have demonstrated scholarship, service, character, and leadership. In one recent application year, for instance, the program asked the following question:

In many communities recently questions have risen about the role of a high school education in today's world. In your opinion, what is the value and importance to students today of completing a high school education, whether in public or private school?

When answering this type of question, don't just pontificate abstractly on the skills students learn through high school, the importance of a diploma in securing a good job, or the societal benefits of secondary education. Although these are all valid points to discuss, you also want to include your personal experiences and perspectives to give the judges more persuasive information about why *you* deserve the scholarship award.

You could, for example, talk about what a high school education has meant to you personally. Perhaps you could mention some specific school-sponsored activities you have participated in (pick the most important ones listed on your application) and describe how this participation has impacted your life. Or maybe you could work in a discussion of your career and life goals by discussing how high school has given you a solid foundation to pursue such dreams. The possibilities are endless.

Whatever you do—and whatever the question—remember that the essay represents one of the few opportunities on the National Honor Society application to place your most compelling personal qualities and credentials in the spotlight. So use this opportunity wisely.

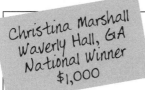

Christina Marshall
Waverly Hall, GA
National Winner
$1,000

SHORT-ANSWER RESPONSE

Winning
Entry

In her response to a question about cheating in the classroom, Christina Marshall relates the topic to a broader discussion of teaching morals and values in the home, school, and community.

In the past, cheating was a rare and shameful occurrence. During those times morals were a lot stronger in the home, at school, and even in the community. People took pride in working hard to achieve their goals. However, today's society has lower values, and people have been pushed by society to DO their best and BE their best. As a result, students struggling to graduate, and even those who are seeking valedictorian status, are going to desperate measures to achieve their goals. Cheating has become their final result.

Cheating in school around the country has grown to "epidemic proportions" because there is a lack of emphasis placed on the values of honesty and pride. If these values were emphasized at home, school, and the community, cheating would not be running rampant in our schools.

At home, parents can begin to reprimand their children for lying and taking items that do not belong to them. Then parents should follow this reprimand with a talk about having high values and morals by emphasizing their importance. This same concept can be applied in schools. When a student is caught cheating, the punishment should not be just a slap on the wrist. A stronger sanction should be administered to make an example. Communities should definitely do their part in up-lifting these values by allowing community members, such as officers and businessmen, to come to schools and discuss the need for higher values in the community.

If all three of these institutions do their part in denouncing educational theft, "cheating," then this "epidemic" will be eradicated.

CONTACT INFORMATION

Keyword
NHSSCHOL

All requests for application materials should be directed to NHS advisers, principals, or counselors.

Scholarship Program Administrators, Inc. (SPA)
National Honor Society Scholarship
P.O. Box 24605
Nashville, TN 37202

Phone: (800) 253-7746
E-mail: dsa@principals.org
Website: www.nhs.us

RELATED AWARD PROGRAMS

For more information on a Related Award Program, enter the associated keyword in the "Enter a Keyword" box located in the Coach's Locker Room section of ScholarshipCoach.com

■ Golden Key Scholar Awards

Undergraduates, graduate students, and professionals who are members of this popular college honor society may compete for grants in the fields of art, writing, education, engineering, and many others. There are also special awards for adult students over 25 years of age. Award amounts range from a couple of hundred dollars to several thousand dollars, depending on the program. Requirements and deadlines also vary.

	Keyword
ScholarshipCoach.com	GOLDENK

■ Junior Achievement Scholarship Program

In addition to receiving leadership and learning opportunities in the business world, members of the Junior Achievement organization can compete for 13 different scholarship programs targeted at high school seniors. Ten of the scholarships are school- or program-specific, while three have broader criteria. Application deadlines, required materials, and award amounts vary, depending on the program.

	Keyword
ScholarshipCoach.com	JRACHVMT

■ National Beta Club Scholarship Program

Local National Beta Club chapters must nominate high school senior members for the various awards offered. Overall, 209 students are awarded $1,000 to $15,000 on the basis of academics, leadership, character, and service. Applications are due in early December.

	Keyword
ScholarshipCoach.com	NATLBETA

National Peace Essay Contest

TARGET RECIPIENT

- High school students

ENTRY REQUIREMENTS

Essay

DEADLINE

- January

SCHOLARSHIP Coach.com	Keyword NATPEACE

Money Matters

Added Bonus

It is the hope of the United States Institute of Peace—a nonpartisan federal institution funded by Congress to promote the peaceful resolution of international conflict—that when a student researches and writes an essay on a global peacekeeping topic, the student will become increasingly aware of international affairs. This awareness, it is believed, builds better citizens.

The National Peace Essay Contest is open to any student in grades 9 to 12 studying in the United States, and also to U.S. citizens studying abroad. Students must write essays of 1,500 words or less on the international affairs topic selected for each year's competition.

Each first-place state winner in the National Peace Essay Contest is awarded a scholarship of $1,000 and will be invited to attend the awards program in Washington, D.C. (all expenses paid). After the state winners have been determined, they compete in the national contest for first-, second-, and third-place prizes of $10,000, $5,000, and $2,500.

Entries are due before the late-January deadline.

A CLOSER LOOK

Entries are first submitted to local contest coordinators (frequently high school teachers) for verification. The coordinators check for grammar and spelling errors and are also expected to verify that all necessary documents (registration form, organization participation form, and multiple copies of the essay and bibliography) are included before an entry is submitted. If there is not a coordinator in an applicant's area, it is up to the student to find someone to fill the position; entries will *not* be accepted unless they have been verified.

Although the official contest topic varies from year to year, students in past contests have addressed such topics as:

Within each main topic, there may be additional subtopics that entrants must also address.

- How human rights violations and/or war crimes have been handled in two twentieth-century conflicts

- What the U.S. national security interests should be and when intervention should take place

- The U.S. military's role in international peace-keeping

- The differences between a peace agreement that was successful and one that failed

Essays must be under the 1,500-word limit or points will be deducted. All essays should be accompanied by a bibliography, and no personal information—such as a student's name or school—may appear on the essay itself. The entry packet should include the completed entry form and four copies of both the essay and the bibliography.

Selected professionals complete the first round of judging on the state level and then each state forwards one winner to the national contest, where the board of directors for the United States Institute of Peace will select the top three winners. State-level judges select winners based on three primary criteria.

When considering the score for *style and mechanics* (33 percent), judges look for solid organization (including a clear introduction, body, conclusion, and bibliography), a clear and coherent presentation of ideas, and minimal grammar, punctuation, and syntax errors.

The second judging criterion, *quality of research* (33 percent), is scored by examining the writer's proper citation of sources, adequate research of facts and different points of view, appropriate use of examples, and overall grasp of the topic.

The final criterion, *quality of analysis* (33 percent), depends upon each student's clear response to the topic at hand, analysis of the question from different points of view, and a synthesis of ideas to find support for any conclusions drawn in the course of writing the essay.

▌ COACH'S ANALYSIS

The essays from past winners in the National Peace Essay Contest have developed much more thoughtful themes than an exposition on "The Origin of the Two-Finger Peace Sign." In fact, most winners have distinguished themselves to the contest judges in at least one of the following three ways.

The first way to distinguish yourself is by using an interesting analytical framework to set forth your argument—a framework that lets you evaluate specific examples from world events in a clear and systematic way. National first-place winner Richard Lee of Columbia, South Carolina, for instance, first described six "tests" used by former Secretary of Defense Caspar Weinberger to determine whether or not to commit U.S. military forces. As he went through both case studies outlined in his essay—conflicts in Somalia and Bosnia—he referred to Weinberger's six criteria and pointed out the extent to which each criterion had been satisfied.

Another first-place national winner, Tim Shenk of Harrisonburg, Virginia, derived his framework from a four-part model of reconciliation (truth, mercy, peace, and justice) presented by a professor of conflict studies and sociology at Eastern Mennonite University. He then

For specific tools and exercises that help you develop an analytical framework in your essay, see the third book in my scholarship trilogy, Scholarship Seeker's Toolbox*.*

compared and contrasted attempts at reconciliation in Bosnia and South Africa by evaluating whether or not truth, mercy, peace, and justice were achieved in these instances. The strength of this framework-based approach is in its clear and intriguing methodology.

A second way past winners have distinguished themselves is through the extent of their research. In recent years, first-place national winners have cited, on average, about 25 bibliographical sources. (The research needed for this essay contest is obviously *not* for the faint of heart.) A good starting point for this research is on the United States Institute of Peace website (www.usip.org), which features the institute's digital library, archives of institute publications (*Peace Watch, Peaceworks,* and *Special Reports*), research papers, and links to leading international affairs websites.

Of special note is the "Guide to Specialists," available online, which lists foreign policy experts with regional and topical expertise. Designed as a resource specifically for professional foreign policy journalists, you can use this list to find experts on your chosen subject matter and then can consult their books or articles, or ask them questions via e-mail. Past winners have also frequently utilized periodicals such as *Foreign Affairs, Foreign Policy, International Affairs, The Economist, New Republic, Current History,* and the *Journal of Conflict Resolution.* (Check your local public or college library, as well as each publication's Internet website.)

Third, past winners have distinguished themselves by creating original historical connections and geographic juxtapositions. First-place winner Joseph Bernabucci of Washington, D.C., for example, went far back in history to link the Treaty of Ghent (1815) to modern-day peace between the United States and Canada, and the Treaty of Sevres (1920) to modern-day disputes between Greece and Turkey—creating an interesting opportunity to compare and contrast the historical ramifications of both. Likewise, first-place winner Elspeth Simpson of Little

Rock, Arkansas, brought together two types of foreign policy issues not usually evaluated against one another—the fight against drugs in Colombia and the fight against nuclear proliferation in North Korea—to show the effect of shifting foreign objectives in two very different (yet surprisingly similar) contexts. What made both of these essays interesting is the way in which the winners made their points through unconventional and intellectually stimulating comparisons.

If you can incorporate an interesting framework, impressive research, and unique linkages and comparisons in your well-written essay, you can leapfrog your entry to the top of the judging stack.

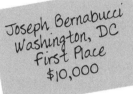

Joseph Bernabucci
Washington, DC
First Place
$10,000

Winning
Entry

A Just and Lasting Peace:
More than the Absence of War

In the following excerpt from his winning essay, Joseph Bernabucci contrasts the causes and effects of two very different historical legacies.

The lives and prosperity of millions of people depend on peace and, in turn, peace depends on treaties—fragile documents that must do more than end wars. Negotiations and peace treaties may lead to decades of cooperation during which disputes between nations are resolved without military action and economic cost, or may prolong or even intensify the grievances that provoked conflict in the first place. In 1996, as Canada and the United States celebrated their mutual boundary as the longest undefended border in the world, Greece and Turkey nearly came to blows over a rocky island so small it scarcely had space for a flagpole. Both territorial questions had been raised as issues in peace treaties. The Treaty of Ghent in 1815 set the framework for the resolution of Canadian-American territorial questions. The Treaty of Sevres in 1920, between the Sultan and the victorious Allies of World War I, dismantled the remnants of the Ottoman Empire and distributed its territories. Examination of the terms and consequences of the two treaties clearly establishes that a successful treaty must provide more than the absence of war.

How do the terms or implementation of treaties determine peace or conflict decades later? Efforts to build a just and lasting peace are complicated not only because past grievances must be addressed, but future interests must be anticipated—even when such future interests were not identified as the cause of war in the first place. Edward Teller, discussing the Manhattan Project, observed, "No endeavor which is worthwhile is simple in prospect; if it is right, it will be simple in retrospect." Only if a nation perceives that continuing observance of the treaty will sustain the state over a long period of time and in changing circumstances, the peace and security promised by the treaty will endure. Machiavelli observed that ". . . fear of loss of the State by a prince or republic will overcome both gratitude and treaties."

* * *

In comparison to the Treaty of Ghent, the Treaty of Sevres can only be described as a short-term success and a long-term disaster. Signed in August 1920 by the representatives of Ottoman Turkey and the Allies of World War I, the treaty dismantled the Ottoman Empire for the benefit of various groups indigenous to the area and, not least of all, British, French, and Italian interests in the Middle East. France received a mandate in Syria, and Britain in Palestine and Iraq. Italy demanded Montenegro as a buffer between its territories and Serbia. Turkey gave up its rights to North Africa and the Arabian peninsula. Kurdestan and Armenia became autonomous. Greece dominated eastern Thrace, the Anatolian west coast, and most Aegean islands. The British, French, and Italian governments controlled the Turkish treasury.

The peace imposed on a captive Sultan did not demand indemnities, but the Turks believed the Treaty of Sevres was so unfair that Mustafa Kemal threatened to overthrow the Sultan. As Allies debated the use of military force to guarantee the Treaty, the United States refused to participate. The Sultan refused to ratify the Treaty, believing his government could not survive if he signed. In 1921, Kemal signed an agreement with Bolshevik Russia that crushed Armenian independence. The Treaty of Sevres rapidly crumbled.

* * *

The Turks, unlike the Americans in 1815, viewed the treaty imposed on them as unfair. Although the Sultan attempted to finesse the Treaty he was dethroned. His successor, Kemal, also known as Atatürk, the father of modern Turkey, commenced hostilities against the Greeks to recover lost territories.

Mediators provided little or no assistance or intervention. Perhaps the Allies didn't have the manpower, the money, or the will to supervise and enforce an imposed peace. The principal issues left unresolved by the Treaty of Sevres remain sources of regional disputes and potential world conflict to this day.

On the other hand, the British and the Americans initially used Russia as a third-party mediator and relied on a boundary commission to set the precedent for successful resolution of twelve subsequent disputes between the United States and what became sovereign Canada. The Treaty of Ghent has never been challenged.

In the future, peace treaties must provide for a great deal more than the absence of war. History has taught us that treaties must represent a "shared willingness" to identify the long-term, as well as the short-term, interests of all parties. Effective treaties must accurately identify such interests, not leave ambiguities or set onerous terms. To that end, in the twenty-first century nations must wage peace more creatively and aggressively than war in the twentieth century. Leaders committed to peace must receive support. A process for mediation, monitoring, and enforcement by a third party, or a mechanism for the resolution of disputes, will preserve the mutual interests of the parties in face of changing circumstances. Initial implementation should be rapid, before national interests, or the perceptions of those interests, change. The Treaty of Ghent satisfied most of these criteria. The Treaty of Sevres did not.

For the complete text of Joseph Bernabucci's winning essay, visit the Coach's Locker Room at ScholarshipCoach.com (Keyword: NATPEACE).

CONTACT INFORMATION

Keyword
NATPEACE

United States Institute of Peace
National Peace Essay Contest
1200 17th Street NW, Suite 200
Washington, DC 20036-3011

Phone: (202) 429-3854
Fax: (202) 429-6063
E-mail: essay_contest@usip.org
Website: www.usip.org/ed/npec.html

RELATED AWARD PROGRAMS

For more information on a Related Award Program, enter the associated keyword in the "Enter a Keyword" box located in the Coach's Locker Room section of ScholarshipCoach.com

■ United States Institute of Peace Fellowship Program

This is a program for doctoral candidates whose proposed dissertations focus on strategies to prevent or end international conflict, to sustain peace, and to explore the sources and nature of international conflict. Qualified applicants submit a summary of the proposed dissertation, a four-page (or less) summary of their background (including education, professional experience, career plans, and recommendations), plus a seven-page project description outlining the intended work. Stipends of $17,000 are paid directly to the winners and must be used for 12 months of writing and researching the dissertation. All applications materials should arrive at the USIP offices by the deadline in early November.

Keyword
USIPEACE

■ U.S. Department of State Fulbright Program

This prestigious program is for graduate students, professionals, and teachers hoping to pursue their studies abroad in order to make a significant contribution to a field of expertise. Emphasis is on fostering international relations during the grant's study and travel period. Submissions require a detailed project proposal. Award amounts vary, and all applications are due in late October.

Keyword
USFULBRI

■ Soros Fellowships for New Americans

This program is for current undergraduates, or students under 30 who hold a bachelor's degree, who are considered "new Americans" (resident alien, naturalized citizen, child of two naturalized citizens). Awards include 30 fellowships for up to two years of graduate study in the United States. Students submit essays, recommendations, transcripts, and activity lists. Semifinalists undergo an interview process. The preliminary deadline is in late November.

Keyword
SOROSFEL

Optimist International Essay and Oratorical Contests

Optimist International, an organization dedicated to bringing out the best in youth, has been helping communities internationally since 1919. In addition to offering childhood cancer programs, awareness programs about general child safety issues, and other various community projects, the organization sponsors two substantial scholarship programs.

To enter the *Optimist International Essay Contest*, entrants submit essays of 400 to 500 words on a topic relating to the principle of freedom. Entrants must be in grades 10 through 12 at a high school in the United States, Canada, or Mexico, or else in grades 10 through 13 in a school in the Caribbean.

After students have advanced through local rounds in the essay contest, winners from each of the 53 "districts" (the 50 states plus Canada, the Caribbean, and parts of Mexico) are awarded $650 each. First-, second-, and third-place international winners ($5,000, $3,000, and $2,000, respectively) will be chosen from among the district awardees. The first-place international winner and his or her parents also receive an all-expense-paid trip to the Optimist International Convention to read his or her winning essay.

The *Optimist International Oratorical Contest* is open to students under the age of 16 in the United States, Canada, and the Caribbean. Applicants must write and memorize a four- to five-minute speech on each year's specified topic. A total of $3,000 is

Entries for both contests may be in English, French, or Spanish, depending on the predominant language of the local Optimist chapter.

allocated for students competing in the oratorical contest at the district level: This prize money is disbursed either as two awards of $1,500 (one each to a boy and a girl) or as three separate awards in the amounts of $1,500, $1,000, and $500. Other prizes may be provided at the club and regional level (generally these awards are up to $500). There is no international round for the oratorical contest; the highest level of competition occurs in the district round.

Entries must be submitted for the essay contest by early January; winners are announced in February. For the oratorical contest, specific deadlines are up to each individual Optimist club participating in the contest. Most local deadlines occur in early June, with students moving on to the district competition doing so by early July. Oratorical winners are announced immediately following each contest.

▌ A CLOSER LOOK

Of the 3,500 Optimist International clubs, more than 1,000 participate in the essay contest, and more than 2,000 participate in the oratorical contest. If your local Optimist club is not participating in either the essay or oratorical contest, you should be able to find a club that participates elsewhere in your district.

The essay topic each year is usually quite broad. Recent essay topics have included:

▌ Are we losing our freedom?

▌ Where would I be without freedom?

▌ When our freedom is threatened

Within this context, past winners have written about freedom from personal, national, and historical perspectives.

Each essay submission should address the topic in a unique way, but the format must conform to the guidelines set forth by contest rules; more specifically, students should pay attention to rules governing the length of the essay (400–500 words) and must include a title page, footnotes, page numbers, and a bibliography.

Oratorical contest topics have focused on how young people can affect the world. Past topics have included:

- If I could change the world

- We are the future

- United we stand in optimism

In the past, winning orators have frequently taken one of two general tacks: They have highlighted things in the world that we should all appreciate and be proud of, or they have discussed current problems and challenged the audience to make things better. Some winners have included both perspectives in their orations.

For both the essay and the oratorical contests, a three-judge panel performs judging duties on both the club and district levels. Judges on the panel are forbidden from discussing a student's essay or oration with each other. Typical judges on the club and district levels include print and television journalists, attorneys, teachers, and government officials.

Students who have won either the essay or the oratorical contest may not participate in the same competition again but may enter the other competition if they are eligible.

JUDGING THE ESSAY CONTEST

Judging for the essay contest is based on a 100-point scale. Two specific judging criteria account for 70 of the 100 points. The first criterion, *material organization* (40 points), assesses the student's logical interpretation of the subject matter, clear presentation of ideas, quality of research, and ability to organize supporting facts. The second criterion, *vocabulary and style* (30 points), assesses the entrant's word choice, sentence structure, and over-all writing style. The remaining 30 points are allocated for *grammar, punctuation, and spelling* (20 points); *neatness* (5 points); and *adherence to contest rules* (5 points). The entrant with the highest grand total of points is selected the winner.

The essay judging procedure also specifies a series of penalties for rule infractions by contest entrants: Five-point penalties are incurred for every 25 words that an essay is over or under the word limit. Five-point deductions are also made for failing to double-space the essay, for forgetting to correctly indicate the total number of words in the essay, and for including a reference within the essay itself that directly or indirectly identifies yourself or your home geographic region (all judging is meant to be conducted anonymously).

The official rules state that an essay's bibliography and title shall not be counted toward the word limit.

Once essays advance to the international round, new judges come into play: namely, the foreign language department at a local St. Louis university (usually the University of Missouri at St. Louis). Because essay entries may be submitted in English, French, or Spanish, having a college foreign language department conduct the judging allows the essay entries to be compared across languages.

Insider Info

At the international level, about 90 percent of the essays are written in English.

JUDGING THE ORATORICAL CONTEST

Like the essay contest methodology, oratorical contest judging is based on a 100-point scale. The official judging score sheet allocates points for *poise* (20 points), *content* (35 points), *delivery and presentation* (35 points), and *overall effectiveness* (10 points). Orators incur one-point penalties for every 15 seconds that their speech is over or under the time limit, as well as three-point penalties for failing to announce the official topic at the beginning of the speech. Deductions of one to five points are also incurred for including a self-identifying reference.

To determine the winners, judges convert their point totals into comparative rankings, in which the orator with the highest point total receives a ranking of 1, the orator with the second highest point total receives a ranking of 2, and so on. Any competitor who is ranked number 1 by a majority of the judges automatically receives first prize. Otherwise, judges' rankings are aggregated for each orator, and the orator with the best overall ranking total wins the top award.

COACH'S ANALYSIS

Because Optimist club members are *not* permitted to serve as judges for either the essay or oratorical contests, the competitions do *not* emphasize the Optimist club philosophy as much as you might expect. As a result, past winning essays and orations have had very diverse subject matter, styles, and tone.

For those entering the essay contest, perhaps the most important thing is to strive for some type of unique approach. "Looking at those who have won," relates Program Director Al Schon, "originality of thought, style and presentation is the key."

How do you achieve a high degree of originality? First, you can do it by adding vivid personal details (but no self-identifying references) to your essay—details that make the essay uniquely yours. No one else in the state, nation, continent, world, galaxy, or universe (let alone the application pile) could have written it, because no one else has shared your unique experiences.

Second, you can add originality to your essay through your intellectual approach. If you can, try to come up with your own unconventional or thought-provoking way of looking at the topic. For instance, if you have to write about the meaning of freedom, try attacking the topic in reverse—by describing a world in which freedom doesn't exist.

Because a college foreign language department conducts final round judging, demonstrating in your essay an appreciation for people of other cultures makes good strategic sense.

Third, you can achieve originality by expressing traditional ideas in novel ways. Past winners have used extended metaphors, historical examples, pop culture references, and illustrative stories to great effect.

For those entering the oratorical contest, a few additional considerations are in order. Not only should you strive for originality in your speech content, but also try to achieve a real comfort level with the material you're reciting. Because the oratorical contest program is for students age 15 and under (with many entrants not yet in high school), the orators who shine are the ones who seem relaxed and natural—qualities somewhat unusual for students of this age. The best way to achieve this level of comfort is by practicing repeatedly in front of family members, teachers, and any other audience that adds some formality (and a bit of anxiety to toughen you up) to the practice session.

"Don't get too nervous or anxious when you start your speech, just relax," suggests district oratorical winner John Coggin of Sanford, North Carolina. "Sometimes my legs felt like they were about to give out. . . . I felt more confident each time I did it."

And once you're comfortable with the material, you can focus on your delivery, and on trying to make a connection with the judges (who are seated among the audience without any identification). "Sometimes you could tell who the judges were because they were taking notes and writing things down," Coggin says. "I would try to make eye contact and look at them more often."

Winning
Entry

WE ARE THE FUTURE

In this winning oration, Kate Slavens discusses the responsibilities and opportunities facing today's young people.

When I was little, I remember thinking about the year I would graduate from high school—2003. 2003? That seemed like a long time away. I mean,

it would be in the next millennium! Well, the new millennium is here, and I am beginning to realize that the future is a lot closer than I once thought. In fact, my class and I, the class of 2003, we are the future.

What exactly does that mean? It sounds like a lot of pressure, actually, to be the future. It definitely is not to be taken lightly. With the future comes responsibility. Responsibility to our parents. Our community. Our country, and anyone who has ever believed in us. We owe it to them to make sure our new millennium will be remembered as a time of peace, equality, and prosperity.

There are so many choices we have to make now that will affect our future. Who we are friends with, what we are involved in, where we want to go to college, and what we want to major in. At times it can seem overwhelming. What we do now does affect our future. We can learn from our triumphs and our struggles, our successes and our failures. Obviously, we want to be successful in everything that we do. But realistically, there are going to be times in life when we fail. To be the future, we must learn and accept both our successes and our defeats.

Let me tell you a story from *Chicken Soup for the Teenage Soul,* edited by Jack Canfield, about a person whose failures ultimately led to his great success. For Sparky, school was all but impossible. In high school, he flunked not only physics, but also Latin, algebra, and English. In sports, he didn't do much better. He managed to get on the school's golf team, but he lost the only important match of the season. However, one thing was important to Sparky—drawing. In his senior year, he submitted a few cartoons to the editor of his yearbook. They were turned down. Despite this rejection, Sparky believed in his ability so much that he decided to become a professional artist. After finishing high school, he submitted some of his drawings to the Walt Disney Studios. He spent a lot of time perfecting the drawings, but when the reply came from Disney Studios, he had once again been rejected. So Sparky decided to write his own autobiography in cartoons. The cartoon soon became famous worldwide. Sparky, better

> *Telling stories works great in orations because the way in which you deliver the story adds a lot of drama.*

known to us as Charles Schultz, created the little boy whose kite would never fly and who never quite succeeded in kicking a football: Charlie Brown. Charles Schultz showed us that whatever our goals, they are possible with determination and perseverance.

As far as our careers, the possibilities seem endless. No more butcher, baker, and candlestick maker. Rather, biochemical engineer, software specialist, and entrepreneur. This cutting-edge technology reminds me of a quote by Muriel Strode. "Do not follow where the path may lead. Go instead where there is no path and leave a trail." I think that in the future our scientists and researchers will definitely leave many groundbreaking trails.

Personally, I am interested in history and the study of people throughout the ages. To some, history in no way connects to the future. But I'm a firm believer that we cannot move into the future until we fully understand our past. After all, America was founded with basic principles. Life, liberty, faith in God, equality, and the pursuit of happiness. To forget that would be like killing a piece of our heritage, a piece of ourselves. We owe it to our forefathers to make the future a place where those ideals are still important.

The future. Neither you nor I, as much as we would like to, have a crystal ball to look in to magically see what it will be like. Instead, we must decide what the future will be by our choices and actions. We Are The Future.

CONTACT INFORMATION

Keyword
OPTESORA

For program details and deadlines contact your local Optimist club

Optimist International
4494 Lindell Blvd.
St. Louis, MO 63108

Phone: (800) 500-5130, ext. 224
E-mail: programs@optimist.org
Websites:
www.optimist.org/prog-essay.html
www.optimist.org/prog-oratoric.html

RELATED AWARD PROGRAMS

For more information on a Related Award Program, enter the associated keyword in the "Enter a Keyword" box located in the Coach's Locker Room section of ScholarshipCoach.com

■ Optimist International CCDHH Scholarships

The Communications Contest for the Deaf and Hard of Hearing invites students through grade 12 who are deaf or hard of hearing to prepare a 4- to 5-minute project that they present orally or through sign language (or both). Entries must relate to a topic provided by the organization. One past topic has been "If I Could Change the World." Awards of $1,500 are given at the district level. Students should contact local Optimist clubs for more information about deadlines and other awards offered.

Keyword
OPTCCDHH

■ Liberty Round Table Essay Contest

To enter this competition, students age 21 and under must write an essay of 1,000 words or less on a topic related to freedom. Applicants are divided into four age categories: ages 13 and under, ages 14 to 16, ages 17 to 18, and ages 19 to 21. First-place prizes range from $100 to $1,000, depending on age group. A wide range of smaller prizes is also awarded. Entries are due in early March.

Keyword
LIBROUND

Principal's Leadership Award

The teacher looked at me and I said I know, it's off to the principal's office I go.

—Young MC
"Principal's Office"

TARGET RECIPIENT

■ High school seniors

ENTRY REQUIREMENTS

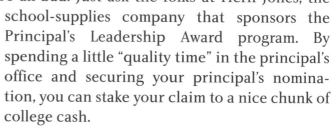

Nomination · Activities & Credentials · Short Answer

Recommendation · Academic Info · Entry Fee

DEADLINE

■ December

SCHOLARSHIP COACH.com

Keyword
PRILEADR

Money
$
Matters

Despite what the old-school rapper Young MC might say, heading over to the principal's office doesn't have to be all bad. Just ask the folks at Herff Jones, the school-supplies company that sponsors the Principal's Leadership Award program. By spending a little "quality time" in the principal's office and securing your principal's nomination, you can stake your claim to a nice chunk of college cash.

Administered by the National Association of Secondary School Principals (NASSP), the Principal's Leadership Award recognizes those students actively demonstrating strong leadership skills, academic achievement, and involvement in community service and extracurricular activities.

Each high school principal from around the nation is encouraged to nominate one outstanding high school senior for the award. Application materials state that nominees should be in the top 20 percent of their class. Of those nominated, 150 win $1,500 scholarship awards.

Applications and nomination forms are due in early December. Winners are announced by late April.

■ A CLOSER LOOK

B ecause the NASSP administers the Principal's Leadership Award, the application bears a striking resemblance to that of the National Honor Society Scholarship (see page 214). Like the NHS Scholarship, the application for this award requires academic information (GPA, class rank, and test scores), student activities (clubs and sports) and leadership roles within those activities, special recognition (awards, honors, and scholarships), and community involvement.

In addition to a school transcript, a principal's recommendation (200 words or less), and a $6 application fee (typically paid for by the nominee's school), the application asks students to write a 300-word essay on a topic related to leadership (which changes each year). One recent question asked:

> *Who exemplifies leadership for you? Identify a living individual in your school, community, state, the United States, or the world at large, who more than anyone else is a model of leadership for you and others. Please focus on those traits or qualities this individual possesses that help make this living individual a leader.*

The judging procedure is also very similar to that of the NHS program. All applications are first forwarded to Scholarship Program Administrators, Inc. (SPA), which assigns points to each section on the application form. Neither the essay nor the principal's recommendation is scored at this phase of judging. SPA compares the scores of applicants from the same state, and the top scorers in each state (about 1,000 to 1,200 students in total) are referred to the NASSP as finalists.

Insider Info

One notable difference from the judging of the NHS scholarship, however, is that 12 principals from around the nation ultimately select the 150 winners.

These principals focus their efforts on evaluating each student's leadership qualities and record. According to David Cordts, who manages the Principal's Leadership Award for the NASSP, the judges "recognize that leadership can be seen in their service and in references to their good character, as well as in their general involvement." Cordts says, "If it comes down to two people who look similar, they identify the one having the strongest demonstration of student leadership."

In the finalist round, the essay and the principal's recommendation are carefully considered. Each applicant is compared solely to other finalists from his or her state—with every state entitled to at least one winner.

■ COACH'S ANALYSIS

Okay, you don't have to be Sherlock Holmes (or even Watson, for that matter) to figure out that providing evidence of your leadership skills is going to help you win this scholarship. When providing this evidence, however, don't just rely on your lists of leadership positions. Instead, *leverage the essay and the principal's recommendation letter to maximize your advantage.*

First, let's tackle how to approach your essay. Regardless of the particular essay question asked in a given year, the judges are really trying to assess, through your response, your leadership abilities and potential. If you are asked to write about a leadership role model, for instance, recognize that such an essay is not really about the person you admire, but rather about *you*. This is because the person you admire really represents a reflection of the leadership qualities and characteristics that you admire most. So if you were answering such a question, you wouldn't want to simply write a biographical piece on your chosen leader. Instead, you should try to relate his or her leadership qualities to your own life and show how you've tried to emulate those qualities in your various leadership roles.

When discussing your leadership skills in the essay, focus your energy on *showing* rather than *telling*. What's the distinction between the two? *Telling* occurs when you make broad statements without backing them up with specific examples. *Showing*, on the other hand, involves describing an activity or relating a story that powerfully illustrates your point. So don't just *tell* the judges that you always "lead by example." Instead, *show* them how you have led others—by describing an activity, event, or scene in which your personal actions encouraged others to act likewise.

Now let's leverage your principal's recommendation. In a contest judged by actual high school principals, you know that this element of the application will carry a lot of weight. Because the recommendation may be a maximum of 200 words, you will need to make sure that each sentence in the recommendation powerfully supports your cause. To facilitate this, provide your principal with something in writing—typically a one-page cover letter, which summarizes your actual credentials and qualities that you are hoping his or her recommendation will address.

If this is your first recommendation letter from your principal, it is probably wise to request a full-length letter (one that's not limited to 200 words) so that it becomes reusable on other scholarship applications for recommendations *without* word limits. Once your principal has completed this in-depth letter, you can select the best passages and construct a compact, 200-word version—a more condensed support statement. Then show it to your principal for approval and signature after, of course, you explain the 200-word requirement.

An added advantage of this approach is that you don't have to rely on your principal to pack maximum content into such a restrictive word limit. Instead, *you* can be the one to review everything your principal has written,

I used this technique when completing my own winning Principal's Leadership Award application.

and then choose the content that most persuasively supports your scholarship candidacy. Think of this process as similar to one that movie studios employ when making trailers for their latest cinematic masterpiece: They look over the full text of what each movie reviewer has written, and then pull out those statements and images that best help sell the movie.

CONTACT INFORMATION

Keyword

PRILEADR

Completed application forms should be sent to the address shown, and not mailed to the NASSP.

Scholarship Program Administrators, Inc. (SPA)
Principal's Leadership Award
P.O. Box 24605
Nashville, TN 37202

Phone: (800) 253-7746
E-mail: dsa@principals.org
Website: www.principals.org

RELATED AWARD PROGRAMS

For more information on a Related Award Program, enter the associated keyword in the "Enter a Keyword" box located in the Coach's Locker Room section of ScholarshipCoach.com

■ Scholar Athlete Milk Mustache of the Year (SAMMY) Awards

The SAMMY Awards encourage high school seniors to maintain high scholastic marks while excelling in sports, academics, and community activities. Students in 48 of the 50 states (excluding Alaska and Hawaii) enter the competition through an online application found at the "Why Milk?" website. There are 25 scholarships of $7,500 each. Preliminary applications are due in early March.

Keyword
SAMMYSCH

■ Boy Scouts Young American Award

Students (both male and female) ages 15 through 25 who have made significant contributions to the community in areas of education, literature, religion, music, science, athletics, business, government, community service, and humanities may apply for the five $5,000 cash grants. (You need not actually be a member of Boy Scouts.) Entry requirements include an activity record, transcript, and recommendations. Applications are due in early December.

Keyword
BSCOUTYA

■ NACA Regional Council Student Leader Scholarship

The National Association for Campus Activities (NACA) Foundation recognizes undergraduate and graduate students for a variety of achievements on campus. There are 13 separate programs (many are regional), with deadlines throughout the year. Applicants are expected to provide evidence of significant participation and leadership. Award amounts, application requirements, and deadlines vary with the specific program.

Keyword
NACALEAD

Profile in Courage Essay Contest

TARGET RECIPIENT

- High school students

ENTRY REQUIREMENTS

Essay

DEADLINE

- January

Keyword
PROFINCO

U.S. citizens enrolled in overseas schools are also eligible to apply.

Money Matters

Added Bonus

Why did Howard Dean, the governor of Vermont, leave a personal message on high schooler Stephanie Dziczek's answering machine? Let's just say that if you had chosen Governor Dean as the subject of your winning essay in the Profile in Courage Essay Contest, your answering machine might have been blinking, too.

Sponsored by the John F. Kennedy Library Foundation, the subject matter of this essay contest is derived from Kennedy's Pulitzer Prize–winning work, *Profiles in Courage*—a book that highlights the principles, integrity, and political bravery of eight U.S. senators.

Eligible students must be in grades 9 through 12 at a school (public, private, parochial, or home school) in the 50 states, District of Columbia, or U.S. territories. To enter the contest, students write an essay of less than 1,200 words about a current elected official in the United States, or an elected public official in post-1956 America, who has courageously addressed a political issue on the local, state, national, or international level.

The first-prize winner in this contest receives $3,000 and a trip to the John F. Kennedy Library in Boston, Massachusetts, for the official award ceremony. In addition, the foundation awards one second-place prize of $1,000 and five finalist prizes of $500 each.

Essays are due in early January, with winners notified in May.

In this historical photo, then-Senator John F. Kennedy signs his book, *Profiles in Courage,* for eager students.

A CLOSER LOOK

In addition to the 1,200-word essay itself, students must submit a complete bibliography, citing all sources consulted in writing the essay. Submissions without a bibliography will be automatically disqualified.

Submissions are put through four different rounds of judging. In each round, submitted essays are judged on two basic criteria: originality (60 percent) and the clear communication of ideas (40 percent). For the first round, graduate students in English, political science, and education, along with John F. Kennedy Library members and staff, read all qualifying entries. Every essay is initially read by two readers and each reader rates it on a scale of one to five. Based on these scores, the top 200 entries are forwarded to a judging panel composed of public-service leaders and other professionals, who whittle the number down to the top 25 to 30 essays.

After a new panel, composed of members of the education department at the Kennedy Library, reviews these essays and selects the top 10 essays overall, the essays are

Insider Info

If there is a large point discrepancy between the two readers, a third judge will be asked to review the entry.

forwarded to the final judging committee, which includes such notable figures as Caroline Kennedy, U.S. Senator Edward Kennedy, former CBS News president David Burke, and historian David McCullough.

■ COACH'S ANALYSIS

To a large extent, how you do in the Profile in Courage contest is determined by what you do *before* you ever pick up paper and pen—namely, in your *choice of an individual* who embodies political courage. No matter how well you have crafted your essay, if the individual you have chosen doesn't resonate with the program's judges, your chances of winning are low.

So what types of individuals and topics work well for this competition? First, look for individuals who are *less* well known on a national level. Part of the challenge in this competition is standing out from the crowd. Choosing prominent national figures makes your job that much more difficult, because other entrants are likely to select such individuals as well. Choosing a lesser-known individual, however, demonstrates your creativity and originality (and remember, that's a whopping 60 percent of the judging criteria). According to Lisa Menéndez Weidman, education director at the Kennedy Library, essays are quickly eliminated from the competition if the writer "picked a topic that has already been rehashed."

If you do feel compelled to select a well-known individual, try to focus your essay on a lesser-known event in that leader's political career.

First-place winner Tyler Boerson, a resident of Haslett, Michigan, chose Michigan Congressman Bart Stupak—a politician who, despite representing a congressional district that vehemently opposed any type of gun-control legislation, defied the National Rifle Association (NRA) on a key vote.

"It took me a few weeks to find a suitable person. I didn't want it to be a typical choice . . . [instead, I wanted] someone who goes more unnoticed because that's how

First-place winner Stephanie Dziczek (shown here with Caroline Kennedy, Senator Ted Kennedy, and her family) estimates that she spent 45 percent of her time on research and 55 percent on actually writing her essay.

Stay away from obscure state laws or issues relevant only to people from a certain geographic region.

Another advantage of more current issues and individuals is that more information is easily accessible over the Internet (but make sure that the website is a credible and accurate source).

courage often is," Boersen explains. "Look outside of the major figures in politics. Look locally and for someone who had an impact on a smaller level."

Second, as you search for such unsung heroes, focus on individuals whose courage involves issues relevant to the nation as a whole. Even though an individual isn't well known beyond the local level, that doesn't mean that his or her issue doesn't have national implications. Avoid topics and issues that are of interest only in your local area—topics likely to be of little interest to national judges. Instead, seek out individuals who embody political issues that are relevant and timely. Although both present-day and historical examples can work well, if you can't make up your mind between a current political leader and a more historical figure, go with the more contemporary individual.

First-place winner Stephanie Dziczek of Covington, Kentucky, wanted to write about someone related to civil-rights issues, but she wasn't sure which individual to choose. After substantial research, she decided to pass up more historical figures to write, instead, about Vermont Governor Howard Dean, a contemporary politician who signed a state law legalizing same-sex unions:

In his campaign for reelection to a fifth gubernatorial term, an ambitious Dean could have focused on health care, taxes, or any of a number of "safe" political platforms. However, disturbed by Vermont's reaction toward gay civil unions, Dean made the "extension of the rights and benefits of the [Vermont] constitution to all Vermonters, regardless of their sexual orientation" the heart of his campaign for acceptance and understanding.

Dziczek chose Governor Dean, in part, because his actions seemed more relevant to current policy issues. "I wanted to write about something really current," Dziczek relates. "It just seemed to matter more."

Third, don't forget the political leanings of your audience. As you would expect, past winning entries for this contest generally lean to the political left. A library foundation named after President John F. Kennedy, a liberal Democrat, is not likely to embrace individuals who embody politically conservative issues. Dziczek, for instance, chose the issue of gay rights for this competition, even though she "wouldn't have written about it if another organization, like a veterans' group, were running the contest." If your own personal political views differ from the ones likely to be embraced by the judges, search for essay subject matter that both liberals and conservatives can agree upon. (Yes, such issues are out there!)

Finally, if you are still struggling to find an individual who meets the foregoing criteria, employ the following methods to jump-start your thinking: Watch television news programs and read the newspaper, scanning for ideas. Ask for the suggestions of parents, teachers, coaches, mentors, and other individuals you respect. Read Kennedy's *Profiles in Courage* and think about which individuals could also have been included in Kennedy's Pulitzer Prize–winning work.

You might want to read Profiles in Courage anyway—it's a great book!

If you're still striking out, try turning the process on its head: First determine an issue that you're passionate about; once you've got that nailed, search articles or reference material related to that issue for a person who has demonstrated courage in support of it.

Tyler Boersen
Haslett, MI
First Place
$3,000

REPRESENTATIVE BART STUPAK

Winning
Entry

Tyler Boersen develops his own definition of courage by discussing the political heroism of an elected official who stayed true to his beliefs despite the efforts of a vocal and powerful opposition.

Many associate the word courage with a comic book or stereotyped Hollywood hero. A larger-than-life character that somehow survives great destruction, braves great peril, and works against evil—often against incredible odds. Most, however, don't understand the true definition of courage is to do what one believes is right, no matter what another says or does. To stand alone in spite of ridicule, and believe without avail in a cause. The cause does not have to be anything great, and the act of courage does not have to be a grand gesture. A single vote can change the minds of a lot of people. Congressman Bart Stupak of Michigan must understand this definition because he did just that. Despite the voiced opposition of constituents and one of the country's most powerful lobbying arms, he chose to vote for what he believed, and even though his vote ultimately did not carry the day, his voice of courage was carried further into the minds of the populace.

* * *

In the summer of 1999, shortly after the Columbine High School massacre, Stupak proved that money and personal experience does not ensure every vote. He was willing to think in terms of the greater good—America over the special interest; nationalism over sectionalism. He was reportedly wavering on a major gun-control issue. The NRA targeted his district because his vote would be key in defeating the minor gun controls proposed (safety locks and background checks) and approving what would be a major blow to gun-control advocates. They sent letters to

Boersen says that once his research was complete, his essay took about six hours to write. In the first two to three hour writing session, he tried to get a draft down on paper without stopping to edit.

Coach's Comments

constituents urging them to call Stupak and tell him how to vote. Handgun Control, a group pushing for the reforms, also courted Stupak's vote. Television and radio ads aired in the district, thousands called Stupak's office, and newspaper reports quoted angry constituents. Nevertheless, Stupak continued to search his soul for the answer, and eventually came up with one: "If you're going to have a check system, then it has to apply equally to everybody" became his philosophy when he decided to vote for the control.

One of Stupak's Michigan colleagues, Rep. John Dingell, sponsored an amendment that would mandate 24-hour background checks as opposed to 72 hours on the original bill. Already passed by the Senate, the bill Stupak supported was designed to help prevent youth crime. The amendment would effectively destroy the intent of the crime bill. In the early morning hours of June 18, 1999, Stupak voted no on the amendment. He was the only one of the 31 NRA-backed Democrats that voted against the amendment. It passed; the final bill did not.

The vote was a minor action, but the results had the potential to be devastating. His constituents felt like they were no longer heard, like he was no longer representing them. "They feel that whatever the government does [on guns], it just takes away more of their rights," Stupak told *USA Today*. Soon, he would have to answer to his constituents on the phone, in letters, and through the media. But with 600,000 constituents and the second largest district east of the Mississippi, it would be impossible to face every angry constituent one-on-one. Stupak said that when he had the chance to explain his vote, his constituents understood. "I certainly don't want to take away anybody's right to bear arms though," he said. But he still faced the challenge of the 2000 election. The NRA abandoned Stupak and endorsed his opponent, businessman Chuck Yob. But as his story went national, with appearances in major newspapers and an ABC News special, *Peter Jennings Reporting: The Gun Fight,* he began to emerge from the deep end, and he earned back constituent trust. They felt that he was able to make decisions for himself; he was looking out for the good of the country. He won reelection by almost 20 percent, losing only one county. He won without a single contribution from the NRA.

For the complete text of Tyler Boersen's winning essay, visit the Coach's Locker Room at ScholarshipCoach.com (Keyword: PROFINCO).

CONTACT INFORMATION

	Keyword
SCHOLARSHIP COACH.com	PROFINCO

John F. Kennedy Library
Profile in Courage Essay Contest
Columbia Point
Boston, MA 02125

Phone: (617) 929-1204
E-mail: profiles@nara.gov
Website: www.jfkcontest.org

RELATED AWARD PROGRAMS

For more information on a Related Award Program, enter the associated keyword in the "Enter a Keyword" box located in the Coach's Locker Room section of ScholarshipCoach.com

■ National History Day

Students in grades 6 through 12 can submit projects in any of the seven catgories: individual exhibit, group exhibit (2–5 people), individual documentary, group documentary, individual performance, group performance, and individual paper. Each project category has specific guidelines, but all projects should relate to the broad theme established for the contest year. Past themes have included "Rights and Responsibilities in History," "Taking a Stand in History," and "Revolution, Reaction, Reform in History." Awards range from $250 to $5,000 at the state and national levels. Deadlines vary by state and category. The national competition is held in June.

	Keyword
SCHOLARSHIP COACH.com	NATHIST

■ ACLU Youth Activist Scholarship Award

Graduating high school seniors are eligible for this award, which recognizes students with a strong commitment to civil liberties. Applicants are required to submit a personal statement that reflects their dedication to activisim in their school or community. Students compete for nine $4,000 scholarships ($1,000 awarded annually over four years). To apply, students must first be nominated by their high school's ACLU program administrator.

	Keyword
SCHOLARSHIP COACH.com	ACLUACTV

Prudential Spirit of Community Awards

TARGET RECIPIENT

■ Grades 5–12

ENTRY REQUIREMENTS

Project   Short Answer   Activities & Credentials

DEADLINE

■ October

KEYWORD

Keyword
SCHOLARSHIPCOACH.com   **PRSPIRIT**

Money Matters   Added Bonus

They've spearheaded recycling programs and gathered books for homeless shelters. They've helped raise money for public museums and brought joy to the lives of children with cancer. And they've all been recognized as part of the Prudential Spirit of Community Awards.

Open to students in grades 5 through 12 in the United States and Puerto Rico, the program seeks to recognize students who have "demonstrated exemplary community service." To apply, interested students summarize their work on a particular service project, write four short essays, and obtain verification from a local contest administrator.

The program is organized into two separate divisions: a middle school division (grades 5 to 8) and a high school division (grades 9 to 12). In total, 104 students (two from each state, plus Washington, D.C., and Puerto Rico) are chosen as "state honorees" and each receive $1,000 and a trip to Washington, D.C., for an awards ceremony and other special events. From among these state winners, ten students—five from each age division—are chosen as "national honorees" and receive an additional $5,000 award.

Applications are due by the late-October deadline.

Winners of the Prudential Spirit of Community Awards come from all types of backgrounds and all corners of the United States. They are also good at posing with large medals.

▋A Closer Look

Membership in Girl Scouts or 4-H is not required to apply through those organizations.

Homeschoolers may apply through the Citizens' Scholarship Foundation of America (CSFA). One homeschooler will advance to the subsequent judging rounds.

Students may apply through one of three outlets: their middle or high school principal, their local Girl Scout Executive Council, or their county 4-H agents. For every 1,000 students in the school or organization, two students may be selected to proceed to state-level judging (one for each grade division). If applications are not submitted through one of these three channels, however, they will be automatically disqualified.

Students must focus their applications on one community service activity in which they have played a "significant role." This role could entail holding a leadership position, or simply could mean making a large contribution to a group effort. Students must apply individually, however. Group applications will not be accepted.

In completing a brief summary of this activity, applicants are asked to describe in a few sentences not only the service activity itself, but also how they became involved, the role they played, the time they invested, and the impact the activity has had on other people. Students are then asked to expand upon their summary in four short-answer responses (each a half page in length) that communicate the inspiration for the project, the individual effort they invested in the endeavor, the positive impact the project made, and the personal growth they experienced through it. The application form provides about half a page for each essay response, and additional sheets may *not* be included.

The judging process at the state level begins as the Citizens' Scholarship Foundation of America (CSFA), an organization that helps administer numerous scholarship programs, reviews each applicant's submission. According to Connie Fiorito, the contest administrator at the National Association of Secondary School Principals (which co-administers the program), submissions are judged on "how they are written, how much involvement students actually had, and how much self-initiative was put into the project, rather than it being guided by adults." She also notes that "what kind of roadblocks they had to go through to initiate their project" is also specifically considered. Each one of the four essays is judged with equal weight.

While the CSFA chooses state honorees, a separate judging panel actually selects the ten national winners. Made up of representatives from organizations supporting the program, the panel has included the head of the Points of Light Foundation, the CEO of Prudential, a representative from the American Red Cross, the national director of the Girl Scouts, and members of service groups such as America's Promise and Kids in Distressed Situations. Leading politicians and celebrities also frequently serve on this judging panel.

Insider Info

Kids in Distressed Situations also gives $25,000 in children's products for each of the ten national winners to distribute to kids in their communities.

COACH'S ANALYSIS

In presenting your service project, it is essential to powerfully communicate where your motivation to pursue the project comes from, and why this motivation makes you so devoted to the particular service endeavor. Communicating the source of your drive to follow through with the volunteer effort adds credibility to the depth of your service commitment. This puts your service efforts in a context that judges can understand, relate to, and better appreciate. (It's also something that the public relations department for the Prudential Spirit of Community Awards specifically highlights in the press release they write on each winner.)

To help organize your thoughts on the subject, try asking yourself the following questions:

▮ Was there some event in your life that motivated you to pursue the particular service endeavor?

▮ Why did you pursue this particular service project and not some other type of volunteer work?

▮ Did you know someone personally who would benefit from the program?

▮ How do they get the cream in those Twinkies, anyway? (Just making sure you're still awake!)

Once you've considered such questions, try to relate your underlying motivation clearly and directly to the service project you've undertaken. National winner Kay Lauren Miller of Vienna, Virginia, for instance, discussed in her application how overcoming obstacles in her own life led her to create Reach Out and Read (ROAR), an organization that distributes used books to homeless shelters:

Winning Entry

The mission of ROAR is to help encourage reading by children regardless of their current economic circumstances. I know how important reading is because I was diagnosed with dyslexia when I was eight years old and through a lot of hard work and help from my mother, I have been able to overcome this. I really want other children to have the same chance.

Miller, who won in the high school division, noted that all of the other national winners had related a compelling story about how they came to be interested in their particular volunteer projects. "All of the national honorees had a strong motivation for why they wanted to do the volunteer work, why they wanted to pursue this type of volunteering rather than another type," Miller states. "I think it's real important to add this in your application, if something really important happened in your life that made you go on this track towards volunteering."

As you relate the impact your service project has made, discuss the effect on both the aggregate and individual levels. Include statistics about your project to give the judges a sense of the big picture (figures on how many people your project has helped

Not only has Kay Lauren Miller (above) made a great impact on her community—and on Prudential judges—but she has also had the opportunity to travel to the Bahamas to work on a literacy project.

or how many dollars you have raised are great), but also describe how your program has impacted someone or something on a very specific level. For example, national winner Amanda Waas, a high school sophomore from Miami, Florida, described in her application an event that occurred when she first launched her "Positive Packs" program to help young cancer patients endure their long hours of medical treatment:

Winning
Entry

My initial goals were accomplished the day we brought our first 25 or so backpacks into the clinics. I watched as a crying little girl picked one up and asked us what it was for. We told her and she was so excited that her mother almost cried. I was still there a few hours later when the girl was finished. She put the bag back in the lineup of all the pretty colors, said that she will see us next week, and gave me a big hug. That's when I knew the project was going to be a success!

Amanda Waas' program provides clinics and hospitals with colorful backpacks stuffed with toys, art supplies, and other fun items for children to play with while undergoing treatment. (Man, that's some good stuff!) Waas has been invited to serve as a national judge for the awards next year.

In describing the individual impact of your program, as well as the motivation behind it, Waas advises that you should make a special effort to include your heartfelt feelings in your writing: "Put in your emotion and show why this is so important to you and why you are working so hard at it. It shows how much you are a part of a project and how the project is such a big part of you."

Finally, don't forget to project the impact of the program into the future. Discuss your goals for the future and how you plan on your program growing and expanding. To show that these plans aren't just pipe dreams, describe some of the specific steps you've already taken or plan on taking to help bring about such objectives. If you've already contacted an individual or group that is important to your program's future, mention it. If you've already begun the legwork necessary for expanding the geographic range of your service efforts, explain it. By showing that you have already thought through the specific action steps needed—and combining that specificity with your program's prior record of progress—you can vividly illustrate that the *only* thing separating you from your program goals is the *time* necessary to make them a reality.

Kay Lauren Miller described in her application how she had already contacted a famous author and the Washington Redskins football team about helping her organization.

Winning
Entry

Amanda Waas
Miami, FL
National Winner
$5,000

IMPACT

Amanda Waas illustrates the impact of her program through facts, figures, anecdotes, and a discussion of the program's underlying psychological value.

I feel the project accomplished many goals, one of the most important being the psychological needs of the children and parents. Positive Packs were named such for modeling a positive attitude toward illness and treatments. My goal or impact was getting kids to see at least one positive thing about having to go to the hospital, even if it was only a toy pack they would get to play with during treatment. This might seem simplistic, but in reality, play therapy and its place in pain management, has been proven time and time again. When a child is distracted from pain by something they perceive as fun, then the pain is

perceived as decreased. I definitely loved reading many psychology books along the way. The parents and grandparents who always were there with the kids, now had a little break or sometimes even saw it as a way to interact with the kids. Parents would be thankful as to not have to remember to take toys along with them, as there was enough to worry about.

The fund-raising portion was very successful. With almost $30,000 collected and distributed to the American Cancer Society and The Children's Cancer Fund, that number does not include the donated items (backpacks, toys, games, dolls, art supplies, journals, markers, pens, the donation of the embroidering on all the backpacks and shirts that we wear into the hospitals) and the hundreds of other little things that go into making a project work. Our expectations were met often, but sometimes getting items donated was very difficult. I tried the major backpack companies first, but found that the local vendors were much more interested in working with us.

I am sure this project will continue on in the future. I am always involving more and more adults and students that I feel will want to continue when, or if I no longer can. I also hope Positive Packs will go national or possibly international (especially after the program won a special award from the Disney Corporation, where it was basically introduced to the world!).

PERSONAL GROWTH

Winning
Entry

In the text below, Waas discusses the important skills she learned from the Positive Packs program and some of the project's most memorable moments.

This project has taught me to see everything from the patient's side. What we might want may not necessarily be what the patient wants. I have learned to be an excellent listener, with the attitude that change is good and other people's ideas count just as much as mine. The learning part of the experience came at every door. There was never a day that went by that I did not learn something about myself or the way I could improve the project. People were always willing to teach me things as if I was a grown-up. I appreciated the confidence they showed in my skill and choices, and in return I made sure that everything was done properly. There was one Child Life Specialist that one day had to point out gently to me that I must get thank you notes out a little quicker. She was right, a week was too much time to go by. I thank her all the time for her knowledge, for she was thinking of people's feelings. The skills I acquired were many, but the most important to me was interviewing techniques. What to say, how to say it and how much to say, were things I had to learn with trial and error. It felt so good trying to stay focused and get the message out so that everyone could understand and be moved to help. Public speaking is a necessity in presenting your product.

The most memorable part of this project was the first time my mom was able to feel well enough to participate in one of the walk-a-thons. She had lost almost 35 pounds and had no hair, but she wanted to show me how much she cared. I think I cried the entire five miles. Another memorable part was one I mentioned before in this application, it was the parent telling me their child no longer cried and screamed when they had to come get their chemotherapy. The mother said that all the little girl talked about was which of the packs she was going to pick up that day. Now, that is success you can measure!

I would tell other young people to go ahead and challenge themselves. It is the simple joys in life that can be found in a child's smile, laugh or giggle. Go ahead, get involved, be creative and what is the worst that could happen . . . success!

CONTACT INFORMATION

Keyword
PRSPIRIT

The Prudential Spirit of Community Awards
CSFA
1505 Riverview Road
P.O. Box 297
St. Peter, MN 56082

Phone: (888) 450-9961
Websites: www.prudential.com or www.principals.org

RELATED AWARD PROGRAMS

For more information on a Related Award Program, enter the associated keyword in the "Enter a Keyword" box located in the Coach's Locker Room section of ScholarshipCoach.com

■ Angels in Action Awards

The program recognizes ten students (ages 8–15) who have aided a charity, cause, or their community in an exemplary way. Entry into the competition requires a nomination. Nominees are judged on their acts of selflessness, commitment to the cause, and the relevance of their deeds to the Angels in Action program. Winning students are awarded $5,000. Entries are due in late June.

Keyword
ANGINACT

■ Youth in Action Awards

Just as Prudential recognizes students who have the initiative to begin far-reaching community service projects, the Youth in Action Network targets students between the ages of 16 and 25 who have initiated projects and have demonstrated measurable results. Entrants submit summaries of their youth-initiated service projects and are eligible for a number of $1,000 awards. Entries must be submitted by late March.

Keyword
YOACTION

Scholastic Art and Writing Awards

With a judges' roster that has included the likes of humorist Garrison Keillor, author Judy Blume, and internationally recognized artist Lesley Dill, you know that the folks at the Scholastic Art and Writing Awards mean business—as in the business of identifying and rewarding creative young artists and writers.

Administered by the Alliance for Young Artists and Writers, the program is open to students in grades 7 to 12 who are enrolled in schools in the United States or U.S. territories, or in United States–sponsored schools abroad. Entries may be submitted in 16 different art categories and ten separate writing categories.

More than 900 awards (over 600 art awards and 300 writing awards) are offered at the national level—the most prestigious being a $20,000 Art Portfolio Award and a $10,000 Achievement Prize for Student Fiction. Additionally, nine scholarships of $5,000 each are offered to graduating high school seniors in various subcategories. A wide variety of awards are offered for each artistic or writing subcategory, with prizes ranging from $100 regional awards to $1,000 national prizes.

Each entry should closely follow the guidelines specific to each art or writing category. Entries must also be accompanied by an application fee, which varies by region and discipline.

TARGET RECIPIENT
- Grades 7–12

ENTRY REQUIREMENTS

Writing Sample

Art and Graphics

DEADLINE
- January

Keyword
SARTWRIT

Money
$
Matters

Because many more paintings and drawings are received in the arts division, and a greater number of short stories and poems are submitted in the writing division, these are the categories that are allocated the largest number of cash prizes.

Entries are due at various dates in January, depending on your location and the type of art or writing submission. National winners are notified in May.

A CLOSER LOOK

Each category in the Scholastic Art and Writing Awards has slightly different entry guidelines. For artistic events, the program specifies size limits and mounting guidelines as well as instructions for shipping. Although there are no limits on the length of writing entries, in many cases students are encouraged to enter excerpts rather than full-length manuscripts.

Unique among the entry categories are categories for art and writing portfolios. Each writing portfolio must include between three and eight works, a table of contents that lists the category and title for each piece, and a "statement of purpose" of 500 words or less explaining why each piece was chosen or stating how the student approaches writing. To submit art or photography portfolios, entrants must include eight work samples, with specific requirements depending on the type of art. At least three drawings must be submitted in the art portfolio competition, and matted prints must be used for those entering photography portfolios. (Coach's Hint: Do not submit any depictions of dogs playing poker.)

Students may enter in as many categories as they desire, but each individual work of art or writing may be submitted to only one category (the only exception being the portfolio categories).

Most students submit entries to one of 90 regional competitions that cover geographic areas as small as a city and as large as a state. Prospective entrants should visit the Scholastic Art and Writing Awards website (www.scholastic.com/artandwriting) to

This entry, entitled *Morocco 2*, was submitted as part of the photography portfolio of Silver Award winner Jono Brody-Felder.

ART AND WRITING CATEGORIES

Art Categories

- Architecture and Environmental Design
- Ceramics and Glass
- Computer Graphics
- Drawing
- Graphic Design
- Jewelry and Metalsmithing
- Mixed Media
- Painting
- Photography
- Printmaking
- Product Design
- Sculpture
- Textile and Fiber Design
- Video, Film, and Animation
- Art Portfolio*
- Photography Portfolio*

Writing Categories

- Dramatic Script
- Humor
- Journalism
- Novel Writing
- Personal Essay or Memoir
- Poetry
- Science Fiction or Fantasy
- Short Story
- *Short* Short Story
- General Writing Portfolio*

*Only high school seniors may enter the portfolio competitions.

obtain the specific mailing address for their regional programs. For those who live in areas outside established regions, "at-large" entries should be sent directly to the Alliance for Young Artists and Writers. A teacher or school program coordinator, rather than the student, must submit the entry. The entrance fees for regional and at-large programs vary. In general, the fees typically range from $3 to $5 per entry. Regional judging panels are generally composed of local English and art professors, professional artists and graphic designers, and journalists.

The top regional submissions, about 15,000 entries in total, advance to the national judging round. At this round, there are three judges per category—each judge a well-known or well-respected figure in that field. According to Chuck Wentzel, associate director for the Scholastic Art and Writing Awards, the judging methodology for each art or writing category is mainly left up to the discretion of the individual judge. "We ask them to use their best artistic sense, their best personal aesthetic as a visual artist or a writer as they look at this work," says Wentzel.

For visual arts entries, judges compare each category of art directly to others within that category. "For the visual arts panels, we surround [the judges] with tables, and can get about 100 pieces of artwork out at one time," Wentzel notes. "They can walk around and look . . . and really see it [the artwork] side-by-side." For writing entries, each of the three judges scores the entries and then combines the scores. The highest combined scores receive the top awards.

In an intriguing use of perspective, Benjamin Persson highlights the majesty of New York's Empire State Building. His entry was recognized with both a Silver Award and a Pinnacle Award in the architecture and environmental design category.

■ COACH'S ANALYSIS

For both the art and writing portions of this awards program, you should approach your submission with a three-item mental checklist. This is because the entries that most often stand out are the ones that, according to Wentzel, (1) are unique and original, (2) exhibit "a certain level of technical proficiency," and (3) contain "a sense of the young person who created the work." Of these three criteria, perhaps the most daunting is to create something that truly stands out in its fresh approach.

Lisa Randolph, a contest winner from Farina, Illinois, stood out from the rest because of her use of an original artistic medium: Although she had submitted seven different paintings to the competition, the one that ended up winning both regional and national honors was *not* a traditional oil on canvas.

Struck with inspiration, Randolph decided to glue small, white beads on a large canvas, then paint a self-portrait on top of the beads—resulting in an unusual and interesting textural creation. "Look to experiment with unusual ways of doing things," Randolph advises, crediting the use of the unusual artistic medium with her success in the program. "The texture drew people in and made me stand out. It was entirely different than the other portraits."

On the writing side of the contest, Steven Seigel of Denver, Colorado, demonstrated his originality in a similar way. As an entrant in the poetry category, he showcased his bilingual writing skills by submitting both English and Spanish versions of his poem, *Atlantis,* and doing the translation himself.

Lisa Randolph called this self-portrait *Am I Only Jewelry?* to express her feeling that in some romantic relationships, "guys just want to show [you] off and for you to be an accessory to them."

See page 267 to read Seigel's poem.

As for demonstrating technical proficiency, perhaps the most significant action step you can take when preparing your submission is to show it to others you respect, seeking their feedback. Because the contest is judged on the local and national levels by educators and professionals in artistic and writing fields, do your own "trial run": Show the works you might submit to art or writing instructors at school, to college or university

To learn additional ways to develop your art and writing skills, see my special guide, If Loving the Arts Is Wrong, I Don't Want to Be Right! *(for more info, visit ScholarshipCoach.com).*

professors in your town, or to local artists or writers. Get their feedback about what aspects of your work best showcase your technical skills.

For many students, the third item on your checklist, demonstrating your personal vision and voice, is the most difficult quality to capture. It's kind of like stumbling upon a nude beach—you don't know it until you see it! This vision or voice manifests itself in the truly individual and personal perspective reflected on the canvas or page. Writing portfolio winner Eric Larson from Santa Fe, Texas, set forth his personal voice through the vibrancy of his word choice and the skillful use of an extended metaphor:

> *The documents and institutions that we officially classify as a government are nothing more than a lifeless skeleton, and we the people of the United States of America are the organs, the heart, the mind and the soul of our nation. This body of freedom thinks with the varied opinions of American culture, breathes with the influence of civil involvement, its heart beats with an active participation in democracy and it moves towards justice on the feet of constant social reevaluation. This, then, is the future role of Americans; to keep our nation alive, to force blood through its established veins, to infuse its metabolism with our enthusiasm.*

Had Lisa Randolph (above) entered these paintings as part of the portfolio category she would have won an additional prize. The moral: If possible, submit your work in several artistic categories.

Finally, you should leverage your chances to win by applying in as many categories as possible. Don't sell yourself short by assuming that you're not good enough to compete. "I didn't enter the portfolio competition because I thought it was too much work and I wasn't good enough," relates Randolph, still an avid painter. "They had only three applicants [in her region] and I was told that based on my work [in other artistic categories] I would have won, had I entered."

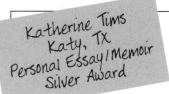
Steven Seigel
Denver, CO
Poetry
Gold Award

Winning
Entry

3: ATLANTIS

Steven Seigel submitted both Spanish and English versions of the poem below, performing the translation himself.

3: Atlantis	3: Atlantis
Me gusta oír	I like to hear
su cuchichea callada	your hushed whisper
cuando	when you
duermes in mis brazos de cedro,	sleep in my cedar arms,
rojo y duro,	red and tough,
durante el noche negro,	during the black night,
salpicada de estrellas,	splattered with stars,
luna hallada.	discovered moon.
Te leo,	I read you,
en astronomía de ojos,	in astronomy of the eyes,
una cancion.	a song.
Existo	Do I exist
en los mares,	in the seas
entre acantilados, algas y un par	between cliffs, algae and a pair
de albatros?	of albatross?

Winning
Entry

Katherine Tims
Katy, TX
Personal Essay/Memoir
Silver Award

FREEDOM ALTERED

In the following excerpt from her winning entry, Katherine Tims, age 13, describes an eventful trip to the bathroom during her preschool years.

My eyes darted between my preschool classmate's circle to the teacher. Should I ask her, I thought? Should I interrupt her? My mind had been running through these thoughts since before playtime. I mean if I had to ask her, it couldn't be during my cherished playtime. Ever since then, I had been trying to summon up my courage to ask her. Oh why, oh why, couldn't I have gone before with the rest of the class? Finally, when I couldn't wait any longer, my hand slowly and very timidly rose.

"May I go to the potty room?" I asked. My teacher tilted her head in what looked like deep thought. This is my lucky day! She seemed not to have noticed that I interrupted her!

"Well . . . I can't go with you now . . . it's only" (she let her eyes smoothly glide down to her gold plated watch) "less than 10 minutes till time for you to be picked up. But if you really need to go . . . wait . . . I think Mrs. Shields' class is there—do you know your way?"

With a moment's hesitation my chin tilted up and down in a small, child-size nod.

At this response, she smiled and said, "Okay. Then you can go, but please try to hurry." I was instantly stunned. Me . . . go by myself???

When she saw the twisted, confused look on my face, she said in a softer, kinder voice, "You can do it. Just go down the hall like we always do, and if you get lost, just ask the nearest adult."

Summoning my innermost "chamber of confidence," I awkwardly rolled to my knees. Then with a bounce of energy I stumbled to my feet, and strutted out of the room. In the hall my first ten steps were shy and conservative, but slowly I gained confidence. I was free, I will be famous! My stiff walk relaxed into a leisurely one, until I remembered what Mrs. Naglieri had said about hurrying, and my feet broke into a trot on the polished, square gray tiles. I must be the first preschooler ever to be walking down the hall alone! At this thought my trot turned into a springing skip. I began to softly sing my favorite song, "Mary had a lit-tle lamb, lit-tle lamb . . ."

All too suddenly, I came to a short halt for amid all the brightly painted plastic doors with four-inch window panes was an unwonted oak door with a tiny teal sign with the figure of a white stick girl on it. (I couldn't read, but everyone knows what the silent girl was meant to say!) Before I could push it open, it shook as if by magic. The massive oak door slowly creaked in a moan of protest and swung open. A teacher was standing there holding the three-inch-thick door as a tall girl in a blue polka-dotted dress with short blond curls and a small look-alike rag doll came striding out, wiping her hands on her dress doing so. The teacher did not notice me, and I could barely hear her, but she was mumbling something about the children in her classroom. Knowing that she was talking to herself, I marched into the bathroom and into a pale pink flimsy stall with no lock.

"Waushshshsh"—the cool metal handle snapped back into place a moment or two later. I hurried, shoving the door of the stall so that it made a satisfying "bam!" as it collided with the other door on the left. I ran to the children's sink which was a full eight inches lower than the big-person sink. I hate bothering with washing my hands. Why in tarnation was I doing it now? I guess because Mrs. Shields would make sure I did . . . I stole a glance around the room. There was no one there. I hadn't realized it, but the oversized wooden door had slowly been closing during this time. The door was shut; the stalls all open. It didn't really sink in right then what the consequences might be. Hot dog! "Squeak!" before adding soap, the water was off, and I skidded back to the monstrous oak door.

Now, I didn't like the idea of being alone in here. I pulled the door. "It won't budge!" I thought. I must not be pulling hard enough. Trying to reassure myself, I yanked with all my might. The door moved about two centimeters, then sank back into place before I could do anything.

*   *   *

During the time I was trapped in there I learned to be wary of sudden freedom because you never know when your luck may change and moments later you may find yourself locked in the girls' bathroom. To myself I quietly promised that I would never ever go to the bathroom or in the halls alone again. Though I didn't realize it then, in a few years I would be breaking this solemn promise.

However, hopefully, I will be ready for more freedom because every day I am growing. And every day that I grow, I gain knowledge. As I add knowledge, I gain caution. For knowledge and caution are the doorstops to the big wooden door that tries to close in an effort to alter my freedom.

To read more from Katherine Tims' winning entry, visit the Coach's Locker Room at ScholarshipCoach.com (Keyword: SARTWRIT).

CONTACT INFORMATION

Keyword
SARTWRIT

The Scholastic Art and Writing Awards
c/o Alliance for Young Artists and Writers
555 Broadway
New York, NY 10012

Phone: (212) 343-6493
E-mail: a&wgeneralinfo@scholastic.com
Website: www.scholastic.com/artandwriting/

RELATED AWARD PROGRAMS

For more information on a Related Award Program, enter the associated keyword in the "Enter a Keyword" box located in the Coach's Locker Room section of ScholarshipCoach.com

■ Imation Computer Arts Scholarship Program

One student from each high school can enter a piece of graphic art in this competition. Submitted through a school administrator, the art must be less than 1MB and should be submitted in JPEG format via the Imation website. The program awards 25 students $1,000 each for producing original, creative, and technically exemplary pieces of graphic artwork. Entries are due in mid-December.

Keyword
IMACOMPU

■ Young American Patriotic Art Awards

This is a competition for high school artists (sponsored by the Ladies Auxiliary of the VFW) in which original artwork is submitted along with a brief explanation of the patriotism expressed in the art. There are specific size, frame, and subject requirements, including accurate portrayal of the flag. Awards range from $2,500 to $10,000. Completed entries are due in mid-December.

Keyword
YOUNGPAT

■ L. Ron Hubbard Writers and Illustrators of the Future

Amateur writers (of any age) may submit any body of prose under 17,000 words in genres of fantasy, science fiction, and horror (with fantasy elements). Entries are judged every three months and prizes of $1,000, $750, and $500 are awarded for each three-month period. Amateur illustrators may submit science fiction and fantasy illustrations only, and judging will also be done by quarters. Three $500 awards are given during each quarter. There is an annual grand prize of $4,000 for each contest (winners are chosen from among quarterly first-place winners).

Keyword
LRONHUBB

Sons of the American Revolution Scholarships

TARGET RECIPIENT

- Rumbaugh Oration: Grades 10–12
- Knight Essay: Grades 11–12

ENTRY REQUIREMENTS

Essay   Performance

DEADLINES

- Rumbaugh Oration: Varies
- Knight Essay: December

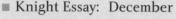

Keyword

SARSCHOL

Money Matters

The Sons of the American Revolution is a patriotic fraternal organization formed to encourage interest in the history of the American Revolution and the enduring institutions of American freedom.

Who is buried in Grant's tomb? What color is George Washington's white horse? What year was the War of 1812? If you're not stumped by these historical "brainteasers" and can write an oration or essay on a historical theme, then perhaps the two scholarships sponsored by the Sons of the American Revolution (SAR) are right for you.

In the Joseph S. Rumbaugh Historical Oration Contest—a program open to high school sophomores, juniors, and seniors—entrants deliver five- to six-minute speeches on a person, event, or document related to the Revolutionary War. For this contest, the program awards a $3,000 first-place prize, a $2,000 second-place prize, and a $1,000 third-place scholarship, as well as various other prizes ranging from $200 to $300.

Likewise, in the George S. and Stella M. Knight Historical Essay Contest, a competition open to high school juniors and seniors who are U.S. citizens or legal residents, students submit 750- to 1,000-word essays on topics related to

the founding of our nation. For this contest, the SAR gives a $7,500 first-place award, a $2,500 second-place award, and a $1,000 third-place award, in addition to various prizes offered at the local level. The first-place national winner also receives an all-expense-paid trip to the SAR Annual Congress.

Local, state, and national entry deadlines for the Rumbaugh contest vary depending on the date of the national convention each year. Entries for the Knight program are due in late December.

▮ A CLOSER LOOK

RUMBAUGH HISTORICAL ORATION

Entrants in the Rumbaugh contest may choose any topic related to the Revolutionary War, as long as the student discusses the relationship of the topic to the present day. Not every chapter of the SAR sponsors the oration contest, so if there is not a contest at the local level, students may proceed directly to the state level. In the event that there is not a contest in their home state, students may approach other states for sponsorship. For a student to go to the national contest, however, an individual SAR chapter must sponsor him or her.

The national competition is held in various states each year. A recent contest was held in Louisville, Kentucky.

The three members of the SAR who serve on each level's Rumbaugh judging panel evaluate each student orator based on six criteria: composition, delivery, logic, significance, general excellence, and adherence to time restrictions. According to contest rules, delivery is given the greatest weight in the judging process, and judges are told to "look for enunciation, sincerity, and persuasiveness." Entrants should be able to deliver their speeches without long pauses, stutters, or prompting.

If a student needs to be prompted, he or she will be out of the running for advancement in the competition.

As for the allotted time, students should be careful to keep their speeches within the five- to six-minute range. According to Rod Hildreth, the chairman of the competition, after six minutes has passed a student is allowed to finish his sentence without any point deductions, but if he continues beyond that he will be penalized.

KNIGHT HISTORICAL ESSAY

Entries for the Knight contest should discuss an event, philosophy, person, or ideal relating to the American Revolution, the framing of the U.S. Constitution, or the Declaration of Independence. Each essay must include a title page, a bibliography (which cites at least three references), and a one-page personal biography. According to Richard Sage, director of the competition, the biography is *not* judged. It is for administration and promotional purposes only.

The number of judging rounds depends on the participation of each local SAR chapter; some essays will be evaluated at the local level, while other student entries will be entered into an "at large" category. At each level of judging, students are evaluated according to five equally weighted criteria: historical accuracy, clarity of thought, organization and proven topic, grammar and spelling, and documentation. When checking the word count, students should be aware that one- or two-letter words will not be counted; in addition, footnotes, the bibliography, and the biography will be excluded from the total word count.

Put the World Book *or* Britannica *down! If you cite an encyclopedia as a source, your entry will be disqualified.*

Although I'm not sure about the favorite colors of most members of the Sons of the American Revolution, if I had to guess I'd choose red, white, and blue.

▌ COACH'S ANALYSIS

Compared to other scholarship oratorical and essay contests, the Rumbaugh and Knight competitions have traditionally placed a greater emphasis on in-depth research and a formal organizational structure. For this reason, you'll want to come up with three or four key ideas and then include numerous historical facts, anecdotes, and quotes to support each idea.

If you're struggling to find a structure for your essay or oration, a proven way to go in this competition—and in most contests, for that matter—is the three-part format. In the first part, the *introduction,* you frame the subject matter to be covered in the piece and then try to capture the judges' attention in an interesting way. For both the Rumbaugh and Knight competitions either a historical anecdote or a present-day example could work well.

See the full text of this entry on page 276.

For instance, Micah Kubic, a first-place Rumbaugh winner from Kansas City, Missouri, began his oration by describing a personal experience in which he observed an elderly woman making the effort to vote, despite having to walk several blocks through a heavy downpour. Not only does highlighting this story make Kubic's oration much more personal in nature, which enables his oration to stand out from other entries, but evoking the image of a civic-minded 70-year-old woman makes good strategic sense in a contest in which the average SAR member (and, therefore, oration judge) is of retirement age. "I tried to connect my oration to the present day," Kubic explains, "in a way that the audience could associate with."

The second part of your essay or oration, the *body,* is the place where you develop your main points and ideas. Follow a logical progression and streamline your ideas to eliminate the "belly-button fuzz"—the extraneous bits of information you just don't need. Many past winners of the Rumbaugh and Knight competitions have organized the body of their essays and orations into a series of paragraphs, with each paragraph devoted to a single core idea.

Finally, in the third part, the *conclusion,* you should not only summarize your main points but also extend the concepts in some way—if possible, tying them back to the anecdote, example, imagery, or original idea presented in your introduction.

Once you've figured out how to organize your essay or oration, deciding which facts are the most important to include will be one of your most challenging tasks. To do this, I recommend drafting your oration or essay moderately long—perhaps seven and a half minutes for the Rumbaugh oration and about 1,250 words for the Knight essay. Then force yourself to pare things down, getting rid of extraneous information and, especially, wordiness.

For Marisol Trowbridge, a third-place Knight essay winner from Sedgwick, Maine, taking this approach made a huge difference: "When I wrote the essay, it was way too long—but I learned not to be afraid of that," relates Trowbridge. "Because it was long, I could sift through and pick out the most important things. I could pull out what was less important and get a more condensed, concise version of what I was trying to say in the first place. . . . The editing process is probably what did it [won a top award] for me."

When choosing what information to include, be sure not to rely too heavily on quoting other people. While a well-placed quote can go a long way toward bolstering your points, using quotes excessively can make it seem that you don't have any opinions of your own but are merely parroting others.

"Whenever I use a quote, I ask myself, 'Does it really add to something that I have said, or can I say it in my own words just as well?'" emphasizes Knight essay second-place winner Sam Wedes of West Bloomfield, Michigan. "Don't depend too heavily on quotes, because the judges want to hear what *you* have to say."

THOMAS PAINE:
CHAMPION OF LIBERTY

Winning
Entry

In this excerpt from his winning oration, Micah Kubic discusses Thomas Paine's important contributions to the American Revolution and the cause of liberty.

Last year, during the election, I was standing inside of my school building to escape a heavy rain when I saw a woman coming towards me. She was about seventy years old, and I had seen her before. She lives a few blocks away from my school and I know that she doesn't own a car. When she emerged from the building, she proudly wore an "I voted" sticker on her shirt. That woman was, to me, the model citizen. She exercised her rights, even under harsh conditions.

Like we all should, she understood that the rights and privileges we have been given were not easily come by. Men and women of courage were required to fight for the freedoms we have.

One such champion of liberty is the man who inspired the masses to abandon their loyalties to Britain, Thomas Paine. Without his pamphlet, *Common Sense,* broad popular support for the Revolution would never have been drummed up. Born in England in 1737, he met Benjamin Franklin in London and was able to travel to Philadelphia with a useful tool for that city, letters of reference from Franklin himself.

Paine worked for a magazine, submitting short essays that immediately tripled the readership. His ability to simplify complex concepts, turning even the most abstract of ideas into powerful emotional arguments, appealed to the colonists. Unfortunately, the owner of the magazine was opposed to causing trouble and refused the more sensational essays the author penned.

Paine captivated the imagination of the oppressed American colonists, and his best work was yet to come. Although many residing in America were upset with British rule and excessive taxes, few were ready to leave the Empire. Even the most vocal opponents of British actions, like Benjamin Franklin and Continental Congress member Benjamin Rush, had not called for independence. They feared moving too early, lest the population not support them.

Paine had no such qualms. He was a courageous man, willing to risk his own future for the sake of the country he wished to build. His fear of an eternal suppression of natural rights was far greater than his fear of moving too early. Wanting to test the waters for support of independence, Paine wrote a pamphlet enumerating all of his arguments for independence.

Kubic suggests choosing a topic for your oration or essay that isn't as well known. "Definitely don't pick George Washington," he advises.

Paine worked tirelessly from fall of 1775 until January of 1776. He would slave over every word, stopping only rarely. When he was finished, he had written a 47-page masterpiece entitled *Common Sense*. The public heartily agreed. In the first three months alone, 120,000 copies were sold.

Common Sense was the single greatest factor on the colonists' part in moving towards revolution. Until its publication, few talked of independence. Newspapers refused to print articles discussing it. Paine's pamphlet forced them to reconsider, and soon independence was the only topic of discussion. The timing could not have been better; George III made a speech to Parliament denouncing American acts of treason.

Paine's arguments put the issue in terms average people could understand, and used graphic and inflammatory language to anger the colonists. He labeled George a brute who relished his children, the Americans, as his main course, "even brutes do not devour their young." He denounced not only the monarch, but monarchy itself. Monarchs "have little more to do than make war and give away places at court. Americans should not feel any obligation to a crowned ruffian who sanctions war against them." He declared, "Let this republican charter be brought forth placed on the divine law, the word of God. Let a crown be placed thereon, so that the world may know, that in America THE LAW IS KING."

To read the conclusion of Micah Kubic's winning oration, visit the Coach's Locker Room at ScholarshipCoach.com (Keyword: SARSCHOL).

Sam Wedes
West Bloomfield, MI
Second Place
Knight Essay
$2,500

Winning
Entry

THE U.S. CONSTITUTION:
DOES IT STAND THE TEST OF TIME?

In this essay excerpt, Sam Wedes demonstrates how the U.S. Constitution is indeed a living document that adapts to the needs of an evolving nation.

In 1835, less than half a century after the ratification of the U.S. Constitution, Alexis de Tocqueville observed in his famous book, *Democracy in America,* ". . . The social state of America is a very strange phenomenon. Men there are nearer equality in wealth and mental endowments . . . than in any other country of the world or in any other age of recorded history." Indeed, by

Tocqueville's time, America had already begun to live up to the legacy that the Founding Fathers had ardently expressed in the Constitution: that America be the exemplar of freedom and equality. Today, America continues to grow and prosper from these ideals of democratic governance. And in so doing, the Constitution lives on as it regulates and adapts to new generations and new ideas.

Much of the Constitution's flexibility can be attributed to the elastic clause (Article I, Section 8), which gives Congress the power to make all laws that are "necessary and proper" to carry out the laws explicitly listed in the Constitution. Such implied powers allow Congress not to be limited solely to the expressed powers of the Constitution and have been used throughout history as a means to adapt to a rapidly changing culture. For example, in the landmark case, McCulloch v. Maryland (1819), the controversy regarding whether Congress had the power to charter a bank was brought to the forefront. Albeit the Constitution made no explicit reference to a national bank, Marshall declared that chartering a bank was among the implied powers of Congress "necessary and proper for carrying into execution the foregoing powers [such as taxation, borrowing money, and regulating commerce]," thus allowing the Constitution to evolve along with the changing needs of the nation.

Another means by which the Constitution lives through today is the amendment process. As James Madison explained, "It guards equally against that extreme facility which would render the Constitution too mutable; and that extreme difficulty which might perpetuate its discovered faults." The first ten amendments are known as the Bill of Rights, which were added to the Constitution to "reassure the people that the vastly strengthened federal government would not oppress them and to secure individual rights for the long term." For example, Amendment I guarantees the freedoms of religion, speech, press, assembly, and petition. Other amendments include the abolition of slavery (Amendment XIII); the rights of citizens, including due process of law and equal protection under the law (Amendment XIV); and women's suffrage (Amendment XIX). Some amendments reflect issues unheard of at the time that the Constitution was ratified, but that became prominent as the country and society progressed. For example, Amendment XXVI, ratified in 1971, lowered the voting age from 21 to 18 after people complained during Vietnam that if they could be drafted into the army at age 18, then they should also be able to vote. Throughout the course of American history, the Constitution has been amended 27 times, allowing it to become one with the ever-changing American identity.

For the complete text of Sam Wedes' winning essay, visit the Coach's Locker Room at ScholarshipCoach.com (Keyword: SARSCHOL).

**CONTACT
INFORMATION**

Keyword
SARSCHOL

Rumbaugh Oration / Knight Essay Contest Chairman
c/o NSSAR Headquarters
1000 South Fourth Street
Louisville, KY 40203-3208

Websites:
www.sar.org/youth/rumrules.htm
www.sar.org/youth/knight.htm

RELATED AWARD PROGRAMS

For more information on a Related Award Program, enter the associated keyword in the "Enter a Keyword" box located in the Coach's Locker Room section of ScholarshipCoach.com

■ Americanism Educational League Private Enterprise Essay Contest

This youth-oriented public-service foundation offers undergraduate students the opportunity to write 1,500-word essays on patriotic topics. In past contest years, topics have included "Why the Electoral College Best Protects Voter's Choice" and "How Best to Combat Today's Religious Terrorism." Cash awards total $12,000—with individual awards ranging from $500 to $5,000. Entries must be submitted by early March.

	Keyword
SCHOLARSHIP**C**OACH.com	**AMEDUENT**

■ Daughters of the American Revolution Good Citizens Award

As the female answer to the SAR, the DAR competition provides awards to high school seniors who have been nominated by their schools based on their leadership, service, dependability, and patriotism. Participants are required to submit an activity list, a transcript, recommendations, and a patriotic essay (completed in a two-hour, verified writing session). Prizes in the national competition range from $100 to $3,000.

	Keyword
SCHOLARSHIP**C**OACH.com	**DARGOODC**

Target All-Around Scholarship

When one of America's major retailers sets its sights on rewarding those students who altruistically perform and initiate important community service work, you've got a scholarship program that really hits the bull's-eye.

Each year, the administrators of the Target All-Around Scholarship hunt for worthy American high school seniors and undergraduate students (under the age of 25) who pursue community service activities with a passion—doing work that significantly improves some aspect of life in their communities.

The application process is straightforward: Entrants list community service activities, leadership positions, and awards and honors, and complete a one-page essay. To be considered for an award, students must have a minimum 2.0 GPA. All students in the United States, except those in Alaska and Hawaii, are currently eligible to participate.

Grand prizes of $10,000 are awarded to four students each year, while about 2,100 other students each receive $1,000 (two awards for each Target store).

Applications are due in early November. Winners are usually notified by the end of February.

TARGET RECIPIENT

- High school seniors
- Undergraduates under age 25

ENTRY REQUIREMENTS

Activities & Credentials | Essay | Academic Info

DEADLINE

- November

	Keyword
ScholarshipCoach.com	**TARGALLA**

Money $ Matters

▪ A CLOSER LOOK

The application process starts by first obtaining a form from a Target store or from the company website. The completed application forms are to be submitted to Citizens' Scholarship Foundation of America (CSFA), the group that manages the selection of the final scholarship recipients.

To apply, students must compile a list of community volunteer service activities they have participated in during the past two years. Each service activity listing should contain five pieces of information:

- ▪ The name of the activity

- ▪ How the student participated in the program (including leadership roles)

- ▪ Total hours for the first year

- ▪ Total hours for the second year

- ▪ Contact information for the volunteer supervisor

If you have an existing community service résumé, simply reformat it to fit the application guidelines.

Applicants may attach additional pages, but such pages should match the format of the application form.

Although recommendation letters should *not* be submitted, an "applicant appraisal" is required from a project supervisor, volunteer coordinator, or community leader. The appraisal is a short form, with four brief questions about your service involvement and three lines for additional comments. In addition to a current transcript, applicants also must submit an essay—no more than one page in length, double-spaced—focusing on one of the volunteer experiences listed on their service activity form. In the essay, entrants are encouraged to discuss how the activity benefited others and how their own lives, or the lives of their families, were changed as a result of the experience.

In a recent application year, some grand prize winners had upwards of 1,000 hours of community service (the highest being about 1,500!).

The number of community service hours documented by the student factors heavily in the judging process, but other less-quantitative attributes, such as the quality of the service, can compensate for fewer raw hours. According to Pei-Loh Lo, who coordinates the program for CSFA, "There might have been people who had a higher number of hours, but based on the other elements of the application, they were not ranked as high." In addition, Lo says that judges do give preference to applicants who live in a community that has a Target store.

COACH'S ANALYSIS

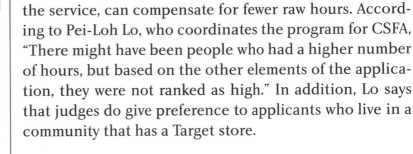

To score big in this scholarship program, you are *not* required to have top grades. This is because once you've met the minimum 2.0 GPA requirement, says Lo, grades aren't considered at all in the judging process. So if your grades aren't as high as you would like, don't let the fact that you have to submit your school transcript and GPA discourage you from applying. Laura Lockwood of Bradenton, Florida, for instance, won a national award of $10,000 from the program, despite having a GPA that, she says, "was the lowest possible to graduate from high school in Florida."

What Lockwood did have, however, was a very strong record of community service. To put your own service record in the best possible light, think of your Target All-Around Scholarship application as a sturdy house that you're trying to build (an especially appropriate metaphor if your service project happens to be related to the Habitat for Humanity program). To build this house, you need four types of "raw materials."

First, you need *commitment,* as demonstrated through your volunteer work. The yardsticks typically used to measure commitment include the total number of hours spent on all community service activities, the number of hours per week devoted to a particular project, and the number of months or years you've worked on that project. If the time spent for your particular service work isn't as impressive as you would like, also try to demonstrate commitment more qualitatively. For example, in your application essay, try to discuss ways that you have demonstrated a commitment to service other than just your time. If you can persuasively convey your underlying motivation and inspiration for doing a particular community service project or can mention other service awards and honors, you can bolster your demonstrated commitment.

Second, you need to show *impact*. Since commitment alone doesn't communicate the results of your work, measuring your impact assesses the positive effect of your efforts. Include the number of people you've helped, the amount of funds you've raised, or the total dollar value of services you've contributed. Impact can also be demonstrated by describing specific instances that epitomize the results of your efforts. Target national winner Clayton Keenan, of Wheaton, Illinois, for instance, described the impact of his service on one particular individual because "a specific, tangible example gives you a good feel for what really happened." He also included quotes from the individual he and his church group helped. "When you hear someone's actual words," Keenan says, "you get a sense that he is a real person." To an experienced program administrator and judge, this level of detail is perhaps even more important. "We find that the ones that are more personal, really do make better essays," Lo says.

Lockwood, also the winner of several other prominent community service awards, suggests taking things a step further by projecting the future impact of the program. She paid special attention in her application to describing how she hoped to expand her youth volunteer program and how it was already starting to be replicated across the country. "Showing how it's replicable is important when you're going for national recognition," she states. "What good is it if I'm recognized for something I've done if people can't take that and run with it in their communities?"

The third raw material is *individual initiative*. Individual initiative can be demonstrated if you've founded your own service program, of course. But it can also be shown by how you have taken action steps to expand on an existing service endeavor. The main thing is to demonstrate some steps you've taken as an individual, distinct from other members of the volunteer group, to extend the scope of the service effort.

To work *leadership*, the fourth raw material, into the Target application, don't just state official positions you have held; also describe your role in organizing an activity, assuming responsibility for implementing the program, and recruiting others to participate. This type of information should specifically be included under the "What Did You Do?" heading on the volunteer service activity list.

Great things to mention include the actions you've taken to recruit more volunteers and how many volunteers you've recruited.

If you can include compelling information in at least *two* of these four areas, you'll have a good chance of getting close to the "target." If you can demonstrate excellence in all *four*, you'll have an outstanding chance of hitting a bull's eye.

Winning
Entry

ESSAY SUBMISSION

In the text below, Clayton Keenan discusses his community service involvement by describing its positive impact on one appreciative homeowner.

One of the more poignant moments in my life occurred in the heart of the South, in the town of Greensboro, Alabama. I was a student leader of a team of about thirty teenagers and adults. We had been working on various projects in the community for about a week. Although we had plenty of work projects, enough to fill both weeks we were going to be in Greensboro, we found an unexpected project that we couldn't pass up. While one of the trip's adult

leaders, Amy, was doing some laundry at a local laundromat, she met a man named Hillard. When he found out we had been working on local homes, he mentioned that his house needed some work. Describing his home, he said that it was "all right in the summer, but a little cold in the winter." When we went to investigate his house, we were shocked to discover the deplorable condition the house was in. The house, or should I say, shack, was, quite literally, falling apart. The reason the house was cold in the winter was because the walls were just one inch-thick, with no insulation or siding. The porch was held up by a couple of two by fours, and the slightest shove would cause it to come tumbling down. The walls and roof did not meet in some places, so you could see directly inside the house. We couldn't pass up this opportunity to help someone who really needed it. We only had time to put insulation and siding up on Hillard's house, but we did as much as we could in the last week we were there. On the day before we left, as we finished up our work, I had the chance to talk with him. As we walked around his yard, looking at the new siding, he commented, "I was considering just scrapping the house because it needed so much work and I couldn't do it all, but now I have a home that I can be proud of."

That moment stays with me, remaining one of the most meaningful moments in my life. It helped me realize how some care and a little work can give someone hope and restore some dignity. It made all of my service efforts seem worth it.

CONTACT INFORMATION

Keyword
TARGALLA

Target All-Around Scholarship
Citizens' Scholarship Foundation of America, Inc.
1505 Riverview Rd.
P.O. Box 480
St. Peter, MN 56082-0480

Phone: (800) 537-4180
Website: www.target.com

RELATED AWARD PROGRAMS

For more information on a Related Award Program, enter the associated keyword in the "Enter a Keyword" box located in the Coach's Locker Room section of ScholarshipCoach.com

■ **Yoshiyama Award for Exemplary Service to the Community**

This award, named after a former chairman of Hitachi, Ltd. (the Japanese electronics company), targets high school seniors who have gone above and beyond what most students consider sufficient community service.

Applicants must be nominated by an adviser or community leader and must submit recommendations and an outline of their service activities. The $5,000 prizes are awarded to ten winners. Applications are due before the fall of each year.

Keyword
YOSHAWRD

■ **Sam Walton Community Scholarship**

Named after the founder of the Wal-Mart retail chain, high school seniors living in the vicinity of a Wal-Mart store may apply for these $1,000 scholarships. Selection is based on test scores, academics, work experience, financial need, plus community and school involvement. Applications are available from local stores, and the deadline is in early March.

Keyword
SWALTCOS

Toshiba/NSTA ExploraVision

TARGET RECIPIENT

■ Grades K–12

ENTRY REQUIREMENTS

Project | Short Answer | Art and Graphics

DEADLINE

■ February

Keyword
TOSHNSTA

Typically, the greatest number of entrants is in the grade 7 to 9 age group, followed by the grade 4 to 6 division. Fewer entries are submitted in the grade 10 to 12 range, and grades K to 3 have the fewest.

Money $ Matters

Wouldn't it be great if bandages could diagnose illnesses, clean wounds, and monitor your vital signs? Wouldn't it be nice to have a small alarm that reminds you when your library books are due, with a tracking device to help you find them? Wouldn't it be cool if your contact lenses gave you super-human sight? According to winners in the Toshiba/NSTA ExploraVision contests, who submitted each of these futuristic ideas, such advances are possible within the next 20 years.

Administered by the National Science Teachers Association (NSTA), the ExploraVision competition rewards those who can set forth a convincing vision for a future technology. The program is open to students in kindergarten through 12th grade who attend school in the United States, U.S. territories, or Canada.

To enter, students form two- to four-person teams and each team prepares a written description of a futuristic technology and five sample illustrations of potential Web pages that would explain the technology. National awards are given in each of the four divisions: grades K to 3, grades 4 to 6, grades 7 to 9, and grades 10 to 12. Each team member on the four first-place teams (one from each division) will be awarded $10,000. Members of the four second-place teams will each receive $5,000.

Projects must be submitted for the first round of judging by early February.

▌ A Closer Look

So what do you have to do, exactly? In creating written descriptions, students must include:

▌ The history of the topic

▌ An outline of the present technology

▌ Future possibilities for the technology

▌ Any breakthroughs necessary to make the proposed advances

▌ Positive and negative consequences the technology could have on society

The description must follow a specific format, outlined in the application, and must include a complete bibliography of sources used to research the chosen technology.

Students are also required to submit sketches of five project Web pages that could be created if they are selected as finalists. Students have a nine-inch by five-inch area (that's 45 square inches of pure visual power!) to convey the ideas for each Web page, and there is space available for a written description of potential special effects. Sample Web pages should support the description of the technology and should draw material directly from the written description.

How are these entries evaluated? Each part of the application has an assigned point value:

▌ History (10 points)

▌ Present technology (15 points)

▌ Future technology (20 points)

▌ Breakthroughs (15 points)

- Consequences (15 points)

- Web page graphics (20 points)

- Bibliography (5 points)

After entries are submitted to the NSTA, they undergo an initial screening process in which the applications are examined to confirm compliance with all rules and regulations. (Note: Failing to have the proper margins or double-space the essay, for instance, could cause an entry to be disqualified.)

Entries that pass the initial screening are sorted according to grade level and geographic region, and then are distributed to the first-round judges—50 science educators, ranging from elementary teachers to college professors, from all across the United States. The judges gather in Washington, D.C., for a full weekend of judging, during which each application is examined by four judges, working in pairs.

Insider Info

The first-round judges devote special attention to determining a reasonable standard of achievement for students of a particular grade level. The judges first remove the applications that do not reach this standard of achievement. Applications that are deemed competitive are assigned point values and are debated until a ranking of the top four groups in each grade level in each of six regions is identified. In this way, 96 teams advance to the next round of the judging.

These 96 applications are then submitted to a second-round judging panel consisting of a dozen research scientists and engineers, including representatives from NASA, the National Institutes of Health, and the National Science Foundation. According to Arthur Eisenkraft, the head judge for the program and the former president of the NSTA, this second-round panel evaluates only the scientific merits of the technological breakthrough. "They're looking at 'Is this possible within a 20-year time frame?'"

Students from winning teams are permitted to participate in the contest in subsequent years as long as each member forms a new team with different students.

For regional winning teams, working websites are due in mid-April.

Eisenkraft emphasizes. "We don't want the scientists to be looking at the quality of writing and age appropriateness of the entry." Based on this criterion, the panel works together to select the best entry per age division for each region, thereby identifying the 24 regional winning teams.

Each of the 24 regional-winning teams must then draw upon their original entry and create a working website that includes a prototype of their technology—a website that can be viewed in its entirety in approximately five minutes. In the final round of judging, the submitted websites, as well as the original entries, are reviewed by the NSTA Board of Directors. After reviewing materials and complete judging scoring sheets on an individual basis, the Board of Directors gathers for two days of discussion and debate—eventually selecting the first-place and second-place teams.

■ COACH'S ANALYSIS

As you might expect, the judging standards in the Toshiba competition get tougher as you climb up the age-division categories—with more scientific latitude given to younger kids and more comprehensive research and scientific sophistication expected of older entrants. But regardless of the age category, there are three important ways you can make your application materials rank among the very best.

The first way is to pick a topic that is just plain *cool*. Eisenkraft says that in his ten years as head judge, three of the winning technological concepts that most stand out in his mind include:

- ■ A futuristic refrigerator that keeps an accurate inventory of its contents, offers meal ideas based on the ingredients on hand, and suggests healthier alternatives when you have a case of the munchies (grades K–3)

▌ A robot that could stop playground fights and mediate other schoolyard disputes (grades 4–6)

▌ A toilet of the future that helps you diagnose illness by performing urine and stool analyses and keeping detailed medical records (grades 7–9)

If you and your teammates are having problems coming up with an idea, try first defining a problem that currently exists and then brainstorming ways that you could help address it if you had the right technological tools. To determine the "coolness quotient" of your project, pitch your future technology idea to family, friends, and teachers and judge their reactions. In a competition where only your imagination provides the limits, some of the best projects are the ones that draw the biggest "oohs" and "aahs" when people hear the conceptual idea.

One of the biggest mistakes students make, Eisenkraft says, is to copy the ideas of prior winners. In general, keep in mind that the judges for the competition are mostly the same from year to year. Even if you didn't know about prior winners, if your project is similar to those that won a year or two before, the judges might assume otherwise. The safest bet is to review the project ideas that have won in recent winning entries (you can do this on the program website), and if your idea is similar to a prior winner, pick something else.

The second way to leverage your chances is by getting feedback from an expert on the technological concepts you're proposing. That's exactly what fifth-grader Travis Gingerich of Anchorage, Alaska, did when he and teammates Shayna Cott, Isaac Park, and Grahm Nelson were trying to get feedback on their "Eagle-Eyes" idea—an advanced contact lens that could give wearers superhuman sight. "We found an expert in town who was an ophthalmologist," says Amos Gingerich, Travis's father.

"He helped advise them on their project." Because the scientists and engineers who form the second-round judging panel specifically assess the technology's feasibility within the specified 20-year time frame, an expert in the field can help you anticipate and address potential criticisms ahead of time.

Third, pay special attention to the parts of the application that have the greatest influence on your chances of winning. Eisenkraft notes that most teams do well on the Present Technology and History sections. As a result, these sections usually have a minimal effect on the eventual contest outcome. (Translation: Focus the bulk of your efforts elsewhere.) On the other hand, Eisenkraft says that, in the Consequences section of the application, many applicants fail to thoroughly address the potential negative consequences because "students are usually enamored with their idea." In addition, he singles out the Future Technology and Breakthroughs sections as two other areas in which the eventual winners typically distinguish themselves. Armed with this knowledge, you should invest more time in these high-leverage sections of the application.

A SAMPLER OF WINNING PROJECTS

To get a better idea of what types of technologies and projects have scored well in the Toshiba competition, let's take a look at some past winning entries from each age division.

Grades K–3:

■ Students at Metairie Park Country Day School in Metairie, Louisiana, devised a technology they could really sink their teeth into—the "Cavity Zapper." Featuring fiber optic bristles that sense cavity-causing bacteria, the device would also include a screen that points out specific areas to brush and floss.

■ Looking to do away with unpleasant throat swabs, students at Irving B. Weber Elementary School in Iowa City, Iowa, came up with the concept behind the "Strep Throat Home Tester." After breathing on a hand-held "strepalyser," users would be notified whether or not they have an infection, as well as other pertinent health information.

■ To remedy the frustration of misplacing your keys, students at Holmes Elementary School in San Diego, California, suggest "Finders Keepers"—a microchip that could be attached to keys to locate them at a moment's notice.

■ Students from French Road Elementary School in Rochester, New York, got on their librarian's good side with their idea for the "Book Beeper and Tracker." This device would feature a small alarm to remind users when to return their books, as well as radio wave technology to help them locate misplaced books.

Grades 4–6:

■ Pickens Academy students in Carrolton, Alabama, could practically smell the success of their Toshiba entry titled "Operation Odor Eater: Taking the Stink Out of Hog Farming." According to these students, such technology could convert hog waste into fuel for electric power generation, filtering the air along the way.

■ The "Allerscan"—a miniaturized gas chromatography unit envisioned by students at Leeds Elementary School in Arlington, Wisconsin—allows users to test foods at the supermarket for allergens. Furthermore, a laser bar code reader notifies users if there are any dangerous foods nearby.

■ Bandages of the future will be no mere Band-Aids according to students at Barrett Elementary Center in Cresco, Pennsylvania. These bandages, equipped with microchips, would be able to clean wounds, stop bleeding, diagnose illnesses, and relay vital signs to a database.

■ According to students at Rogers Park Elementary School in Anchorage, Alaska, contact lenses of the future will allow wearers to zoom in and out of objects, acting as both a pair of binoculars and a magnifying glass. Equipped with a tiny battery and an adjustable lens, these contacts would be fully controllable by the user with a single thought.

Grades 7–9:

■ Designed to offset the symptoms of osteoporosis sufferers, the "Woven Engineered Bone System" was brainstormed by students at Point Grey Mini School in Vancouver, British Columbia. After studying electromagnetic technology, these students came up with an idea for a non-organic substance that would harden, forming a strong and sturdy web around delicate bones.

■ Students at Kate Collins Middle School in Waynesboro, Virginia, explored custom-fit knee replacements that could serve as substitutes for more invasive knee replacement procedures. Their technology—titled "In Vivo Cartilage Implants: The Technology Application of Tissue Engineering to Regenerate Articular Cartilage"—would restore full performance in only six weeks.

■ The "Cardio Mate," concocted by students at St. Luke Lutheran School in Santa Rosa, California, would both detect heart failure and administer treatment. Inserted in a coronary artery, the device would apply medicinal and electronic remedies and alert health care professionals using a tiny Global Positioning System.

■ Students at DeForest Cooperative Middle School in DeForest, Wisconsin, formulated the idea behind the "Photo-Electric Eye Prosthesis." Using technology similar to a digital camera, sensors would collect light that enters the eye and transmit it to the main section of the cerebral cortex, correcting many types of vision problems.

Grades 10–12:

▪ Students at the University of Detroit Jesuit High School and Academy in Detroit, Michigan, conceived a "SMAART" technological advancement. Standing for "Shape Memory Alloys in Airplanes Reduce Turbulence," SMAART technology would make jet travel faster, more affordable, and more comfortable.

▪ Longer swimming time for scuba divers is possible according to students at Providence Academy in Katy, Texas. Outfitted in "AquaGill" dive suits, divers would benefit from artificial hemoglobin tubing that attracts free oxygen molecules in the water, thereby allowing longer dive times.

▪ Students at South Salem High School in Salem, Oregon, sought to better treat Attention Deficit Disorder (ADD) with "biosensing technology." According to these students, ADD treatment would include placing a miniature microprocessor on the frontal lobe of the brain and joining it with nearby nerve cells.

▪ The "Electro-Lipid Propulsion System"—a combustion/electrical engine thought up by students at Don Mills Collegiate Institute in North York, Ontario—would use lipids instead of gas to power engines that normally require explosive force and numerous cylinders.

CONTACT INFORMATION

Keyword
TOSHNSTA

Toshiba/NSTA ExploraVision Awards
1840 Wilson Blvd.
Arlington, VA 22201-3000

Phone: (800) EXPLOR-9
E-mail: exploravision@nsta.org
Website: www.toshiba.com/tai/exploravision

RELATED AWARD PROGRAMS

For more information on a Related Award Program, enter the associated keyword in the
"Enter a Keyword" box located in the Coach's Locker Room section of ScholarshipCoach.com

■ Craftsman/NSTA Young Inventors Awards Program

This competition (from the same administering organization as the ExploraVision program) seeks students in grades 2 through 8 to submit ideas for an invention or modification of a tool that is self-contained, portable, and usable without supplementary equipment. Submissions require project descriptions, "inventor's logs," and pictures of the students using the tools. Scholarships are U.S. Savings Bonds ranging in value from $250 to $10,000. Submissions are due in mid-March.

Keyword
CRAFTINV

■ Discovery Young Scientist Challenge

Students in grades 5 through 8 are nominated based on their participation in a science fair affiliated with Science Service. Selected nominees receive a week in Washington, D.C., for age-appropriate scientific activities. Program awards (based on problem solving, leadership, communication skills, and the science project) range from $500 to $15,000. The entrant's science fair participation must occur before early June to be nominated for the program.

Keyword
DISYOSCI

Truman Scholarship

TARGET RECIPIENT

■ Undergraduate juniors

ENTRY REQUIREMENTS

Nomination | Academic Info | Activities & Credentials

Short Answer | Interview

DEADLINE

■ January

ScholarshipCoach.com | **Keyword** **TRUSCHOL**

Money Matters

Senior undergraduates attending schools in Puerto Rico, the Virgin Islands, Guam, American Samoa, and the Northern Marianas may also apply.

Do you want to attend grad school in preparation for a career related to public service? If this is indeed the case, let Harry—as in the 33rd U.S. president, not the fictional boy wizard—come to the rescue.

Each year, the Harry S. Truman Scholarship Foundation seeks out students who show the same dedication to public service as the program's namesake. Students nominated for these scholarships are undergraduate juniors who have distinguished themselves on campus—through leadership, service, or academics—and who have firm plans for graduate study. Between 75 and 80 students receive these $30,000 awards ($3,000 for the senior undergraduate year and $27,000 for graduate study).

Each college or university may nominate four juniors as well as two students who have transferred from two-year programs and are currently third-year students. Nominees must be U.S. citizens or nationals.

After faculty representatives have nominated qualified students, each nominee submits an application detailing his or her academic record, community service, work experience, public service, and leadership positions. Students are also expected to write short essays about future plans, submit a "policy proposal" memo, and include transcripts and recommendation letters with the completed applications. Finalists chosen from the preliminary applications undergo an interview process.

Applications are due in late January.

A Closer Look

Nominators select students in the top 25 percent of their class who have demonstrated an interest in some aspect of public service. The nomination process is different for each school. Generally, students who wish to be nominated submit to the faculty representative their application materials, and a panel at their school selects the strongest applicants to forward to the national competition.

The program is geared toward students who want positions in the government, nonprofit, and advocacy sectors. This can include serving in local, state, or federal government as an elected official or policy writer; teaching at any level; practicing law as a district attorney or public defender; or pursuing a medical degree with the express purpose of aiding the unfortunate. Students selected as Truman Scholars are those who demonstrate that they are the most likely to make a difference in society.

To do this, students not only are asked to fill out an application detailing their school record and activities, but they also must write a short essay about one example of their leadership ability. There are also a number of short-answer questions requiring applicants to detail future plans and other personal information that may be pertinent to the judges. Past questions that applicants have answered include:

▪ What do you hope to do and what position do you hope to have upon completing your graduate studies?

▮ What do you hope to do and what position do you hope to have five to seven years later?

▮ Describe the problems or needs of society you want to address when you enter public service.

After the applicant has identified the intended area of public service and detailed how he or she will achieve those goals, the applicant will be asked to write a one-page policy proposal, outlining a policy problem or issue in the intended area of public service. The proposal should be executed in a memo style and addressed to the government official who could most directly address the problem.

The proposal should be in three parts: (1) problem statement, (2) proposed solution, and (3) major obstacles/ implementation challenges. The presentation of the problem should include statistical data and major sources that support statements about the policy. The proposal is expected to be concise, to be neatly presented, and to include a page of references, exhibits, and footnotes.

Also included with the application should be college transcripts and three recommendations—each focusing on a *different* aspect of the nominee's potential to effect positive change through public service. According to contest literature, one recommendation should support the applicant's leadership example, another recommendation should detail the applicant's commitment to a public service career, and the final recommendation should discuss the nominee's potential success in graduate school based on his or her academic and intellectual capabilities.

Scholarship winners are selected in two rounds of judging. The first-round judging panel is made up of professionals from the academic and government sectors, including elected public officials, U.S. attorneys, and deans and professors from leading universities. This judging panel narrows down the applicant pool to 200 finalists.

To do this, the judges evaluate applicants based on their policy proposals, leadership records, public-service records, graduate study proposals, writing and presentation, and likelihood of acceptance into graduate schools (based on prior academic records). Each criterion is rated on a scale of 0 to 3 points, with bonus points available. According to program literature, if students are to advance to the next round, they will need:

- Very enthusiastic nomination letters from faculty representatives

- Sustained participation in activities (community or campus activities, government internships or employment, partisan politics and campaigns, public or nonprofit board or commission)

- Demonstrated public policy–related ambitions

- A very great likelihood of admission to graduate programs

- An understanding of the intended career field and an ability to tackle a complex problem (shown through the policy proposal)

After the written applications have been judged, students who have advanced to the finalist round will be assigned an interview date and location. This time and place *cannot* be changed: If a finalist cannot attend the assigned interview, he or she will be out of the running for a Truman Scholarship.

Regional selection panels (each composed of five judges, also from the academic and government sectors) conduct 20-minute interviews during which the applicant will be asked questions based on answers provided in the written application. The questions will generally require students to defend priorities, opinions, and statements made in the initial application and should establish their breadth of knowledge, analytical abilities, and understanding of issues.

The regional panels of judges are not required to select winners; if a winner is not chosen in a given state, the money will carry over to the next year's competition.

One scholarship is available for residents of each of the 50 states, the District of Columbia, Puerto Rico, and the islands (as detailed earlier). Up to 30 additional winners are chosen from the entries at large—resulting in an annual selection of 75 to 80 Truman Scholars.

COACH'S ANALYSIS

Because the Truman Scholarship has such an involved written application process, with numerous application components, the quality that most distinguishes the winners is their ability to make the parts of the application work together to tell a cohesive narrative—one that is credible with the judges.

To do this, you need to think of each part of the application *not* as an individual component but, instead, as part of a unified whole, with each element reinforcing other elements. For example, if your stated goals involve public service to help protect the environment, you need to (1) chronicle a history of service and work with campus, community, and government environmental groups; (2) write a policy proposal on some aspect of environmental policy that demonstrates a deep level of personal knowledge; (3) illustrate your heartfelt motivation for wanting to protect the environment; and (4) include recommendation letters that bolster and support all of the aforementioned areas.

"The most important thing is that everything about your intent, background, and goals needs to make consistent sense," offers Truman Scholar Richa Gulati of the University of Texas at Austin. "It looks odd if you've been working for a financial brokerage, then all of a sudden you want to do public service. They can tell people who've concocted a story."

Once you've established the main theme of your application (such as the theme of "environmental activism") you also want to include credentials that fall *outside* this spotlighted area. Avoid becoming a single-issue applicant by including interests and credentials beyond your proposed career path. You should try to come across as someone with a breadth of interests and abilities; you don't want to be categorized as the proverbial "one-trick pony."

Honestly, I've never seen a pony do tricks . . . but I bet that one trick is spectacular!

Insider Info

Another frequent mistake made by many Truman applicants is to put too great an emphasis on the policy statement. Don't spend so much time on your policy statement that it limits the time you can spend on other application elements. According to information provided by the Truman Foundation to faculty representatives, your responses to application questions about leadership experience, past service, academic plans, and personal qualities are far more important to the overall judging than the policy statement itself.

Your written personal statement is perhaps the most important. The personal statement is the place to put your entire application in the proper context, make an emotional connection with judges, and let them know about the intangible qualities you possess that might not be demonstrated in the rest of the application.

Gulati's personal statement, for instance, supported her stated public-service goals—to help create better economic and human rights conditions for women in India and other developing countries—by emphasizing her bicultural upbringing and contrasting her privileged life here in America with that of her cousins in India. "It puts what I want to do into perspective," Gulati stresses. "It helps make my motivation clear and gives my goals credibility, makes them more real. My personal statement was the strongest part of my application because it was intensely personal."

Once you've been named a finalist, be prepared for the judges to ask challenging questions and probe your positions. "The nature of the interview was very hostile," relates Gulati. "They take absurd positions and force you to concisely argue the opposing point of view. The goal of the interview is to find your weaknesses, and if they can't find any, that's good."

Past finalists have suggested practicing for the interview with some of the following questions:

- What is a political position you feel strongly about? Now argue the other side.

- What would be your alternate "life plan" if the one you plan on does not work out?

- What makes you tick and what ticks you off?

- How would Harry Truman respond to your proposed policy?

Because judges expect you to have a working knowledge of world affairs, don't forget to stay abreast of current events—especially in the period immediately prior to your interview. And remember, each interview is quite short. If you are struggling to answer a particular question, don't get bogged down in it and use up all your time. Keep your answer concise, cut your losses, and give the judges an opportunity to ask you a question you can answer more convincingly.

Winning
Entry

PERSONAL STATEMENT

In this well-crafted essay, Richa Gulati puts her public service goals in perspective by juxtaposing the quality of life she experienced in America and India.

I make the same mistakes every summer in India out of habit. Entering a room, I automatically flip the switch for the lights. It usually remains dark—electricity only comes for a few hours of the day. I turn the faucets on for water; nothing comes out. I go to buy vegetables at the market but the vendor has already sold out his meager supply for the day. I used to think it was fun, when I was little, to sleep on the roof. Now older, I know that we did so only to escape the stifling heat of our crowded concrete apartment. Toilets? Roads? And this is the life of the upper middle class.

> *Notice how Gulati focuses on these everyday details to help the reader visualize life in India. Sometimes the details make the difference.*
>
> Coach's Comments

I was born, raised, and educated in the United States and have benefited from the material prosperity common to the West. Yet I have spent significant time outside of the United States in the village of Yamunanagar, Haryana, in India with my extended family. Although my memories of India are filled with joy, many of them are peppered with images of a hopeless poverty in unimaginable conditions. It is not, however, just the nameless poor in India that have motivated my responsibility to better the lives of others, but also those vividly painful discussions with my two cousins, Pooja and Gauri. Talking to both women is often like hearing my own thoughts, opinions, and aspirations. Yet despite such striking similarities, the opportunities available to those like my cousins whose academic successes are no different than my own are terribly scarce. They often feel that emigration—so unlikely for most women in India—is the only way to realize their dreams.

I have yet to discover the reason why I am the only female out of a family of 16 aunts and uncles to be born in the United States. Listening to these frustrations from cousins whose faces are mirror images of my own, I often question my luck in being an American. Why can I quench my thirst for water any time of day? What difference besides geography do I have with any other woman in India? By what twist of fate am I here and Pooja there? How can I, or anyone, ignore that? For me, a life without basic necessities is a vacation I take during summers with the knowledge that I can return to enjoy every comfort of home. For this reason, I have committed myself to ensuring that people like Pooja and Gauri can one day enjoy a decent standard of living that I as an American have.

CONTACT INFORMATION

Keyword
TRUSCHOL

Students must *be nominated for this award and submit applications in conjunction with designated Truman Scholarship Faculty Representatives at their schools.*

Truman Scholarship Foundation
712 Jackson Place NW
Washington, DC 20006

E-mail: office@truman.gov
Website: www.truman.gov

RELATED AWARD PROGRAMS

For more information on a Related Award Program, enter the associated keyword in the "Enter a Keyword" box located in the Coach's Locker Room section of ScholarshipCoach.com

■ Andrew W. Mellon Fellowships in Humanistic Studies

Prestigious Mellon Fellowships are awarded to students entering graduate programs leading to doctorate degrees in the humanities. Eligible study areas include history, philosophy, women's studies, foreign language and literature, cultural anthropology, and English literature. Eighty-five students are awarded $17,500 stipends in addition to enough money to cover first-year tuition and fees. The online application is due in mid-December.

Keyword
ANDWMELL

■ Beinecke Scholarship Program

This program offers undergraduate juniors the opportunity to pursue graduate study in the social sciences, humanities, and the arts. To be eligible, students must be recipients of financial aid and attend one of the 100 participating colleges.

The 20 awards provided by the Sperry Fund consist of $2,000 given before graduate study begins, with an additional $30,000 awarded while students are in graduate school. Scholarships must be used within five years of receipt of the award. Nominations are due in mid-March.

Keyword
BEINSCHO

■ Jacob K. Javits Fellowship Program

This program is for undergraduate seniors and graduate students working toward a doctorate or MFA degree in the social sciences, arts, or humanities. Awards are up to $29,000 for each year of graduate study. Students complete an extensive application outlining future plans, academic accomplishments, and activities. Materials should be received by the U.S. Department of Education by late November.

Keyword
JAVITFELL

U.S. Foreign Service National High School Essay Contest

Many high school students might feel a little out of place waiting in line with a bunch of high-powered U.S. ambassadors. But that wasn't the case for Marguerite Gabriele, a high school sophomore from Dallas, Texas.

That's because Gabriele had been selected as the first-place winner in the United States Foreign Service National High School Essay Contest, an honor that includes not only thousands of dollars in college cash but also an opportunity to receive recognition at a special award presentation. "It was his [U.S. Secretary of State Colin Powell] day for granting ambassadorships," relates Gabriele, with a slight giggle. "Right before me they were granting the ambassadorship for Germany!"

The American Foreign Service Association (AFSA), which sponsors the program, awards cash prizes to the top three essay writers: a $2,500 first-place prize, a $1,250 second-place prize, and a $750 third-place award. The first-place winner also receives an all-expense-paid trip to Washington, D.C., for the special award ceremony (Gabriel's family also got to come) and the opportunity to have his or her essay published in *Foreign Service Journal,* a magazine for foreign affairs professionals. In addition, the top winner's high school or sponsoring organization receives a $500 check. (They'll love you!)

TARGET RECIPIENT

■ Grades 9–12

ENTRY REQUIREMENTS

Essay

DEADLINE

■ March

Keyword
USFOSERV

Money
Matters

Added
Bonus

To enter this annual essay contest, applicants must be in grades 9 through 12 and enrolled in a public or private school, parochial school, or high school correspondence program in the 50 states, District of Columbia, or U.S. territories. Although U.S. citizens attending schools overseas may also apply, children of members of the U.S. Foreign Service may not participate in the competition. To be considered for an award, essays must be between 750 and 1,000 words in length and must adhere to each year's specified essay topic.

Entries are due each year by early March, and award recipients are usually announced in late June.

A CLOSER LOOK

Each year's essay topic, which is usually broadly defined, relates directly to the role the U.S. Foreign Service plays in international affairs. Past essay topics have included issues related to global challenges, long-term diplomacy, and the role of the Foreign Service in the promotion of U.S. interests. Entry guidelines state that students are expected to spend a significant amount of time researching the topic and should formulate an answer that includes both scholarly opinion and independent thought. In addition to the essay, entrants must submit a comprehensive bibliography and a completed registration form.

Before essays are sent to the official judges, they are first screened for contest rules violations. According to Program Director Perri Green, "As many as 50 percent of the essays are rejected because students do not follow the established guidelines." Green states that the most common rules infractions include failing to attach a bibliography, forgetting to obtain the required signature of a sponsoring teacher, and including the entrant's name or

Marguerite Gabriele (right) is all smiles during her award presentation with Secretary of State Colin Powell. Gabriele estimates that she spent about 12 hours on her winning essay, spread out over the course of one month.

school name on pages other than the registration form (essays are judged anonymously).

After contest administrators screen the submissions, a panel of 10 to 15 judges—composed of educators from the Washington, D.C., area, former ambassadors, and other members of the AFSA—reviews each essay. Program administrators assign each judge a portion of the entries, and the judges score each essay according to four basic criteria:

- Analysis and quality of research (30 percent)

- Originality of thought (30 percent)

- Clarity of expression (30 percent)

- Syntax (10 percent)

Insider Info

The top five essays from each judge advance to the finalist round. Here, five judges read each essay, and program administrators rank each entry based on the cumulative scores from all five readings—with the top three in the rankings taking top honors. Although Green notes that there has never been a tie, she says that in such an event, each essay's cumulative score on the "originality of thought" criterion would determine the winner. (Translation: That's probably the most important judging factor.)

▌ COACH'S ANALYSIS

To start planning your essay, think strategically. Gabriele says that when writing her winning essay, she tried to think about the essay contest from the perspective of the sponsoring organization itself—contemplating the organization's motivation for giving away the money.

"You have to ask yourself, 'Why is the AFSA giving away this money?'" Gabriele explains. "It seemed they want to gain the interest of people who are not in the Foreign Service and to spread the knowledge about the importance of the Foreign Service."

To do additional detective work, Gabriele spent a few hours on the AFSA website trying to learn everything she could about the organization and its members. Gabriele then tried to emphasize, especially in the conclusion of her essay, the many diplomatic contributions of AFSA members to the well-being of the nation. More than just paying lip service, Gabriele brought credibility to her argument by backing it up with facts, figures, and quotes that supported the position: "I needed to show that I understood what the AFSA is all about. I figured they would display the first-place essay on their website. . . . My essay put the AFSA in a very good light." If you can cite such facts and figures from a source that other applicants would likely overlook, more power to you!

For more strategies on how to research the motivation of a scholarship's sponsor, see the first book in my scholarship trilogy, How to Go to College Almost for Free.

In addition, Gabriele employed another key tenet of effective scholarship essay writing: *Make your essay personal.* Although she did not refer to her grandfather in the initial draft of her essay, she added a description of her grandfather's military service to the version she eventually submitted. In fact, her essay potentially could have benefited from an even greater use of personal examples, anecdotes, and perspectives. The best thing about incorporating these personal details is that it makes the essay uniquely yours and helps your composition stand out better in the application pile.

TODAY'S GLOBAL CHALLENGE OF PEACEKEEPING: A LONG-TERM EFFORT OF DIPLOMACY

Winning
Entry

Marguerite Gabriele stresses in this essay excerpt the need for long-term diplomacy and the important work of America's diplomatic corps.

"Those who do not learn from history are doomed to repeat the mistakes of history." George Santayana first uttered this statement, as have countless historians and statesmen after him. More recently Madeline Albright, as the U.S. Secretary of State, reconfirmed Santayana's warning in an October 2000 interview with NBC's *Meet the Press*.

Repeatedly, statesmen and politicians have admonished us to heed the lessons of the past by pointing to World Wars, territorial disputes, and crimes against humanity. I see no reason to dispute their warnings; I can only venture a step farther exploring this issue: throughout our history, it is obvious that the efforts of peacekeeping require patient and long-term diplomacy and not only the intense bold strike of military intervention.

If America is to succeed in its efforts to end wars and to prevent crimes against humanity on a global scale, one bold strike is not enough. Rather, patient, long-term diplomacy is needed to obtain and sustain lasting peace. One can look to the past, as Santayana recommended, to discover why this is so. After World War I, Germany and some other countries were financially devastated and spiritually demoralized. They received no outside help to repair the damage the war had done to their way of life. The misguided efforts of some dictators in Germany, Italy, and Russia eventually led to the outbreak of World War II, just one generation later. Again, much destruction occurred: Nations were destroyed.

However, after the Second World War, leaders in the United States joined with other countries to rebuild the war-torn nations who had lost their governments and infrastructures to the bombings and fighting. Alliances were formed and programs were put in place to help millions of people throughout Europe and other parts of the world rebuild their countries and regain their prosperous way of life. Then U.S. President Harry S. Truman believed that the best way to further the cause of world peace and freedom and to protect America's role in world affairs was to take a strong international stand. Farsighted leaders such as Truman and Winston Churchill of Great Britain avoided the mistakes of the past by learning from it, as Santayana had advised. After much negotiation, preparation, and international cooperation, the Marshall Plan and the Truman Doctrine were put in place. As a result, the reconstruction of Europe and some Mediterranean countries became a reality.

Who helped to rebuild and to repair the devastated property and lives that the war had destroyed? In part, some of the U.S. servicemen promoted peace by remaining at their posts. My grandfather was one of the members of the American military who remained at posts overseas to ensure that peace and stability would be maintained long after the armistice was signed.

*   *   *

In the fifty-some years since the end of the Second World War, the members of the American Foreign Service have worked "quietly behind the scenes to achieve diplomatic and economic goals through skillful and subtle diplomacy that may take years to yield success." By their efforts of quiet diplomacy foreign service officers have "fought" during the Cold War, during the conflicts of Korea, Vietnam, and most recently in Croatia. About 12,000 U.S. employees and 9,500 foreign nationals at some 165 embassies and 100 consulates abroad comprise today's Service.

The need to remain diligent in peacekeeping efforts continues even today. While speaking to U.S. troops in Norfolk, Virginia, President George W. Bush emphasized the need, not only for military readiness, but for continued diligence in peacekeeping efforts. "We're witnessing a revolution in the technology of war, powers increasingly defined not by size but by mobility and swiftness," he said. "We will cooperate in the work of peace," he continued, assuring our allies worldwide that the United States will continue its ongoing, long-term commitment to global peacekeeping.

While heeding Santayana's words to learn from history yet keeping an eye to the future, one can conclude that our military servicemen, and no less importantly our Foreign Service officers, have helped to maintain global peace in the years since World War II. Day by day, task by task, Foreign Service officers report on and analyze political and economic developments, maintain good relations with host countries, negotiate international agreements, and interpret U.S. policies and interests for foreign governments. The members of the Foreign Service lessen the need for a strong blow of military force by standing silently, yet strongly, for peace.

For the complete text of Marguerite Gabriele's winning essay, visit the Coach's Locker Room at ScholarshipCoach.com (Keyword: USFOSERV).

CONTACT INFORMATION

Keyword **USFOSERV**

National High School Essay Contest
American Foreign Service Association
2101 E Street, NW
Washington, DC 20037

Phone: (202) 338-4045
Fax: (202) 338-6820
Website: www.afsa.org

RELATED AWARD PROGRAMS

For more information on a Related Award Program, enter the associated keyword in the "Enter a Keyword" box located in the Coach's Locker Room section of ScholarshipCoach.com

■ UNA-USA National High School Essay Contest

High school seniors compete with an essay of 1,500 words or less on a topic provided by the United Nations Association of the United States. Past topics have included "How can the nations of the world work together multilaterally to successfully address the problem of global warming?" and "The United Nations and the protection of human rights." Prizes range from $500 to $1,000. The deadline is in mid-April.

Keyword **UNAUSAHS**

■ Rotary International Ambassadorial Scholarships

Undergraduate juniors and seniors, graduate students, and professionals in any country with a local Rotary chapter are eligible for this travel award as long as a local Rotary club endorses the application. Students compete for approximately 1,000 awards of up to $25,000 each for study abroad. Local deadlines vary from March to July, but district applications are due by mid-December.

Keyword **ROTINTLS**

USA TODAY
All-USA Academic Teams

TARGET RECIPIENT

- High school seniors
- Two-year college students
- Undergraduates

ENTRY REQUIREMENTS

Activities & Credentials | Academic Info | Short Answer
Essay | Recommendation | Nomination

DEADLINES

- High school: February
- Two-year college: December
- Four-year college: November

| | Keyword |
| SCHOLARSHIP COACH.com | USAALLAC |

Money Matters

How would you like to join a high-profile team that recruits its members from all over the country, doesn't require you to wear a uniform, and doesn't even have any meetings or practices ... but *still* awards a fair amount of scholarship money to its members? Sound too good to be true? Well, it's not, if you're talking about the All-USA Academic Teams—three separate scholarship programs sponsored by the *USA TODAY* newspaper.

For each competitive program—one for graduating high school seniors, one for community and junior college students, and one for students at four-year institutions—20 top students are selected as "First Team" members. Each receives a $2,500 cash award. Additionally, 40 more students receive recognition as members of the "Second Team" and "Third Team," but do not receive any monetary awards.

Students must complete a written "nomination form," which includes a student essay, letters of recommendation, activity lists, awards and honors lists, and a transcript. High school applicants must also submit their SAT or ACT scores and a list of past and current enrollment in academically rigorous courses (such as honors, advanced placement [AP], International Baccalaureate [IB], or college-level classes).

High school juniors planning to graduate early may also apply.

To be eligible for the All-USA High School Academic Team competition, entrants must be high school seniors attending accredited U.S. high schools (including non–U.S. citizens and exchange students), home-schooled students pursuing a high school–level curriculum within the United States, or U.S. citizens enrolled in an accredited high school outside the United States. The application deadline for the high school competition is typically in mid- to late February, with the winners announced in mid-May.

To enter the All-USA College Academic Team competition, students must be full-time undergraduates at a four-year U.S. institution. However, U.S. citizenship is not required. Program rules classify a student as a full-time undergraduate if he or she is carrying at least 12 credits toward an undergraduate degree or, if not carrying the credit load, anticipates earning an undergraduate degree at the end of the current academic term. Entries for the college contest are due in late November, and the winners are announced in late February.

For the All-USA Two-Year College Academic Team competition, students must have completed at least 12 semester hours, must have a minimum 3.25 GPA, and must be expecting to graduate with an associate's degree by late August of the award year. Unlike the high school and four-year college competitions (which are administered directly by *USA TODAY*), the two-year college program is administered by Phi Theta Kappa, an international honor society for such colleges. Applications for this competition are due in early December; winners are announced in early April.

▌ A CLOSER LOOK

To apply for this program, students must be nominated. Most nominations, however, are traditionally a result of student initiative—the students *themselves* seeking out a nominator, rather than the other way around. In the high school competition, teachers and advisers nominate students, while for the four-year college program, professors serve as nominators. Community, technical, and junior college presidents may nominate up to two students for the two-year college competition. The high school and four-year college programs follow the same application and judging process, but the two-year college program follows a different procedure.

HIGH SCHOOL AND FOUR-YEAR COLLEGE PROGRAMS

To apply for the high school or four-year college programs, students must submit the following materials as part of their written nomination form:

- A 500-word description of the entrant's most outstanding intellectual endeavor

- A nomination letter written by the nominator

- Two additional letters of recommendation

- Lists of awards, honors, and extracurricular activities

- A description of individual academic and professional pursuits (such as internships, summer programs, research, and published work)

- An official transcript

The nominator's letter must address the merits of the specific intellectual endeavor selected by the student. If the endeavor happens to be a group project, the program requests that the student's individual role in the project be highlighted. The other requested recommendation letters are designed to give judges a more complete picture of the student and should cite specific examples that demonstrate how the applicant is exceptional.

Application materials specifically mention that students should not submit a prepackaged résumé instead of answering the specific questions in the specified format.

When providing the various lists requested in the application, applicants should list only the number of items requested—and should list them in order of importance. Listing more than the requested number of items could result in disqualification, and in any event, judges are instructed to read only the requested number of items. (So steer clear of this temptation!)

Each credential should be listed only once on the application. For example, an activity in which a student also won an award should be credited in only *one* list. Furthermore, according to competition guidelines, the brief description for each item listed should be limited to a sentence or two.

Officials from national education associations and representatives of colleges and universities serve as judges for the program. In the past, this has included officials from the American Association of School Administrators, the National Association of Secondary School Principals, the Department of Education, the National Education Association, the National Association of College Admissions Counselors, and the American Association of University Professors, to name just a few.

During the first round of judging for the program, the panel will use a scoring sheet when evaluating the applications. Points are assigned for each piece of information requested. For example, students will be given more points if they have both a high GPA and AP or IB courses, rather than just one or the other; the judges are scoring students on both their level of achievement and the comparative difficulty of the courses. The student's essay on his or her most outstanding intellectual achievement carries the greatest weight in the judging process. When reviewing each essay, judges evaluate originality, level of difficulty, potential or actual result, and significance to society.

TWO-YEAR COLLEGE PROGRAM

Because Phi Theta Kappa both administers the program and oversees the judging process, the application and judging criteria for the two-year college program is quite different from the other two *USA TODAY* teams. Students are expected to submit:

- A biographical questionnaire (interests, background, and future plans)

- Lists of leadership roles, community service, other activities, and honors and awards (do not duplicate listings)

- Three recommendations—one focusing on academic abilities, one on leadership abilities, and another on community involvement

- A transcript

- A 500-word essay about one educational experience at the two-year college that transformed the way the applicant thinks about learning and the future

- Essay responses to discussion questions on topics such as leadership examples you are most proud of and your most satisfying experience

The applications are evaluated in three different rounds of judging. The judges of each round score the nominations based on the lists of activities and recognition (worth up to 20 points), responses to the discussion questions (20 points), the essay (20 points), the transcript (5 points), and the recommendations (5 per recommendation).

During round one, three judges independently score each nomination, and the top 100 highest scorers are sent for the second round. Three more judges then independently score the nominations, and their top 60 nominations are forwarded to the third group of judges—12 judges who examine the 60 finalists and determine which students will comprise the First, Second, and Third teams.

COACH'S ANALYSIS

I've focused this Coach's Analysis on the high school and four-year college programs. For more tips on the two-year program, see the Coach's Locker Room at ScholarshipCoach.com (Keyword: USAALLAC).

As you might imagine, this scholarship program places a considerable amount of weight on such academic metrics as GPAs, standardized test scores, and advanced coursework. However, the part of the application that really does make or break your scholarship candidacy is the essay on your most outstanding intellectual endeavor.

What types of intellectual endeavors work well in the essay? Traditionally, those who have written essays about extensive research projects have dominated the winner's circle. Because this emphasis on research tends to apply best to students pursuing laboratory- or technology-based scientific inquiry, a high percentage of past winners have been accomplished scientists; many have also received recognition from the Intel Science Talent Search program, for example.

That being said, this *doesn't* mean that students who don't fit this profile can't bring home the scholarship bacon ("soy bacon" if you're a vegetarian). So to plan the strategic approach that is right for you, let's tackle this essay in three different ways: first from the perspective of a student who has done extensive scientific research, second from the perspective of a student who has done research in non-science fields, and third from the viewpoint of someone who hasn't done any research at all.

For those who have logged their share of hours in the science lab, make sure that your essay powerfully communicates your relentless intellectual creativity. Don't just focus on what the research was, but also discuss how you came up with the idea for the research, how

Keep in mind that the judges aren't scientists, so you want to be extremely clear in communicating your work, being sure not to rely on scientific jargon.

you intellectually overcame obstacles and challenges that surfaced during your research, and how your research was based on a new way of thinking that hadn't been done before.

"A lot of people could have done the actual research I did . . . they could have collected samples," states Ashley Hinerman-Mulroy, a First-Team scholarship winner from Wheeling, West Virginia, who wrote an essay about her research on biomining techniques for cleaning water pollution. "What made me unique is that I thought of the project on my own without someone having to tell me. It wasn't the physical research, it was coming up with the idea for the research."

For those who have done research in the humanities, you have the added challenge of showing that the academic rigors of your work are on par with that of science researchers. To do this, stress the intellectual and analytical processes behind your work, such as how you formulated your underlying research questions and how you proceeded to advance your thinking in a systematic way. Emphasize the aspects of your research that are well beyond anything that would be attempted as part of a class project, paper, or assignment.

Sherwin had undertaken this project as part of the National History Day competition (see page 251). Along with his project partner, Sherwin took second place nationally in the history contest.

First-Team winner Matthew Sherwin of Venetia, Pennsylvania, for instance, who wrote his essay about the process of creating a trifold display on a 1968 coal mine disaster, described in detail the process of personally interviewing disaster survivors, victims' families, politicians involved in reform legislation, and members of the media who covered the event. "They [program judges] are looking for students who have passion . . . for in-depth research and investigation," Sherwin explains. "I tried to show them this wasn't a rinky-dink display I slapped together the night before."

Sherwin also suggests highlighting the importance of your chosen field or research so that the judges can understand the greater implications of your work. Sherwin says that he "tried to stress in the essay why history is as important as science or technology, why studying history and having a knowledge of the past is important for us in society today."

If your most outstanding intellectual endeavor isn't at all research-based, the way in which you construct your essay is even more critical. One common mistake made by such entrants is describing their endeavor as an organizational, managerial, or leadership challenge, rather than as an intellectual, inventive, or academic one. To emphasize the intellectual aspects of the endeavor, you need to explore the analytical and investigative process behind the project you have pursued. If you chose to discuss a major community service undertaking, for instance, emphasize how your academic and intellectual abilities have been tested and challenged. If you can point to research others have done (such as in social science fields) that helped shape the underlying theory and philosophy behind your service project, this can also be an extremely effective strategy.

Past winners who fall into this category have pursued endeavors in the arts, journalism, website creation, public policy, and community service.

No matter which of the above categories you fit in, keep in mind that when scholarship judges ask you to discuss something that you have accomplished, the specifics of the accomplishment are only *part* of the story. Seek to explain not only *what* you did, but also *why* you did it. Try to demonstrate a sense of passion and enthusiasm to the judges, and illustrate how this attitude toward your field of interest has fueled your extensive endeavors. Remember, the "why" is just as significant as the "who," "what," "where," and "when."

ESSAY SUBMISSION

Winning

Entry

In response to a question about his most outstanding intellectual endeavor, Matthew Sherwin chose to detail his work on an in-depth historical research project.

> "When I try to understand what is happening today,
> I try to decide what will happen tomorrow;
> I look back; a page of history is worth a volume of logic."
>
> —Oliver Wendell Holmes

To take control of its future, a society must know from whence it came. Unfortunately, my generation often recognizes history solely as bland textbooks instead of a vibrant summation of our people's experiences. In order to satiate my drive to "understand what is happening today," I undertook an extensive research project last year regarding one of our nation's most important yet least discussed events.

In 1968, a year rife with social unrest and war escalation, a substantial turning point took place in the back-hills West Virginia town of Farmington. The normality of life would be forever shattered by a late November explosion at Consolidation Coal Company's #9 Mine. Seventy-eight miners perished; nineteen remain forever entombed in this "hollow of sorrows." Before Farmington, the coal mining industry ranked as one of the most hazardous in health and safety. After the passage of legislation fueled by the nation's attention acutely focused on Farmington, effective mine inspections and recognition of pneumoconiosis saved the lives of thousands.

My colleague Chris Hefferan and I spent months researching this oft-overlooked watershed. Our studies culminated in the presentation of a six-foot trifold exhibit adorned with artifacts and a bibliography in excess of 30 pages. Initiating our research, we visited Pittsburgh's Carnegie Library to collect secondary sources. Our best form of printed information, though, would come from primary sources—myriad newspapers, the *UMWA Journal,* and Consol archives. Yet to move from mere academic work into the realm of true historical analysis, we looked beyond the vested biases of union, media, and company by investigating first-hand the area so deeply torn by that fateful morning. Chris and I attended the somber memorial atop the portal where the first explosion blew hundreds of feet into the air. We ultimately interviewed individuals involved in every facet of the tragedy—media members, bereaved family, the rescue/recovery attempt coordinator, the Congressman who authored essential reform legislation (West Virginia's current Secretary of State), and the UMWA Secretary-Treasurer. Gary Martin, the last man pulled alive from the mine, offered our most personal interview as he described his ascent from the 600-foot shaft in a makeshift bucket minutes before an explosion utterly decimated the mine.

Chris and I made a formidable team; my roles included writing the bibliography, formatting/constructing the exhibit, initiating and conducting research, and presenting our findings to the National History Day panel. While our exhibit did take second place in the nation, we believe a much greater feat was accomplished. Awareness of the turning point increased throughout our school (where the exhibit was displayed), community (where our research was documented), and \ our nation (where NHD presents the most original and difficult historical research). Our exhibit will eventually be displayed in a museum in Farmington, where we hope it will honor the men who sacrificed their lives and remind our generation of the "volume of logic" shared in our collective history.

CONTACT INFORMATION

High School and Four-Year College:

All-USA Academic Team
USA TODAY
7950 Jones Branch Drive
McLean, VA 22108-9995

Phone: (703) 854-5890
E-mail: allstars@usatoday.com
Website: www.usatoday.com/life/academic/hsform.htm

Two-Year College:

All-USA Academic Team Competition
Center for Excellence
1625 Eastover Drive
Jackson, MS 39211

Phone: (601) 957-2241 ext. 560
E-mail: Clancy.Mitchell@ptk.org
Website: www.ptk.org/schol/aaat/announce.htm

RELATED AWARD PROGRAMS

For more information on a Related Award Program, enter the associated keyword in the "Enter a Keyword" box located in the Coach's Locker Room section of ScholarshipCoach.com

■ Josephine de Kármán Fellowship Trust

This program awards undergraduate seniors in any major and graduate students beginning the last year of any Ph.D. program. Application materials include recommendations, activity lists, a 250- to 300-word statement about long-term objectives and proposed research, and a two-page statement with additional information. Ten $8,000 awards are given each year. Applications should be postmarked by a deadline in late January; Fellows will be notified in mid-April.

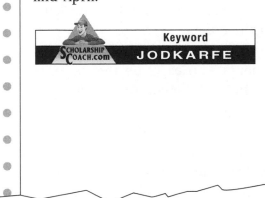

Keyword
JODKARFE

■ Toyota Community Scholars Program

High school seniors are selected based on leadership, scholastics, and community service. Students compete for 100 awards ranging from $10,000 to $20,000. Submission materials include information about academic activities, school participation, community service, and awards and honors, as well as a transcript, recommendation letters, and test scores. Entrants are also asked to write short-essay responses to questions. Recent questions have included "Which one of the activities listed do you find most rewarding or personally satisfying?" Preliminary applications are due by early December; semifinalist applications are due in late March.

Keyword
TOYOCOMM

Voice of Democracy

Those who say talk is cheap evidently haven't entered the Voice of Democracy "audio essay" contest—a lucrative awards program sponsored by the Veterans of Foreign Wars (VFW).

The premise for this contest is straightforward: Students write an essay on a patriotic topic that will be three to five minutes long when read aloud. The entrants then record themselves reading the essay and submit the tape to the VFW competition.

Open to high school students in grades 9 through 12 (in public, private, parochial, or home-study programs), the contest is not only for those who are natural public speakers: At no point in the competition are entrants asked to give a live speech.

Students who excel on the national level, after advancing through local and department levels, can receive a first-place $25,000 prize, a $16,000 second-place prize, or various other top-level awards. Approximately 30 other national winners will each receive $1,000, and various other awards will be given to students at the preliminary levels. First-place award recipients from each VFW department receive a trip to Washington, D.C., for a tour of historic landmarks and a chance to interact with other winners.

The audio essays are due in early November. Winners are contacted in February.

TARGET RECIPIENT

■ Grades 9–12

ENTRY REQUIREMENTS

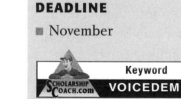

DEADLINE

■ November

Keyword
VOICEDEM
SCHOLARSHIP Coach.com

Money Matters | Added Bonus

There are 54 VFW departments, including all 50 states, the District of Columbia, Europe, Pacific areas, and Latin America.

▌ A Closer Look

Each entrant's 3- to 5-minute audio essay is expected to address each year's unique essay topic. Past topics, which are always very general, have included "Reaching Out to America's Future," "My Voice in Our Democracy," and "America's Role for the Next Century."

Because judging for this competition is based solely on the audio essays, each submission is expected to be of good quality—clear, understandable, and free of static and other noises. Gordon Thorson, the program director for the Voice of Democracy contest, recommends recording the tape at a local radio station, if possible. In fact, some VFW posts have set up recording arrangements for entrants with local broadcasters. Many national winners have scored well, however, using home recordings. Entrants are also permitted to re-record their audio presentation as many times as needed throughout all levels of the competition—for example, after advancing to the next round of judging—as long as they follow their original script.

Past winners of the Voice of Democracy competition include Charles Kuralt, the late CBS television news broadcaster.

Students should be sure to follow the time guidelines set by contest administrators, although entrants are given a 5-second grace period in meeting the time restrictions. Note that anything more than a 5-second discrepancy will result in automatic disqualification.

The official judging scorecard for the Voice of Democracy contest uses a 100-point scale in which *originality* and *content* are each worth 40 points and *delivery* is worth the remaining 20 points. The judges score the originality of the student's audio presentation according to three basic subcategories: *imaginative approach* (15 points), *positive message* (15 points), and *human interest* (10 points). Likewise, judges evaluate the content of the presentation according to three subcategories: *relates to theme* (15 points), *theme development* (15 points), and *clarity of ideas* (10 points). Finally, the oral delivery of the essay comprises two subcategories: *clarity of expression* (10 points) and *believability* (10 points). "For those who win on a national level," said Thorson, "most every judge has scored them 85 or better."

On the local level, contest judges typically include individuals with backgrounds in broadcasting, teaching, journalism, and law. All contestants are judged solely on the basis of their audio presentations; although speech scripts are submitted, judges are not permitted to evaluate the spelling, punctuation, or sentence structure of the speech script itself. Before judging the current year's contestants, judges frequently listen to a tape of last year's winners. (This is a great idea for you, too.)

On the national level, two different judging panels score the presentations over a two-day period. On the first day, 10 to 12 judges—including representatives from the English departments at American University and Georgetown University, the editor of the official VFW magazine, and past heads of the VFW and VFW Ladies Auxiliary—listen to the audio presentations of the 54 winners from the 50 states plus four other regions. Although judges are permitted to discuss and debate the presentations, they typically score the presentations without any discussion. In totaling the first-day judges' ballots, both the highest and lowest scores are thrown out, and the scores of the remaining eight to ten judges are added together. The contestants with the top five scores advance to the second day of judging.

For the second day of national judging, a new "blue ribbon" panel is convened. Such judging panels have included U.S. Senator John Glenn; Federal Communications Commission (FCC) Director Michael Powell; and individuals from major television broadcast networks, the U.S. State Department, and the U.S. House of Representatives. A tabulation of the second-day judging scoresheets determines the prize levels of the five top winners.

For audio clips of winning Voice of Democracy entries, see the Coach's Locker Room at ScholarshipCoach.com (Keyword: VOICEDEM).

Insider Info

■ COACH'S ANALYSIS

An analysis of past winning Voice of Democracy entries reveals that the top winners have usually been the best storytellers—individuals who could make an emotional connection with judges by communicating an especially poignant, inspiring, or personal story that illustrates important lessons for our nation.

Lindsey Liberatore was awarded first prize for her moving speech entitled "What Price Freedom." Although it would have been fun to take this big check into the bank, she was later given a smaller one to deposit.

First-place winner Lindsey Liberatore of Lakeville, Massachusetts, described the moving experience of visiting the Vietnam Memorial with her father—a veteran who had lost his best friend in the war—as a way of illustrating the true price of freedom. Another first-place winner, Mitchell Warner of Provo, Utah, told the tale of Gail Halverson, a pilot who air-dropped candy to the children of West Berlin, to illustrate the importance of taking simple actions in support of freedom and democracy.

Compared to programs like the American Legion Oratorical Contest (see page 18) and the Sons of the American Revolution Rumbaugh Oration (see page 271), the Voice of Democracy contest places a *lesser* emphasis on researching and citing historical facts or proposing solutions for the future. The style of the oral presentation is also different: For this contest, strive to be less like a political speechmaker and more like a dramatic storyteller. Good role models include Garrison Keillor of National Public Radio's "Prairie Home Companion" or Paul Harvey and his famous "The Rest of

This strategy makes sense given the program's roots: Created and originally sponsored by the National Association of Broadcasters, the Voice of Democracy program was taken over by the VFW in 1960.

the Story" radio segment (although you don't have to be anywhere near as good as these seasoned professionals to win).

When trying to brainstorm a story or narrative to include, try thinking about your own personal experiences; talking to grandparents, parents, teachers, neighbors, and friends; and consulting historical reference materials. Remember that the *telling* of the story itself is only part of your audio essay: The story needs to be directly related to each year's contest topic and, like a parable, should communicate some important truths, principles, or moral lessons.

Remember to practice your delivery repeatedly; because this competition is judged by audiotape, the quality of your voice is extremely important: An emotionally charged, passionate delivery conveys credibility and believability.

"When you read with emotion, you capture the judges' attention and tug at their heartstrings. It's all about the inflection in your voice," emphasizes fourth-place national winner James Smith, who concedes that, compared to the first-place winner, he was still too "elegant and proper" in style.

Insider Info

Finally, to give your entry the best possible chance to win, avoid a common mistake that many prior entrants have made: According to Thorson, many applicants include well-known quotes, such as several by President Kennedy, that have been repeated so frequently that they have become clichés. "The judges will actually keep track of how many times certain quotes are used," Thorson reveals. "Don't use popular quotes. They detract from the essay." Instead, if you want to use quotes, use lesser-known ones that still convey your message.

Lindsey Liberatore
Lakeville, MA
First Place
$25,000

WHAT PRICE FREEDOM?

Winning
Entry

In this transcript of her winning audio essay, Lindsey Liberatore describes the cost of freedom in terms of those soldiers who gave their lives in the fight for it.

Names. Thousands of names, all carved delicately and precisely into panels of marble, and together these names form what is commonly called the Wall. They are the names of those soldiers killed in the Vietnam War. The names of those soldiers, who fought and died for the sake of an idea, for the sake of an idea known as freedom. Like those who came before and after them, they gave their lives to aid in the achievement of this idea. They were killed for fighting for a common cause, and will be forever remembered and honored for their sacrifice.

I first visited this monument when I was three years old. I went with my father, and have always thought that my memories of that visit were a dream. I can remember the way my father looked. He was wearing very dark sunglasses, and was kneeling, touching one of the thousands of names before him. I walked over to his side, and he lifted me up into his arms as we walked away. When we returned home, I recall asking my mother, "What's the matter with Daddy?" She simply said that he was sad, for what reason I didn't understand at the time.

It wasn't until last week that I learned this memory was not in fact a dream but had actually happened. I also learned why my father had been so "sad." I have always known that my father served in the Marines, and was in combat in Vietnam, but never knew the full extent of the ordeal he went through. In 1967, he reported to boot camp on Parris Island in South Carolina. A young man named Steve was also sent to training in the same platoon. Almost instantaneously, the two became inseparable.

They spent every waking minute making light of every situation possible, whether it be scrubbing the mess hall with toothbrushes or having to remake their bunks if a dime didn't bounce to a certain height when dropped onto the surface. They became best friends. The two survived boot camp, but were separated when my father was sent to Vietnam. However, to each one's surprise they met again, and were stationed together during part of their tours.

It was like they never spent any time apart. The jokes and pranks started again, and the good times surpassed the bad. Never did the two think about the distinct possibility that one would make it back home without the other. My father was on a base, making arrangements to report home, when he learned of Steve's death. There was an explosion in the ammunition pit, and Steve was one of the several fatalities. His name now lies on panel twenty-five of the Wall, and it was there that my father knelt, tears streaming down his face unhidden by his sunglasses thirteen years ago.

When I was working on this paper, and trying to determine what freedom really means, and how one can possibly put a price on something that indefinable, my father said something that truly made me think. After telling me his story, he stated that most people might never know the true price of freedom. They will take their freedom for granted, and accept it as a given, until the threat of it being taken away is poised, or until they lose someone they love to the idea of freedom.

My father said that every day he thinks of Steve, and when I was born he thought of Steve, and when he taught me to ride my bike he thought of Steve, and when he taught me to drive he thought of Steve. He thought of what he has been able to experience and Steve could not, and he thought of just how much was sacrificed to obtain freedom for all.

Our world has lost a countless number of individuals to the fight for freedom, and we will give our all to keep it within reach. We mourn for the sacrifices we have all had to make, but we will always work to never lose sight of our freedom. We will always work to appreciate just how beautiful and precious freedom is, in all its definitions. We will always feel blessed to be allowed the chance to express ourselves, and be thankful for our personal freedom. We will always hold what we may not realize close to our hearts—we will hold our freedom close to our hearts.

For all of these reasons, and for many more, for Steve and my father, and all those who have made sacrifices; I have come to the conclusion that the idea, or rather the ideal of freedom is, and always will be, priceless.

AMERICA'S ROLE
FOR THE NEXT CENTURY

Winning
Entry

In his winning entry, Mitchell Warner shows how the simple act of a young pilot sets the standard for America's role on a global stage.

1945. Berlin has been divided. The western sector is cut off from the rest of the free world, surrounded on every side by communist armies. West Berliners look for shelter in bombed out buildings and scramble desperately to find something to eat. Then, almost miraculously, allied pilots, risking their lives, begin to airlift food and supplies every day through hostile communist air space. And Berlin survives.

Among these courageous pilots is Gail Halverson. While unloading supplies, young Halverson is drawn to the barbed wire fence surrounding Templehof Air Base in West Berlin. There he sees the frightened faces of children for whom hope is all but lost.

Wanting to help them, he collects his fellow pilots' gum and candy rations, ties them to handkerchief parachutes, and drops them to the waiting children as he flies over West Berlin. Word spreads of this young pilot's unauthorized generosity. The story of the Candy Bomber captures the world's imagination.

Soon candy companies throughout the free world begin shipping gum and candy to Templehof Air Base. Mailbags filled with thank-you letters and returned parachutes from the children of West Berlin overflow Lieutenant Halverson's mail slot. The operation grows until it becomes a recognized unit of the United States Air Force. During a single year, young Halverson and his squadron drop 23 tons of candy to the imprisoned children of West Berlin.

To those children, the young American pilot gave more than a few moments of pleasure. To them and to the rest of the oppressed world, he gave hope. Day after day, looking up at the American flag painted on the sides of the planes overhead, these children were assured that there is a country that cares. A country where citizens live in freedom, choose their own leaders, and act generously towards the rest of the world. This instilled hope in these children— hope that one day their country too might be free. In the hearts of others around the globe watching the drama in Berlin, a young American pilot's simple act planted hope and the sweet possibility of freedom and democracy.

Today there are still blockaded Berlins. All across the world men, women, and children are yearning to be free. America's role in the next century must be what it has always been—to kindle and fan the flame of hope in oppressed people, and their dreams of freedom might be realized.

As Americans we must combine our simple acts to maintain the standard of freedom and democracy for the world. Simple acts—like making certain that we vote in every election for dedicated people who know the difference between right and wrong. Working to make our communities safe. Learning and passing on the stories from our history that tell of the heavy price that patriots paid for our freedom. Teaching each other the responsibilities of citizenship. Serving as volunteers to help those in need. These are things patriots do. These are things you and I can do. And you know what? They're not that hard. In fact, they are as simple as dropping candy to the children of West Berlin.

I visited with Gail Halvorsen. He repeated the words of children pleading with him as winter was closing in, "Keep flying, even if you cannot land your planes. We can survive without rations, but if we lose our freedom we will never get it back."

Keep flying. That's what the world is asking America still. Keep helping us win and preserve our freedom. Keep doing what you've always done to be an ensign to all who seek liberty.

Every child that caught a parachute caught hope—hope for freedom, hope for democracy, hope for peace. The simple act of a young American pilot responding to the need he saw created hope—the first step towards that nation's freedom. I've come to understand that the simple things you and I do make America the nation that can give hope to all people.

This must be the role of America in the next century: to be the standard bearer of hope for freedom and democracy, to all the world.

CONTACT INFORMATION

Keyword **VOICEDEM**

Students should contact their local VFW post for more information.

Voice of Democracy
VFW National Headquarters
Kansas City, MO 64111

Phone: (816) 968-1117
E-mail: info@vfw.org
Website: www.vfw.org

RELATED AWARD PROGRAMS

For more information on a Related Award Program, enter the associated keyword in the "Enter a Keyword" box located in the Coach's Locker Room section of ScholarshipCoach.com

■ VFW Youth Essay Competition

Students in grades 7 and 8 may enter this essay competition. Applicants' 300- to 400-word essays on chosen themes are submitted to local chapters for judging and forwarding to the national contest. Past theme choices have included "What Freedom Means to Me" and "Is Freedom Really Free?" National winners receive savings bonds ranging from $1,000 to $10,000. Local chapters should have the essays by early December.

Keyword **VFWYOESS**

■ Radio and Television News Directors Association Scholarships

Here's a program for undergraduate students of any major who want to pursue an interest in radio or television. The association awards scholarships ranging from $1,000 to $10,000. The different awards have various requirements (some including minority status, financial need, and grade level). Applica-

tions—including a résumé, three samples of journalistic work, a recommendation, and information about professional intentions—are due by an early-May deadline.

Keyword **RADTVNEW**

■ And Now . . . A Word from Our Planet

Students are invited to become a "spokesperson for the earth" by composing a radio ad intended to educate listeners about the relationship between the environment and human population pressures. The ad scripts should be 30 seconds long and are expected to focus on a short topic chosen by the administrators. Past topics have included pollution, global warming, and shortages. Cash awards of $500 to $1,000 are available. Participants must enter before the February deadline.

Keyword **ANDNOWPL**

Washington Crossing Foundation Scholarships

TARGET RECIPIENT

- High school seniors

ENTRY REQUIREMENTS

DEADLINE

- January

Keyword
WCROSSIN

Money
Matters

When asked about George Washington's crossing of the Delaware River during the American Revolution, many students who have seen the famous painting might ask, "Wasn't he the guy standing up in the boat?"

Not content to allow Washington's decisive and brave action—an action that turned the tide of America's fight for independence—to be remembered only through that one well-known painting, the Washington Crossing Foundation offers valuable scholarships to high school seniors at American schools who want to pursue careers related to government service.

A variety of awards are offered, including at least five awards of $10,000, $7,500, $5,000, $2,500, and $1,500. (Additional awards are usually given each year.) Because Washington crossed the Delaware River in Pennsylvania, residents from this state are also eligible for additional awards of $20,000, $5,000, and two awards of $1,000 each.

The entry requirements for this scholarship competition include a transcript, standardized test scores (SAT, ACT, PSAT), recommendation letters, and a list of activities. Applicants also must submit an essay of 300 words or less discussing their career goals.

Completed applications are due by the mid-January deadline. Winners are notified in April.

▌ A CLOSER LOOK

Applicants for the Washington Crossing Foundation scholarships are expected to demonstrate experience in all types of community and school activities, as well as academic excellence and a dedication to public service. Program guidelines specify that the 300-word essay should be a single-page submission that incorporates:

- ▌ A specific career choice

- ▌ A reason why the career has been chosen

- ▌ A clear understanding of career requirements

- ▌ Steps that have been taken in preparing for the career

- ▌ A statement of how Washington's crossing of the Delaware has influenced the student's career path

Students must also submit at least one letter of recommendation from their principal or school guidance counselor. You may also include additional recommendations from other individuals—something especially important if your principal or your counselor doesn't know you very well.

Entrants also may submit additional supporting materials of their choosing. Some past applicants, for instance, have included a résumé of community service and school activities, along with a list of awards and honors received as a result of these activities. Students have the option of providing additional recommendations from other school and community leaders who can speak knowledgably about their activities.

Every document should be submitted in triplicate and collated into three separate, stapled packets. Nothing should be mailed separately: Recommendations and transcripts should be included before sending off the entire packet.

The initial judging committee is composed of about ten members, including one member from the board of trustees, one former scholarship winner, one educator, and additional members of the foundation. The judging methodology for the contest is subjective; each judge is permitted to use his or her own methodology.

"Our committee runs the gamut of professions," says Walter Robson, scholarship coordinator for the Foundation. "Each judge has his or her own parts that they want to emphasize. Some will look at extracurricular activities, some will look at grades." If a student doesn't have strong grades, Robson notes, other factors can compensate. "Some who have had outstanding preparation for a career can get by with a lesser GPA than some of the others."

As for the essay itself, Robson says that the judging committee generally looks for three things: (1) evidence of how the students have prepared themselves for their intended career through the leadership qualities they have exhibited, (2) their sincere intentions to achieve their stated goal (as expressed through past and current activities), and (3) their honesty about the influence Washington's actions have had on their decisions. Student applications that do not properly address *each* of these areas will be eliminated.

Students that meet the standards of the program are named semifinalists. At this stage in the judging, students *may* be interviewed over the phone if a judging committee member so desires. After the 50 or so finalists are named, *all* students left in the competition undergo phone interviews. Judges conduct interviews individually or in pairs, and then share information with the rest of the committee. The committee as a group then makes all final award decisions.

One past applicant, who hoped to someday serve as a diplomat in a French-speaking country, was interviewed in French.

According to Robson, the questions asked in the interviews are tailored for each individual student. "It can be almost anything. It will be based on what's in their application; it will be based on general knowledge," he says. "There will be some thought-provoking questions to see how well they think on their feet. A common question is to ask applicants to tell us what they would like to accomplish through government."

▌ COACH'S ANALYSIS

To do well as an applicant for any scholarship sponsored by a group with a particularly strong agenda or perspective, you should be able to clearly recognize and understand their unique viewpoint. This is especially important for the Washington Crossing Foundation program.

Not only do members of the Foundation have a deep appreciation for the contributions of George Washington, but many past winners have also characterized them as quite politically conservative. With this in mind, you will want to highlight the aspects of your record that would appeal to a group with these political leanings.

One Washington Crossing winner I interviewed did exactly this: After reviewing literature about the organization and talking to a past winner from his area, he thought hard about "the things I have done that they would value the most." In the application, he decided to emphasize his training as an Eagle Scout—developing an example of how he learned the importance of service to one's country. Characterizing his own political views as "conservative on economic issues, but liberal on social issues," he steered clear of anything that could be especially controversial to the scholarship sponsors, recognizing that "it's a good way to rile somebody up if you pick the wrong thing."

Of particular concern to a good many applicants is the challenge of seamlessly relating their career goals to inspiration derived from our famous Revolutionary War general and first U.S. president. (I'm assuming that you

For the sake of accuracy, I should mention that George Washington's cherry-tree exploits and famed wooden teeth are generally considered to be myths.

Make sure that your historical facts are 100 percent correct. Every year, numerous applications are thrown out because the essays contain inaccurate information. If there's one group that knows the details of Washington's crossing like it happened yesterday, it's the members of the Washington Crossing Foundation!

don't want to be a professional cherry-tree remover or wooden-tooth dental hygienist.) Although there are many creative ways to make this connection in the Washington Crossing essay, the standard method employed by many past winners is to pursue four major objectives:

1. Briefly describe what Washington did in his historic crossing.
2. Highlight the lessons and symbolism of that event.
3. Relate those lessons and symbolism to you and your future career.
4. Describe your future career goals with passion and enthusiasm, explaining clearly how this relates to government service.

One winner, for instance, described how George Washington employed his best judgment, knowledge, and instinct when making his historic crossing of the Delaware River, and then related Washington's bold maneuver to his own efforts to chart a course toward a career as an electrical or computer engineer at the National Security Agency (NSA). He also emphasized how working for the NSA could help preserve the security established by George Washington and help protect American interests as the nation faces new challenges more than 200 years after Washington's feat.

The trick here is to not get bogged down in the "George Washington" aspects of your essay. After all, they aren't awarding the scholarship to Big George himself! So keep the focus on you and your career goals. To instill your essay with credibility, avoid the temptation to overstate the George Washington connection: Unless it's truly the case, it really is not wise to claim that you spend every waking moment contemplating Washington's historic crossing. (Then again, if this is actually true, you may want to consider taking up a hobby or getting a pet.)

If you're still having problems relating Washington's crossing to your career, try this simple exercise: List on a sheet of paper the admirable qualities Washington exhibited, then list alongside those qualities the ways that you, too, have exhibited or intend to exhibit such admirable personal traits. "Read about the event, understand what happened, and treat it as a symbol," another winner advises. "Then ask yourself, 'What is the meaning of this symbol, and how could this symbol be applied to you?'"

CONTACT INFORMATION

Keyword
WCROSSIN

The Washington Crossing Foundation
P.O. Box 503
Levittown, PA 19058-0503

Phone: (215) 949-8841
Website: www.gwcf.org

RELATED AWARD PROGRAMS

For more information on a Related Award Program, enter the associated keyword in the "Enter a Keyword" box located in the Coach's Locker Room section of ScholarshipCoach.com

■ U.S. Senate Youth Program

This program awards two high school juniors and seniors from each state who are serving in an elected position. Winners receive a $2,000 scholarship and travel to Washington, D.C., for a week of interaction with top government leaders. The application process varies by state but is based on student activities and knowledge of U.S. government and politics. State deadlines also vary, but the program's sponsor, the Hearst Foundation, must receive the names of the 104 selected delegates by the early-December deadline.

	Keyword
SCHOLARSHIP COACH.com	USSENPRO

■ James Madison Fellowships

Seeking to bolster education about the Constitution within American high schools, the James Madison Foundation encourages prospective teachers through financial aid packages. Students pursuing an MA, an MA in Teaching, or a Master of Education—all with a concentration related to American history or political science—are eligible to apply. Recip-

ients are expected to teach one full year for every year of the award. Awards can range up to $24,000 per year. Transcripts, recommendations, and a 600-word essay on the Constitution are due by early March.

	Keyword
SCHOLARSHIP COACH.com	JAMADFEL

■ Public Employees Roundtable Public Service Scholarships

Undergraduate and graduate students who are interested in pursuing a career in the public sector can apply for this program. Applicants submit transcripts, lists of all public-service experience, recommendations from supervisors, and a two-page essay on a question provided by the administrators. One past question was "How will your work in the public sector help improve the public image of government employment?" Undergraduate awards are $1,000. Graduate awards are $500. Applications are due before the deadline in late May.

	Keyword
SCHOLARSHIP COACH.com	PUBEMPLR

Young Naturalist Awards

TARGET RECIPIENT

■ Grades 7–12

ENTRY REQUIREMENTS

Project Essay Art and Graphics

DEADLINE

■ January

Keyword
ScholarshipCoach.com **YONATURE**

Money
$
Matters

This program is sponsored by the American Museum of Natural History and administered by the Alliance for Young Artists and Writers, so students should be spot-on with their scientific facts and the writing style of their submissions.

If you enjoy slithering around in the marshes looking for rare insects, exploring caves in search of bat droppings, or squinting into a microscope at tiny critters sandwiched between sheets of clear glass, then lace up your hiking boots and run to the nearest Young Naturalist Awards application.

All students in grades 7 through 12 in the United States, U.S. territories, and Canada (as well as U.S.-sponsored schools abroad) are eligible to explore the natural world through their own earth science, biology, or astronomy expeditions and then submit an illustrated essay about their findings.

At each grade-level category, the program awards various scholarship prizes: Two students from each eligible grade will receive $500 (grade 7), $750 (grade 8), $1,000 (grade 9), $1,500 (grade 10), $2,000 (grade 11), or $2,500 (grade 12). These 12 national winners are also invited to attend an awards ceremony at the American Museum of Natural History in New York. In addition, 36 finalists will each receive small cash awards of up to $50.

Students may submit one of two different types of essays: a narrative essay or an essay focusing on field-journal entries. Essay word limits vary from 500 to 3,000 words, depending on a student's grade level.

Entries are due in early January.

A Closer Look

All 7th- through 12th-grade students who embark on an interesting scientific expedition involving the natural sciences may enter the competition each year—even if they have won the competition before.

Warning: Some past applicants have submitted entries that are not focused on the natural sciences. You may have a great project that could win first place in another competition, but make sure that your entry conforms to the program guidelines.

Students writing narrative essays should communicate their objectives, methods, and findings, but also should describe the expedition and the thought processes behind it in an entertaining way as if the reader were actually coming along for the ride. Entries focusing on field journals should address the same sorts of details by using excerpts from field-journal entries—including field sketches, observations, and details about data collection and results. All projects should incorporate original illustrations, maps, or photographs from the expedition.

As entrants get older, more is expected of their essay submissions. Students in grades 7 and 8 should submit an essay between 500 and 2,000 words, while students in grades 9 and 10 should write a 750- to 2,500-word composition. Students in grades 11 and 12 are expected to turn in the most in-depth projects—essays ranging from 1,000 to 3,000 words. According to program director Chuck Wentzel, older students tend to submit essays with "a more traditional academic feel," and usually demonstrate a better understanding of data collection and interpretation methods.

The judging panel for the competition includes professionals from a variety of fields. Past judges include curators and vice presidents from the American Museum of Natural History, the editor of *Natural History* magazine, and scientists from the National Center for Science Literacy, Education, and Technology. In particular, judges look for evidence of "observation, research, analysis, and interpretation in your writing and visuals." Judges also want to see that the student is accurate and clear, and has developed a strong personal voice.

▮ Coach's Analysis

Many entrants in the Young Naturalist competition never have a chance to win because they pick the wrong type of project topic from the very start. Such students choose topics that don't provide them with an opportunity to flex their observational and investigational muscles. On the contrary, your expedition should be a personal one in which you have the opportunity to collect information on your own, first-hand.

As someone who manages the submitted entries each year, Wentzel notes that, of late, the entrant pool has been "heavy on space projects" even though "most of these students have not been in outer space." Because more *personal* explorations usually win, you should attempt something like a space project only if you have access to samples and specimens (via a museum, perhaps) that allow you to make personal observations and collect your own data.

In looking at past winners of every age, the most successful expeditions have been those conducted very close to home (such as in the entrant's backyard), explorations that were part of school-affiliated field trips (such as to a wilderness area), or projects related to a family vacation in an interesting natural locale. Each of these types has its own distinct advantages. Projects you can do near your house give you the ability to observe things easily over an extended period of time (especially important if you are attempting to write a field journal). Projects that are part of formal school activities allow you to draw upon the knowledge and guidance of teachers as well as resources that you may not have access to as an individual. Projects that are offshoots of family vacations often enable you to travel to more exotic places than you would be able to see otherwise. Young Naturalist winner Frieda Shmuel, a seventh-grader from East Meadow, New York, did her project on the salt of the Dead Sea after visiting

Summer break is a great occasion to conduct your Young Naturalist expedition.

Israel with her family. The bottom line is that you should pick a project area that maximizes the resources you have available to you.

Also consider the artistic implications of the project you choose. If you are a skilled artist, pick a topic that plays to your artistic strengths. (Hand-drawn illustrations add a wonderfully personal touch.) Young Naturalist winner Susan Wiedmeyer, a 10th-grader from Mukwonago, Wisconsin, chose to explore her wooded backyard—an "expedition" that allowed her to showcase her skills in drawing animals. If you're not as comfortable with a pen and paper, pick a project that gives you an opportunity to shoot interesting and communicative photographs. You've heard that a picture is worth a thousand words; choose a project that gives you the best chances at strong visuals.

Once you've chosen your winning topic, the next step is to understand the typical elements of Young Naturalist winning entries. In general, Young Naturalist winners:

The program discourages students from using illustrations or photographs they have not produced themselves. If a presentation will benefit from professional images, they are permitted, but they must be attributed and balanced by the student's own graphics.

After you've incorporated these points, have a teacher review your entry to ensure that all points are fully covered.

- ▌ Provide a vivid description of the environment in which their expedition takes place (usually this occurs at the beginning of the essay and is in the first person)

- ▌ Include scientific data that they gathered themselves (this gets more important as you climb the age-division categories)

- ▌ Document their procedure for gathering this data, paying special attention to the scientific method

- ▌ Perform research into the academic discipline related to their expedition and include relevant facts and figures in their essays (most winners include substantial bibliographies)

- ▌ Convey a sense of amazement at, and fascination with, the wonders of natural science

So get your sunscreen on, your trail mix out, and your notepad ready. This is one fun project assignment that can also yield some substantial college dough.

Frieda Shmuel
East Meadow, NY
Grade 7 Winner
$500

Winning
Entry

AN ESSENTIAL MINERAL

In her entry, Frieda Shmuel, age 12, describes a family trip to the Dead Sea and her explorations into the wonderful world of salt. The graphics on pages 348 and 349 were submitted as part of her winning entry.

After eight days in Israel, a country full of fascinating features, traveling from the Western Wall in ancient Jerusalem to Hamat Gader, where hot springs and alligators are your only cares, I didn't think anything could ever astound me again. That was until I saw the Dead Sea.

I don't think I will ever forget the drive in our van going from Masada to the Dead Sea. I remember very well driving down that mountain and looking at the sea below. There were signs written in three languages—Hebrew, Arabic, and English—all along the way. They said *200 meters above sea level . . . 100 meters above sea level . . . sea level . . . 100 meters below sea level . . . 200 meters below sea level*, all the way down to *400 meters below sea level.*

That wasn't the only thing that occurred that day which was unforgettable. After we, my family and I, arrived at the Dead Sea, we went to a nearby restaurant. After having a small snack consisting of bourekas and a drink of water, we got ready to go into the unrealistically hot water. Stepping into the Dead Sea was like stepping into a hot cup of tea. The average air temperature is 102 degrees F, even in the heart of the winter, and the water temperature reflects this heat.

When we were only up to our knees in the sea, we had trouble keeping our feet down. They would still float up. It was like trying to keep a helium balloon on the ground; if you let the balloon go, it would rise up. When we were into the water up to our waist, we just let go and floated freely.

The Dead Sea is one of the only seas where virtually nothing—plants or animals—can live. This is because it is so salty. The Dead Sea, at 1,292 feet (394 meters) below sea level, is the lowest point on Earth. However, this has nothing to do with why it is so salty. The high salinity level is caused by the increasing evaporation rate.

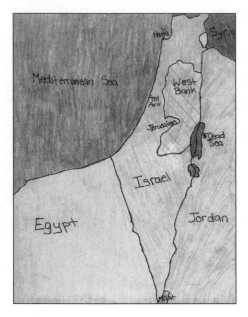

Though seawater has a lot of salt, it has a number of other elements, too. "At least 72 elements are found in the sea-water," said Martina Moran, a receptionist at the Salt Institute, in an e-mail interview. All of Earth's natural elements occur in the sea.

Scientists don't yet have a full understanding of why the ocean is so salty, even though they have been studying it for over a century. All they know is that salt occurs naturally. However, there are many theories why the ocean became this way. One is that, at the beginning of the world, storms, lightning, and rain created seawater that way. Some people believe that it began with the big bang theory.

I have never thought of salt as valuable. It just has always been there. After I did a little research, however, I realized that salt isn't just "salt." Without salt, we wouldn't be able to survive. Human blood has salt, tears have salt, and body cells cannot function without salt because it helps us cry and maintain nerve function. One quote that proves this is: "A civilized life is impossible without salt." This was said by Pliny the Elder, a Roman writer during the Middle Ages.

Common salt is called sodium chloride, or NaCl. These two elements are on the Periodic Table of Elements. The crystals come in the form of cubes. Under a magnifying glass, table salt looks like a bunch of tiny cubes, all combined together. Salt in its pure form can vary from clear to white.

Salt's source is brine from seas, salt lakes, and other bodies of water. Even the underground sources come from brine. Salt found underground is formed by the evaporation of river bodies and inland seas years ago.

The use of salt apparently began way before there was any reported record keeping. As far back as 2,700 BC, historians have found writings about salt published in China. The writing made up probably the first-known treatise on pharmacology. The earliest recordings show that salt was almost universally sought after by man.

I cooked water from the Atlantic Ocean and water from the Dead Sea to make it evaporate so I could see the salt crystals. There were 473 ml of each (16 oz). The Atlantic Ocean water took 10 minutes to evaporate. As I was watching it evaporate, it started to bubble. There were little bubbles of salt all over my stove. When it was done, I put the salt in a bowl. There was approximately one tablespoon and a half of a teaspoon of salt. The salt tasted very bitter, compared to table salt. The Atlantic Ocean salt looked clearer than table salt. The Atlantic Ocean salt was also finer than the table salt.

The Dead Sea salt was very captivating when I evaporated it. It took about 50 minutes to evaporate 473 ml of water. Just as the Atlantic Ocean water did, the Dead Sea water bubbled all over my stove. When there was a little bit of water left, I started to stir it. I took some of the salt from the pot and put it on a spoon and then put it into a different bowl. The salt would form a layer on top and bubble underneath. Taking the layer off was like peeling wax off something. As I looked at the salt in the pot, I could see that it looked exactly like glaze on a doughnut. There was more than a cup of Dead Sea salt. It was very hard and stayed hot for a long time. The Dead Sea salt tasted even more bitter than the Atlantic Ocean salt.

The Atlantic Ocean salt and the Dead Sea salt were the same whitish color, however. I was fascinated by the differences in salt between the Dead Sea and the Atlantic Ocean.

The Dead Sea and the surrounding area are a great example of the importance of salt. I went to visit it as a routine part of our vacation, not thinking much about why the Dead Sea was so famous, and left understanding so much more. I was awestruck at how different two types of salt can be. Now I realize how valuable salt is. The next time I want salt at the dinner table, I'll ask, "Can you pass the sodium chloride, please?"

For the complete text and graphics of Frieda Shmuel's winning entry, visit the Coach's Locker Room at ScholarshipCoach.com (Keyword: YONATURE).

Susan Wiedmeyer
Mukwonago, WI
Grade 10 Winner
$1,500

Exploring a Woodlot's Ecosystem

Winning
Entry

In the excerpt below, Susan Wiedmeyer, age 15, demonstrates that there is more to her wooded backyard—and its interconnected ecosystem—than meets the eye.

Ever since I was a toddler, I have enjoyed exploring in my wooded backyard. Every walk through the woods was an adventure for me. I always found it exciting to learn something new about the wonders my backyard held. To this day, I still marvel at my wooded sanctuary, different from the manicured lawns and city lots of my friends. The aura of my backyard captures my senses and sends me to a whole new place, a place of uniqueness and diversity. I decided to take an inventory of the plants, wildlife, and the non-living components of my backyard to document the diversity and the vast number of different species in my woodlot. After I studied my inventory, I could not help asking myself, "Are all these various woodlot components connected? If so, how are they all connected?" I looked for some reference in the vast field of ecology to guide me in my search for answers. Ecology is a branch of biology that studies the relationships between the organisms and their environment. I learned that in the early 1970's, ecologist Barry Commoner summarized the study of ecology into four basic tenets: "Law No. 1—Everything Is Connected to Everything Else; Law No. 2—Everything Has to Go Somewhere; Law No. 3—Everything Is Always Changing; and Law No. 4—There Is No Such Thing as a Free Lunch." Come along with me as I investigate the inner relationships of the many living and non-living components of my wooded backyard's ecosystem.

Commoner's First Law:
Everything Is Connected to Everything Else

"When we try to pick out anything by itself,
we find it hitched to everything else in the universe."

—John Muir

While exploring my wooded backyard, I have noticed a variety of relationships, including symbiotic relationships, which are close connections between two organisms of different species. I recognize three symbiotic relationships:

interspecific competition, predation, and parasitism. An interesting example of interspecific competition I have observed in house wrens and chickadees competing for the same sources of food, such as cankerworms and caterpillars. The intense competition I have observed between wood ducks, gray squirrels, flickers, and screech owls for the same nesting sites in my backyard is more evidence of interspecific competition. Similarly, all the woodlot animals compete for limited water supplies during dry weather. Another symbiotic relationship I have observed is predation, such as when the screech owl and sharp-shinned hawk consume chickadees and other small birds for the nutrients these predators need to exist. An example of parasitism, the third symbiotic relationship I have observed, is when fungi, such as the hen of the woods, feed on trees and rot the underground parts of them.

Intraspecific competition between two organisms of the same species and the relationships between living and non-living things may not be symbiotic, but they are just as much a part of the ecosystem of the woodlot. For instance, when chickadees compete with other chickadees for the same territory or nesting sites, they demonstrate intraspecific competition. The same is true of gray squirrels competing with each other for nesting sites, acorns, and hickory nuts. An example of a relationship between living and non-living things is that which exists between dead leaves and living trees. This is important because the layers of dead leaves on the forest floor decay and enrich the soil that nourishes the living trees. In another instance, decaying logs and the roots of dead trees support the growth of fungi and even seedlings, supplying them with all the nutrients they need.

Intricate food webs and food chains connect everything in the woodlot. I have observed the red fox during his frequent visits to my backyard. The red fox's diet includes small rodents, rabbits, and young opposums. In the same way, adult opposums may raid great horned owl's nests and eat the owlets, as I sadly discovered early one morning last March. Through examination of the many sporobulus the owls leave behind, I have discovered that their diet consists of rabbits, small rodents such as mice and moles, garter snakes, and small birds. Further down the food chain, rabbits regularly consume vegetation, including grasses and wild flowers. These grasses and wild flowers need the sunlight to produce their food. These examples of the food web and food chain clearly demonstrate the connectedness of the ecosystem.

For the complete text and graphics of Susan Wiedmeyer's winning entry, visit the Coach's Locker Room at ScholarshipCoach.com (Keyword: YONATURE).

CONTACT INFORMATION

Keyword
YONATURE

Young Naturalist Award
c/o Alliance for Young Artists and Writers, Inc.
555 Broadway, 4th Floor
New York, NY 10012-3999

Phone: (212) 343-6492
E-mail: sfewster@scholastic.com
Website: www.amnh.org/youngnaturalistawards

RELATED AWARD PROGRAMS

For more information on a Related Award Program, enter the associated keyword in the "Enter a Keyword" box located in the Coach's Locker Room section of ScholarshipCoach.com

■ Canon Envirothon

Students in grades 9 through 12 who possess basic knowledge about forestry, soils, aquatics, wildlife, and current environmental issues form five-member teams to participate in this competition sponsored by Canon, the Japanese business-machines company. Various national, regional, and state competitions award up to $3,000, $2,000 or $1,000 for each team member. Deadlines vary by location.

Keyword
CANENVIR

■ Federal Junior Duck Stamp Conservation and Design Program

This program, sponsored by the U.S. Fish and Wildlife Service, asks students in grades K through 12 to express in artistic form what they have learned about habitat conservation and environmental science. The winning 9″ × 12″ picture of a North American waterfowl is made into a federal duck stamp; the student artist receives $2,500 and a trip to the adult Federal Duck Stamp Contest. Entries are due in March.

Keyword
FDUCSTMP

Scholarship Award Index and Keyword Master List

All featured scholarships and Related Award Programs mentioned in the book are listed alphabetically in the pages that follow. For your convenience, the page on which an award first appears is shown for each listing, along with the corresponding ScholarshipCoach.com keyword for the award.

To use the keywords, you will need to complete the registration process for the Coach's Locker Room portion of the ScholarshipCoach.com website—a special section of the site for readers of my books and users of my multimedia products. For complete instructions on how to register for the Coach's Locker Room (including information on the access code you will need), see pages 13 and 14 of this book.

Once you have registered and logged into the Coach's Locker Room, it couldn't be easier: Simply type the keyword for each featured scholarship and Related Award Program into the "Enter a Keyword" box. You will then have instant access to a wealth of bonus material, as well as the latest updates to information contained in this book. See you online!

Scholarship Name	Page	Keyword
A ACLU Youth Activist Scholarship Award	251	ACLUACTV
Acton Institute Essay Competition	137	ACTONESS
Amateur Athletic Union Youth Excel Program	119	AAUEXCEL
American Fire Sprinkler Association Scholarship Contest	129	AMFIRESP
Americanism Educational League Private Enterprise Contest	280	AMEDUENT
American Legion Oratorical Contest	18	AMLEGORA
America's Junior Miss	33	AMJUNMIS
America's National Teenager	46	AMNATLTN
Amy Writing Awards	170	AMYWRITE
And Now . . . A Word From Our Planet	335	ANDNOWPL
Andrew W. Mellon Fellowships in Humanistic Studies	307	ANDWMELL
Angelfire Scholarship	32	ANGEFIRE
Angels in Action Awards	260	ANGINACT
Arts Recognition and Talent Search	48	ARTRECOG
Ayn Rand Essay Contests	63	ARANDESS
B *Backpacker* Magazine's Outdoor Scholarship	201	BACKPMAG
Baker's Plays	170	BAKEPLAY
Barry M. Goldwater Scholarship Program	75	BARMGOLD
Beinecke Scholarship Program	307	BEINSCHO
BMI Student Composer Awards	62	BMISCOMP
Boy Scouts Young American Award	243	BSCOUTYA
Burger King/McLamore Scholarship	83	BURGKSCH
C Calgon "Take Me Away to College" Scholarship	163	CALTAKME
Canon Envirothon	352	CANENVIR
Coca-Cola Scholars Program	90	COCASCHO
Coca-Cola Two-Year Colleges Scholarship Program	101	COKE2YRC
Collegiate Inventors Competition	102	COLINVCO
Computer Professionals for Social Responsibility Contest	129	COMPPROS
Craftsman/NSTA Young Inventors Awards Program	297	CRAFTINV
D Daughters of the American Revolution Good Citizens Award	280	DARGOODC
Discover Card Tribute Awards	111	DISCTRIB
Discovery Young Scientist Challenge	297	DISYOSCI
Donna Reed Performing Arts Scholarships	62	DONNARTS
DuPont Challenge	120	DUPCHALG
E Elie Wiesel Prize in Ethics	130	ELIEPRIZ
Elks Americanism Essay Contest	147	ELKAMESS
Elks Most Valuable Student Competition	139	ELKMVSTU

Scholarship Name		Page	Keyword
F	Federal Junior Duck Stamp Conservation and Design Program	352	FDUCSTMP
	Felix Morley Competition	148	FMORCOMP
	FIRST Robotics Competition	110	FIRSTROB
	Fleet Reserve Association Americanism Essay Contest	32	FLEETRES
G	Gates Millennium Scholars	101	GATESMIL
	Glamour's Top Ten College Women	156	GLAMTOPS
	Golden Key Scholar Awards	220	GOLDENKY
	Guideposts' Young Writers Contest	164	GUIDEWRI
H	Hearst Journalism Awards Program	155	HEARJOUR
	Hertz Foundation Fellowships	110	HERFOUND
	Holocaust Remembrance Project	171	HOLREMEM
	Horatio Alger Association	119	HORALGER
	Humane Studies Fellowships	155	HUMASTUD
I	Imation Computer Arts Scholarship Program	270	IMACOMPU
	Intel Science and Engineering Fair (ISEF)	191	INSCIENG
	Intel Science Talent Search	180	INSCITAL
J	Jacob K. Javits Fellowship Program	307	JAVIFELL
	James Madison Fellowships	342	JAMADFEL
	Jane Austen Society Essay Contest	74	JANEAUST
	Jay Shalmoni Memorial Holocaust Art & Writing Contest	179	JSHALMON
	Jaycees Scholarships	147	JAYCSCHO
	Josephine de Kármán Fellowship Trust	325	JODKARFE
	Junior Achievement Scholarship Program	220	JRACHVMT
	Junior Science Humanities Symposium	191	JRSCIHUM
L	Liberty Round Table Essay Contest	237	LIBROUND
	L. Ron Hubbard Writers and Illustrators of the Future	270	LRONHUBB
	Lucent Global Science Scholars Program	213	LUCGLOBL
M	McDonald's Arching into Education Scholarships	89	MCDOARCH
	Mensa Scholarships	213	MENSASCH
	Miss Active Teen Across America	46	MISACTIV
	Morris K. Udall Ph.D. Fellowships	201	MORKUPHD
	Morris K. Udall Scholarship	193	MORKUSCH
N	NACA Regional Council Student Leader Scholarship	243	NACALEAD
	National Alliance for Excellence Scholarships	202	NATLALLI
	National Beta Club Scholarship Program	220	NATLBETA

Scholarship Name	Page	Keyword
National Defense Science & Engineering Graduate Fellowships	82	NATLDEFS
National Foundation for Jewish Culture Awards	179	NATLFJCU
National History Day	251	NATHISTY
National Honor Society Scholarship	214	NHSSCHOL
National Peace Essay Contest	221	NATPEACE
National Science Foundation Graduate Research Fellowships	82	NSCIFGRF
O Olin L. Livesey Scholarship Fund	147	OLINFUND
Olive W. Garvey Fellowship Program	137	OLIVFELL
Optimist International CCDHH Scholarships	237	OPTCCDHH
Optimist International Essay and Oratorical Contests	229	OPTESORA
P Pre-Teen America Scholarship and Recognition Program	47	PRETAMER
Principal's Leadership Award	238	PRILEADR
Profile in Courage Essay Contest	244	PROFINCO
Prudential Spirit of Community Awards	252	PRSPIRIT
Public Employees Roundtable Public Service Scholarships	342	PUBEMPLR
R Radio and Television News Directors Association Scholarships	335	RADTVNEW
Robert C. Byrd Scholarships	213	RBYRDSCH
Rotary International Ambassadorial Scholarships	314	ROTINTLS
S Sam Walton Community Scholarship	287	SWALTCOS
Scholar Athlete Milk Mustache of the Year (SAMMY) Awards	243	SAMMYSCH
Scholastic Art and Writing Awards	261	SARTWRIT
Siemens Westinghouse Science & Technology Competition	192	SIEMWEST
Signet Classic Student Scholarship Essay Contest	74	SIGNCLAS
Sons of the American Revolution Scholarships	271	SARSCHOL
Soroptimist Programs	163	SOROPPRO
Soros Fellowships for New Americans	228	SOROSFEL
T Talbots Women's Scholarship Fund	163	TALBFUND
Target All-Around Scholarship	281	TARGALLA
Toshiba/NSTA ExploraVision	288	TOSHNSTA
Toyota Community Scholars Program	325	TOYOCOMM
Truman Scholarship	298	TRUSCHOL
U UNA-USA National High School Essay Contest	314	UNAUSAHS
United States Institute of Peace Fellowship Program	228	USIPEACE
USA TODAY/All-USA Academic Teams	315	USAALLAC
U.S. Department of State Fulbright Program	228	USFULBRI

Scholarship Seeker's Toolbox

Next-Generation Power Tools for Finding and Winning Scholarships

Whether standing in line after one of Ben Kaplan's scholarship workshops or surfing online at his ScholarshipCoach.com website, thousands of students, parents, and counselors have asked The Scholarship Coach essentially the same question: "Now that we know exactly what we need to do, can you help us actually do it?" In response, Ben has engineered the next generation in scholarship tools and technology—the *Scholarship Seeker's Toolbox*.

Designed to perfectly complement *How to Go to College Almost for Free* and *The Scholarship Scouting Report*, this toolbox features strategic worksheets to complete, useful action steps to check off, helpful exercises to jump-start your thinking, special calendar organizers to post up, and plenty of ready-to-use templates—plus a friendly dialogue style that puts The Scholarship Coach himself right beside you, guiding you through each form, task, and exercise.

Could you benefit from special brainstorming worksheets that help you quickly identify positive patterns in your experiences, and translate those themes into persuasive writing? What about mock judging ballots on which parents, teachers, and friends can help critique your scholarship application drafts? Or how about diagnostic self-analysis tools that help you identify and hammer out application trouble spots? *Scholarship Seeker's Toolbox* has all of this and so much more.

Designed for students and parents to work through on their own, as well as for guidance counselors and teachers who need a curriculum guide and textbook for school-administered courses, this one-of-a-kind resource makes finding, applying for, and winning scholarships a matter of simply turning the pages and following the instructions. By integrating thoughtful exercises with analytic tools, *Scholarship Seeker's Toolbox* actually coaches you, in an interactive way, to better scholarship results.

Published by Waggle Dancer Books

Scholarship Essay Boot Camp

The Ultimate Training Guide for Winning Scholarship Essay Contests

According to Scholarship Coach Ben Kaplan, the process of writing scholarship essays can be straightforward, pain-free, and even (dare we say) fun. No kidding! For students and parents who need to get up to speed fast on effective scholarship essay techniques, this guide is the ultimate kick-start. Ben launches this essay training program by revealing the ten most frequently committed scholarship essay mistakes, and showing you or your child how to fix each of them with a few strokes of the pen.

After further showcasing the nine core ways to "wow" essay judges, Ben launches into an under-the-lens analysis of his own annual essay contest—revealing, for the first time, precisely why the judging panel picked certain essays, while tossing others aside. To top it all off, he escorts you back-stage at ten of America's top scholarship essay contests and parcels out sample winning entries, judges' and winners' commentary, and some fun surprises along the way.

Scholarships That Totally Rock!

Scholarship Programs and College Cash Resources for Your Academic Interests

Have you ever wasted countless hours scouring for scholarships, only to wind up with a list of awards that have absolutely nothing to do with your specific career interests or field of study? If this sounds familiar, then you've come to the right place!

In this special series of guides, Ben Kaplan details the best scholarships, fellowships, contests, and college cash opportunities that match your unique interests; databases, websites, and other resources custom-tailored to your college goals and future plans; and specific application strategies of critical importance to the types of awards you will be applying for.

Each volume in the *Scholarships That Totally Rock!* series is designed for particular categories of students—including separate guides for law students, medical and nursing students, business students, and engineering students. New guides for a growing list of academic and career interests are added on an ongoing basis. Warning: With one of these guides in your hand, you might very well develop the urge to scream at the top of your lungs, "This scholarship isn't just good, it totally rocks!"

Download these multimedia guides at ScholarshipCoach.com

Slash Your Tuition, Baby!

How to Use AP, CLEP, and Other Tests to Save Big-Time College Cash

In this invaluable series of money-saving guides, Ben Kaplan shows you how to save as much as $30,000 in college costs (or even more) by earning credit through Advanced Placement (AP), College-Level Examination Program (CLEP), International Baccalaureate (IB), SAT II, and university-specific testing. In fact, for many of these tests, you only need to answer 40 to 50 percent of the questions correctly to save big-time tuition dollars! Not only does the guide help you determine which tests to take for the maximum savings, but it allows you to instantly compare—via the innovative Scholarship Coach Tuition Savings Calculator™—the college-credit-for-testing policies at your favorite schools.

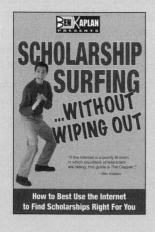

For each school, you'll have at your fingertips an easy-to-read chart of the specific tests that earn college credit, the amount of credit awarded for a given test score, and the hundreds (or even thousands) of tuition dollars you can potentially save by taking each test. You'll know in an instant which schools will reward you with the most credit toward that expensive degree.

Unlike most students who only discover the college credit policies in place at their school *after* they have already enrolled and taken their exams, these guides will enable you or your child to incorporate this critical financial information into your college planning months or even years ahead of time. The result is not only a more informed choice about which college to attend, but also a better decision on which preparatory academic courses to enroll in and which college credit tests to take. You'll also benefit from Ben Kaplan's exclusive Tuition Savings Rating™— a college ranking system that will help you determine, at a glance, how each school measures up.

Organized into handy volumes according to school type, the set allows you to select the information just right for you—including volumes for *Elite Private Universities*, *Top Public Universities*, *Leading Liberal Arts Colleges*, and a variety of geographic regions. Don't enroll without it!

Scholarship Surfing...Without Wiping Out

How to Best Use the Internet to Find Scholarships Right for You

Searching for scholarships on the Internet can be an extremely time-consuming and frustrating process...that is, until now! In this informative guide, Ben cuts through all of the junk pages, broken links, and malfunctioning databases to take you on a private tour of the must-visit and lesser-known scholarship hotspots on the Web. Going beyond the material covered in *How to Go to College Almost for Free*, you'll learn to ride the waves of leading search engines (including how to navigate their powerful, hidden riptides) to locate scholarships specifically for your interests, background, and talents—saving you countless hours while yielding better results. This guide comes complete with case studies, documentation, and insider help tips that will assist you or your kids in avoiding the garbage and surfing for the gold.

Download these multimedia guides at ScholarshipCoach.com

I Love My Bunsen Burner!

Awesome Opportunities for Exploring Science, Technology, and Engineering

In a world where scientific and technological breakthroughs are occurring daily, the possibilities for students to explore the sciences are virtually endless! In this hot guide, Ben Kaplan profiles the very best camps, contests, curriculums, clubs, learning opportunities, and special programs for students interested in exploring the physical and biological sciences, the social sciences, mathematics, computer science, engineering, environmental science, and a variety of technology-related disciplines. From summer programs that explore aeronautics or oceanography to laboratory programs and invention contests that enable young people to flex their problem-solving muscles, this volume is the first step in supercharging your scientific learning and creating stepping stones to future college and scholarship possibilities.

If Loving the Arts is Wrong, I Don't Want to Be Right!

Awesome Opportunities for Exploring the Performing Arts, Visual Arts, and Writing

Finding new artistic adventures and opportunities is as easy as stepping into the spotlight when you have this standout guide. Highlighting many of America's premier learning programs for budding singers, actors, dancers, painters, sculptors, filmmakers, photographers, writers, and musicians, these illuminating program profiles will help you find new and exciting opportunities that spark your creativity. Featuring camps, competitions, festivals, and workshops as well as proven techniques for finding the best teachers, mentors, and learning opportunities in your community and beyond—this volume is the ideal tool for students who want to explore and extend their artistic creativity and abilities.

Can't We All Just Get Involved?
Awesome Opportunities for Exploring Leadership, Civic Affairs, and Community Service

If you haven't explored the wonderful world of student leadership conferences, civic affairs programs, social activism initiatives, and community service opportunities, you're missing the boat! Whether its volunteering your summer to build homes for needy families or spending a week behind the scenes at the United Nations, this guide will help you find key programs that develop important leadership skills even as you are giving something back to society. You'll also learn how to choose leadership and service activities that best position yourself for college admissions and lucrative scholarship winnings, while having a ton of fun along the way.

Around the World in 80+ Pages
Awesome Opportunities for Exploring Foreign Cultures and Languages

How would you like to study 19th century architecture in a quaint Italian village? What about composing lyric poetry off the coast of Ireland? Or maybe just working with other kids from every corner of the globe on a new Internet website? In this must-have guide, you'll discover leading study abroad, foreign language, and cultural enrichment programs both in the U.S. and overseas. Featuring helpful advice from students who have participated in these programs—along with strategies for leveraging your cultural experiences into impressive school projects, compelling college essays, and winning scholarship applications—this volume is the ideal passport for any student and parent who wants the best that the world has to offer.

Dude, Where's My Franchise?
Awesome Opportunities for Exploring Business, Entrepreneurship, and Personal Finance

Whether you raised venture capital for your lemonade stand as a toddler, made major stock trades before your 12th birthday, or just want to explore the possibility of a future career in business, this guide gives you or your kids the inside track on key opportunities that help young people develop their business savvy. Not only will you discover entrepreneurial summer camps and commerce-themed essay contests, but you'll also encounter business plan competitions and investment strategy games. You will also gain valuable insights from other students and their parents as they relate key stepping stones they have discovered, and discuss how to create your own entrepreneurial opportunities from scratch.

Download these multimedia guides at ScholarshipCoach.com

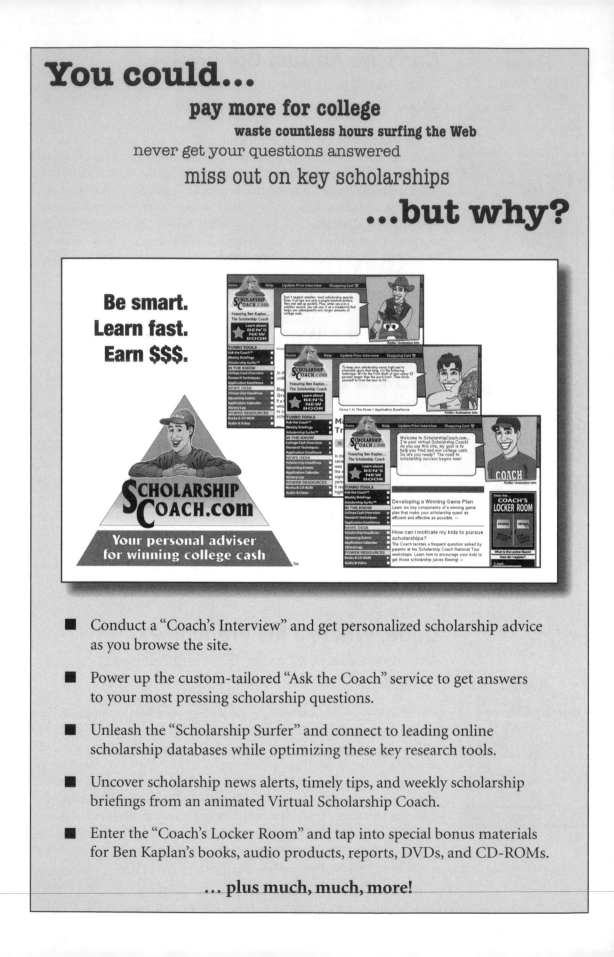

About the Author

Ben Kaplan won more than two dozen merit-based scholarships while still in high school—accumulating nearly $90,000 in scholarship funds for use at any college. In 1999, he graduated from Harvard University magna cum laude with a degree in economics, completing his degree in six academic semesters. Virtually the entire cost of his college education had been covered by his scholarship winnings.

In addition to writing *The Scholarship Scouting Report*, Kaplan is the author of *How to Go to College Almost for Free* and *Scholarship Seeker's Toolbox*—the three books forming an essential paying-for-college trilogy for students of all ages. Kaplan has also written numerous articles on winning scholarships, including columns for *The New York Times* and *U.S. News & World Report*, that have been syndicated in publications nationwide. He has been featured on hundreds of television and radio programs, including appearances on *The Oprah Winfrey Show*, NBC, CBS, CNN, and National Public Radio.

Known internationally as "The Scholarship Coach," Kaplan has advised thousands of students and parents on college scholarships and financial aid. He has served as the resident scholarship adviser at some of the Internet's most popular scholarship search websites, and is the founder of ScholarshipCoach.com, the leading online scholarship advice portal. His annual Scholarship Coach National Tour brings unique college scholarship and financial aid workshops to students, parents, and guidance counselors across the nation.

Besides speaking on college-related matters, Kaplan also energizes and inspires audiences with his dynamic presentations on personal growth, self-empowerment, leadership, opportunity creation, success in school, and a variety of youth-related issues and topics.

Kaplan's eclectic background has included interning for a leading U.S. Senator, crafting speeches for the Nasdaq Stock Market's chief economist, and writing case studies at Harvard Business School. He also co-authored the book and lyrics for the Hasty Pudding Theatricals' 151st annual musical, "I Get No Kick From Campaign."

Prior to college, Kaplan attended South Eugene High School, a public school in Eugene, Oregon. Among other awards, Kaplan was selected the "Top Student Leader in America" by the National Association of Secondary School Principals.

Kaplan currently resides in Portland, Oregon and can be contacted via e-mail at Ben@ScholarshipCoach.com. For more information, visit BenKaplan.com.